THANKS FOR ASKING

Thanks for Asking

By

Bruce H. Williams

First Published in October 2000

Copyright © 2000 by: Radio Merchandise

Radio Merchandise, Inc.

All Rights Reserved.

www.brucewilliams.com

Pictures By: Everlasting Images

Library of Congress Catalog Card Number: 00-092958

ISBN #: 0-9652409-1-6

Printed in the United States of America By:

MARRAKECH EXPRESS

Dedication

It has been said that every guest list is an exclusion list. This is true. I am reluctant to single out people who have been influential in my life and risk the omission of someone important. As a consequence, this book is humbly dedicated to all those individuals who have interacted with me over the last six decades and have made my life so rewarding. I thank each and every one of you. If I was asked to write my own epitaph, and happily I will not, my choice would be the following: *"Before he died, he lived."*

Bruce H. Williams

Acknowledgement

I would like to thank the following people for their combined efforts to help get this book in your hands. Lisa Fallon, whose tireless effort and constant nudging helped to get this book beyond the talking stages and Daniel Puckett, our long suffering editor.

Table of Contents

Introduction

In starting this adventure, I feel a bit like the late Charles Kuralt must have felt when he started motoring across America. No specific goals in mind and yet some kind of a feel for what he was trying to accomplish. Where does one begin? I suppose, technically, the beginning was a million years ago in Newark, New Jersey, when I became the second son of H.R. Williams, and Florence Williams' only child. Perhaps somewhere in this text we'll go back to that time.

But, like many others, I really had a rebirth half a century after the initial biological entry. That rebirth has become a focus for me in the second half of my life, and much of what I have done since is a result of that incident on Sunday, December 5, 1982, at approximately 3:32 in the afternoon.

A few weeks before that date, I had finally purchased my very own airplane. For a short time I was a partner in the ownership of one, but I'd never owned one all by myself. I responded to an advertisement in the local newspaper and found that the owner of the airplane had lost his medical certificate and felt that it was time for him to retire from flying. The aircraft was an exceptionally, well maintained, Cessna 182 Skylane. Almost immediately, we struck a deal in which I paid half down and was to give him the other half in some two years, along with accumulated interest. To both of our sorrows, he received payment for his plane far more quickly than either of us had anticipated. On the morning of December 5, 1982, a friend, Henry Spritzer, called and said he had learned that I had a new airplane; some of his friends would like to see it. I hadn't planned on flying that day, but any excuse is a good excuse, so I arranged to meet Henry and three of his friends at Princeton Airport later that day. All of his friends were pilots; Henry was not. Henry is an attorney who served as our municipal attorney when I was part of the majority of our Town Council and infrequently handled some legal matters for me. I thought of Hank then, and continue to think of him, as a good friend, albeit one I see very infrequently. There was, however, a time after the accident when I had a great deal of difficulty maintaining that relationship.

We met at Princeton Airport and decided we would take two airplanes down to Mammoth County Airport. Henry, one of his friends, and I were in my airplane. The two others were in the other aircraft. We flew down to Mammoth without incident. We landed and had breakfast. We switched places on the way back with one gentleman whom I'd met on several social occasions, and another whom I'd not met until that day and have not seen since that time. The trip back to Princeton was uneventful, but the landing was anything but!

After one missed approach, I managed to blow the second approach and hit a tree at a rather high speed. Fortunately, there was no fire. Clearly, although I was legally qualified to fly the airplane, I'd either had a bad day or was not prepared to fly it. I tend, in retrospect, to think the latter, but that is purely subjective. In any event, my last recollection in the air was the propeller chopping into the trees. My next very foggy recollection was experiencing a great deal of discomfort. I have no idea how I got out of the airplane, whether I was thrown out or crawled out. In looking at pictures, one would wonder how anyone could have survived being in the front of the aircraft, although the back seat was a testimony to the integrity of the construction of the airplane. In any event, my recollections are very sketchy — and perhaps happily so.

I was taken along with the others to Princeton Hospital with an emergency squad that, through a wonderful piece of chance, was involved in a fund-raiser near the accident scene. This reduced the time that it took to get to us with emergency help.

I was the most seriously injured. The other two passengers essentially suffered only orthopedic injuries. I also had broken bones. My left leg was seriously mangled, as was my skull. The more serious for me was the rupturing of my intestines, apparently caused by the seat belt. But as a practical matter, without the seat belt there is little question that my life would have ended at the moment of impact.

My recollection of the next few days is very, very hazy. I remember waking up intermittently in Intensive Care and then in my hospital room. While Christmas was some 20 days after the accident, it was almost two years after the event that I remembered Christmas Day. Strange how things creep into the recesses of your mind. Al DeVries brought in a Christmas tree fully decorated, and another close friend, Ken Langdon, came in a Santa Claus suit. None of that registered for a couple of years.

While I was in the hospital, since my head was pretty battered, my eyes were swollen shut and talking was almost impossible, I had a good deal of time — in my mercifully few fully conscious moments — to think. The recurring thought was, "Why did I survive this accident?" All reason would say that this should have been a fatal proposition. The airplane was a total loss; the firewall and seats literally were smashed together. Yet miraculously, all three of us were spared (of course, they lived to sue me!).

The recurring theme in my thoughts was "Why me?" And I was left with the only obvious conclusion: There must be something left that I am supposed to do in the grand scheme of things. The first thought I had was, "Perhaps I'll have another child who will do something dramatic: make some great contribution, cure cancer, who knows what." But that was only a fleeting thought, and the realities all were that while biologically that might be very possible, the likelihood of that was slim at best.

A little over a year before, I'd begun doing my broadcast, then called "Talknet," for the NBC Radio Network. After a number of other random thoughts that I discarded, I seriously wondered whether perhaps I was meant to influence someone, someone I might never know of, during my radio broadcasts. Over the passing years, I have come to know that I have had a positive influence on a number of lives. I have received letters from folks who said I have encouraged them to go to school, encouraged them to get out of debt, and take other actions that I feel strongly about. There is a good deal of satisfaction in hearing these stories. However, one that happened relatively soon after I began broadcasting again stands out in my mind; I will share that and perhaps a couple of others to put this into some kind of a perspective.

A gal called from California and her opening line was, "You saved my life." Now, that is a throwaway line; oftentimes "You saved my life, you told me about the sale down at the mall," or something of that sort.

But she went on to say, "I was listening to your program, I'd never heard of you before, the radio just happened to be turned on to that station. You were talking with a young woman from St. Louis, Missouri, and she was talking of doing away with herself. You were broadcasting from your home as a result of injuries received in an airplane accident. You talked to the young woman on the telephone about the sanctity of life and how you almost lost yours by doing something incredibly stupid: cracking up an airplane. You offered to send someone to the house which, as I remember you did, and that ended the incident.

"But what was important in my life was that I had just driven my car to the top of the highest mesa in our area and had the car in gear, fully intending to drive it off the edge and end my life. I determined that life wasn't worth pursuing, and this would be the easy way out. As you finished with the young lady, you were reminding her that there were cancer victims, people who had been injured in accidents, who would gladly change with her and accept all of her trials and all of her tribulations in exchange for a healthy body. I listened to your monologue for about ten minutes, decided I'd give life one more shot, put my car in reverse and drove home. The only reason I'm alive today is because of hearing that broadcast."

Now, campers, that has to make you think. We are in an enterprise that allows us to affect the lives of people we have never met and will never know. I was doing a personal appearance one day, and a mother brought over her daughter, a pretty young thing, perhaps fifteen or sixteen years old, but unfortunately wearing a neck brace. Her mother said, "I brought my daughter here to meet you; she wants to thank you." I raised an eyebrow and she said, "For a number of years, when I picked her up from school, I'd listen to your program going home and, of course, she would far prefer to listen to her music. But I insisted that we would listen to the program that I wanted to hear, which was you. Over the years, you constantly said, 'Wear a seat belt. Wear a seat belt. Don't get into a car and not wear a seat belt.' A short time ago, my daughter got into a car with several of her friends, and she wouldn't let them start until she got into her seat belt, having heard you say it so often. All of the other kids laughed and ragged on her, but she insisted that she wear a seat belt. A few minutes later, all of the others were killed in a horrible automobile accident. Only because of the seat belt that she was wearing at your insistence, is she here today."

I would admonish my fellow broadcasters to consider this incident. It is not that I'm hot stuff, nothing of the kind. But all of us, whether we do a local program or are as fortunate enough as I, to do a national presentation, have this effect on people, for good or for evil.

I was doing an appearance one night and after the show a very young woman, perhaps in her early twenties, threw her arms around me and gave me a big kiss. *What's this all about?* She said, "For several years, when I was quite young, I complained because the other kids had clothes that I couldn't afford and could go on vacations that I could only dream about. My Mom put me on to your program because you were constantly saying, 'who said it should be easy? Who said you are entitled to anything but a shot?' Well, I listened to that. I just graduated from college with honors and I've got a great job. I want you to know you were the Father that I never had."

Maybe that's why I was privileged to stick around after my little incident on December 5, 1982, which in my mind, and heretofore have shared with no one, is as much my birthday as February 18, back in the 1930s when I first arrived in Newark, New Jersey.

In this little exercise I am going to reflect on a great many things that have happened to me, but understand, there will be no "kiss and tell." I have been very fortunate: I was married and had a good marriage for 28 years, which, unhappily, didn't make it to the finish line. That is no reflection on either of us. Subsequently, I have had a few relationships that I look back upon with fondness as well. Of course, my second marriage is a sheer joy. There will be little reference to these relationships other than they existed. I have no patience with so-called celebrities who can't wait to lay out every intimate detail of their life for public scrutiny. If that's what it takes to make this a success, then I am doomed to fail.

Beyond that, what you see is what you get. I have come to know a great many people in the entertainment business. However, with a couple of exceptions, I have kept my personal life and my business life completely separate. This is not to say that I haven't met a great many very, very pleasant and interesting people whom I certainly wish every good thing for. But my friends and acquaintances, which I knew before getting involved in this enterprise, are still my friends and acquaintances. I have met two gentlemen, both of whom work for Walt Disney. I consider them friends, and they are a part of my social life. But they are very much the exception, rather than the rule. Many people in this enterprise have two personalities: one on the air and one off. That type of schizophrenia I'm just not capable of handling.

I am as I am. If you like it, fine, if you don't, that's OK too. I am going to tell you how I feel about situations and if you can accept that, OK. If you can't, that's all right as well. But I'm just not capable of maintaining an "on the air" and "off the air" personality. Now, it would be disingenuous to say that my language is necessarily the same off the air. Yes, I use four-letter expletives probably with a greater degree of frequency than I should off the air. Clearly that's not appropriate on the air. But, that minor difference aside, if you listen to me on the radio and meet me in person, I think you will find I'm much the same person. For better or for worse, I'm me.

I am sitting in my home in New Port Richey, Florida. This is the biggest home that I have ever owned. I am looking at the Gulf of Mexico, watching the boats sail in and out from the Gulf. I have an indoor pool, a beautiful piano lounge on the second level of the pool area, a game room with slot machines, a pool table, and all the other accouterments, and a huge kitchen. In short, it's a very gracious way to live.

From time to time, I sit here and ask myself, "How did all this happen? How did I get from a three-family house on 15th Street in East Orange as a child, to relatively luxurious living?" Working on this little piece has caused me to ponder and consider how all of this happened.

I am asked so many times how I got into radio. I was a radio listener well before I was a radio personality and rather hope that I'll be a listener after this sojourn ends.

However, I've been in the radio business for over 25 years. I've done this longer than anything else in my life, vocationally. Most of my flirtations with business are relatively ephemeral; as soon as they are successful, I lose interest very rapidly and would rather move on to some other endeavor. There has been one consistency, however, in the second half of my life: radio. I have no regrets.

I've been listening to the radio for a long time. Going all the way back to my Columbian School elementary days, I used to build crystal sets. After all, we didn't have transistor radios. I would build them in a cigar box and then take them to school. I would string an antenna down the aisle and listen to Ed and Pegeen Fitzgerald on WOR instead of paying attention to the teacher. Of course, from time to time, she would notice the antenna, walk up the aisle and confiscate the radio, antenna and all. But, three or four days later I built another one and started the process all over again.

For a long time, too, I have been a talk radio fan. I remember that I would regularly go out on dates and do my best to seduce the young women — more often than not, unsuccessfully — and then come home and park the car in the garage, and listen to the likes of Long John Nebel, who, in my opinion, continues to be the quintessential example of talk radio. Even though, I suspect were I to listen to some of his shows today, I would find them a bit corny. *The Shadow* and the *Green Hornet* are examples of this marriage of 1940 and 2000: They may seem corny now, but they were very exciting in their time.

In any event, I used to listen to these guys out in the garage in the wee hours of the morning. John Nebel used to broadcast from the transmitter site at WOR, which at that time was not on the Empire State Building, but rather the tower in Carteret, New Jersey. He didn't even get to go to the studios at 1440 Broadway. He interviewed the crazies of the world, the guys who'd been on the moon long before Neil Armstrong made the trip, people who had been talking to extraterrestrials. One guy, who is still around, was a debunker of all these things, the Amazing Randi. I remember those broadcasts as if they were yesterday.

I had a teacher in high school that knew John Nebel. He called me one day and said, "You guys should meet. Between the two of you, you could probably own the world." Unhappily, that meeting did not come about. I did speak to him on the phone and just before his death, had an occasion to meet him at WMCA.

One of the things that John did so well was commercials and, in those days, commercials were not tightly regulated in either content and length. When I do a network commercial now, it is done within a microsecond of the appropriate time, certainly no more than a quarter to a half-second off. John did a commercial until he was tired of doing it. I remember very vividly one of his commercials for the O'Riley Ridge Grill. Now, the O'Riley Ridge Grill was nothing more or less than a skillet with some raised surfaces in the bottom, lines of metal across so that you could fry bacon and the bacon would sit up on top of the lines. The grease would drop into the cracks and be carried away, giving you a very crisp piece of bacon. Long John was Jewish, but that didn't slow him down from doing a commercial for a pan that was to cook bacon. These commercials would last for something in the order of three minutes. Well, when he got done, there were rabbis calling up wanting to buy this skillet in which to cook bacon. He was that good a salesman.

One of the more popular nighttime programs for years was the Art Bell program, which originated in the West Coast. I have no way of knowing whether Art Bell knew of Long John Nebel and simply knocked off the style, (which by the way is no crime), or developed it on his own. There is no question in the mind of those people who have heard both perform, that Mr. Bell's show is surely a copy of Long John's. Why not! It worked. People wanted to hear about the crazies of the world, they wanted to hear about people who talked to dolphins, landed on the moon, or had been captured by aliens. Frankly, that sort of activity only goes so far with me. Clearly, the public enjoys it. John gave it to them during his lifetime and Mr. Bell provided the same type of entertainment with a great deal of success.

There were others who were on late at night. Big Joe Rosenthal's Happiness Exchange appealed to the geriatric set. Among other things, he sold some kind of a salve that I am absolutely persuaded was nothing more than petroleum jelly with a little sulfur in it. Big Joe's Salve (or something of that nature) would cure everything including venereal disease and cancer for about $6 or $7 a jar.

There were other "talkers," some of whom I have come to know, such as Barry Farber, and still others who were nothing more than a voice over the air: Gene Sheppard, Big Wilson, the aforementioned Ed and Pegeen Fitzgerald, and John B. Gambling. These were the people I listened to. Oftentimes I am asked, "Well, did you always want to go into radio?" Never had that random thought. Never gave it even a passing thought either as a child or as a young adult.

When I was discharged from the military in November 1954, I moved back home with my Mom and Dad. I was twenty-two years old, full of testosterone, vim, and vigor — no more and no less than today's twenty-two year olds. The difference was that I never had a thought about getting my own apartment. My best recollection is that the only guys or girls I knew who had their own places didn't have any parents or, alternatively, had some kind of a falling-out. But anybody who was getting along with their parents lived with their parents until they got married. That's just the way it was. It was culture-based, not financial. That isn't to say we didn't go out and raise hell and do all the stuff that today's kids are doing. Well, the fact is that there were a lot of things you could do, and a lot of things that you weren't allowed to do. The one thing you surely didn't want to do, if you wanted to stay healthy, was walk into my Father's house and flip the radio on at 2 or 3 o'clock in the morning. That just wasn't done.

My Mom would listen with great interest, (earplug in ear) to a guy named Barry Gray. Dad used to call him "Barry Pink." Years later, I got to know Barry since we worked together at

WMCA. Shortly after I began my experience with WMCA, we were all told to appear at a premiere of a movie, 1978's *Movie Movie,* which starred George C. Scott in two entirely different roles. We all showed up, including the new kid on the block. I remember so vividly Mrs. Ellen Strauss (about whom you will hear more elsewhere in this book) introduced Barry as "my star." He was the star at WMCA; he had many years in broadcasting, beginning his career in Florida, for years broadcasting from Chandlers Restaurant. Barry had what amounted to his own studio, he was always impeccably dressed, never carried anything in his pocket that would bulge, and, out of fashion of the time, he carried what amounted to a purse. Barry in that day, like Larry King today, interviewed the makers and the shakers, politicians, the social set, and some with some high degree of notoriety. He was a fixture in talk radio, beginning his career after the military in the middle 1940s.

In 1996, I nominated Barry for the Talk-Show Host of the Year and it was my privilege to present it to him at the annual meeting of the National Association of Radio Talk Show Hosts. Retrospectively, I am very pleased that I made the nomination when I did, as Barry passed away a short time later in his early eighties.

I mentioned that my Dad, many years ago, called him Barry Pink for his left-wing leaning. He and Walter Winchell, a very influential commentator and columnist of the time, had an ongoing battle that went well beyond the usual "I don't like him, he doesn't like me" sort of thing. As a matter of fact, Barry had accused Winchell of having thugs beat him on the way to work one day. Whether this is true or not, I don't know. There is no question that Barry came a lot further toward the center, and even toward the right, before the end of his broadcast days. He finished his career with WOR, a 50,000-watt powerhouse in New York City.

My first interest in performing came in the early 1970's, when listening to WCAU from Philadelphia. My wife was a member of the Catholic Church. I had agreed, before our marriage, to raise our children Catholic. That was a condition of being married in the Catholic Church, and I had no problem with that. I did not, however, agree to become Catholic, and I did not, and have not since. I did take my children to Sunday School every Sunday and rather than go home, I would sit out in the car. While they were receiving their religious education, I would listen to the radio.

One of the shows I listened to regularly was a fellow named Bernard Meltzer. Bernie Meltzer was an officer during World War II, a Democratic politician in Philadelphia (he never said Philadelphia, it was always "Phyllemdelphia"), and a member of the Planning Commission. He did not have a radio voice; he broke all the rules and still had a gangbusters program. He began on WCAU, moved over to WOR in New York, and became one of the prime money earners for that station for many, many years. He also worked on our Talknet for a short time on weekends.

Back in 1981 when NBC called to offer me a contract, they wanted me to come in that afternoon. I said I couldn't manage because I was having dinner with a former professor, Dr. George Gens. George was a talk show fan and somehow or other stumbled on me in New York City. He called me and we talked — would you believe on the air — about old times. He and his wife invited me to dinner at their home, so I couldn't go into New York to sign a contract. I said, "Nope, sorry fellows, I'll have to come in tomorrow." It was around the 17th or 18th of October 1981.

During the course of our dinner, George talked about Bernie Meltzer because he was a fan. You should know Dr. Gens was a speech pathologist of major repute. It was his opinion, after listening to the speech pattern of Bernie Meltzer, that he was suffering from arterial sclerosis. There's no question. Even the casual listener, at the end of Bernie's career, knew this was not the same guy who had been so articulate years before. In the '90s WOR dropped the program and a smaller station, WEVD in New York City, picked it up. Bernie clearly was declining and eventually had to be relieved of his broadcast duties. He was confined to a nursing home where he passed away in April of 1998.

Bernie was a guy who did everything wrong according to program directors, general managers and, of course, the sages of our industries: consultants. The problem was, the public never knew he was doing those things wrong and they enjoyed him. He was clearly the Father of Advice Radio. Sure we put our own little spin on it, but he really was the first one unless you can count Mr. Anthony of the 1940s. Mr. Anthony did an advice show purely by mail given the fact there was no two-way radio as we currently understand it.

Bernie did essentially the same type of program that I am doing, except he was the Jewish Grandfather, where I am the Hip Uncle.

I wanted to be the Hip Uncle. The more I listened, the more I determined in my own mind, "I can do that." Of course, making that pronouncement and making it happen took a long time, but that was my first inclination toward, "Gee, that's something I might like to try."

So that's who I listened to, and that's how I decided to get into the business. One thing I brought to radio was a fairly wide range of knowledge. I am often asked on my program, "How did you learn so much?" or "How come you've done so much?" and my flip answer has always been, "Well, I really can't keep a job." However, there's a little more to it than that. We are all a product of our total experiences and, in reflecting on this, I have had more than my share of experiences, some by design, and some clearly by accident. Shortly after high school, they threw in a war, and I couldn't let them have a party without me; as a consequence, college was not a serious consideration. When I got out of the Air Force, I was far more busy thinking about making my first or second million than I was about going to school. But eventually I did go on and earn my degree, and still went on to make those millions.

What follows are some of the experiences I had along the way, and some of the lessons I've learned — a triumph or two and my share of failures. To anyone whose recollection differs from mine, I can assure you that I have made every effort to be accurate but the mind does remember selectively. There may be many inaccuracies and I hope that you understand that they are inadvertent.

I am indebted to you, my listeners, for posing these kinds of questions, because they forced me to be introspective about my own life, which at times has been disquieting but overall a worthwhile experience.

Thanks for asking.

What It Takes

Everybody wants to go to heaven, but nobody wants to die. There's a homily that would sit pretty close to most people.

People often have goals they want to reach — a better job, a better house, a better life in general — but they can't seem to find a way to get there. They think that they've never had a chance to get ahead, or that life's demands and obligations such as family or work, keep them from living the way they'd like to live. So they ask, "What can they do?"

The specific answer always has to come from inside. Each person has to figure out how he will manage his life better, how he will make opportunities for himself, and how he will satisfy the obligations he has undertaken, while setting aside time and energy for getting ahead.

The general answer is always the same: It's *your* life, and if it's going to change, *you* have to make it happen. No one else will.

Doing so takes some qualities of character — some virtues, if you will. Along the way, I've learned that they're essential if you're going to get what you want.

1
Self-Discipline

Self-discipline is what separates what I might have been tempted to say was "the men from the boys," but now in order to be totally politically correct, "the children from the adults." (Probably the last time I can be counted as PC-positive.)

From my early childhood I remember very distinctly my Dad's Friday night poker excursions. He'd play with the neighbors; I don't know the exact stakes, but they were enough to make it interesting. I remember very well overhearing Dad and Mother talk about the fact that he simply couldn't afford to play anymore because he couldn't afford to lose. At the time, I had no idea how painful it must have been for him to tell his friends he couldn't play. Whether he told them he couldn't afford it or made some other excuse, I will never know. But I do know that he opted out of the Friday night poker games and, to my knowledge, never got back in. More than a half a century later I still have the chips he played with.

It's funny how things come full cycle. As a young adult with five children, I too played in a Friday night poker game, which, at the time, was high stakes, given our incomes. I was not a half-bad poker player. On occasion, I won substantial amounts on these Friday night adventures. But on the other hand, there were those nights when no matter what I did, I came up one card short and, as a consequence, I left a good deal of money in somebody else's pocket.

In the middle of this, I suffered some business reverses and some expansion expenses and it became clear that while the winning nights were great, I simply couldn't afford to lose. And I, too, 30 years later, had to call my friends and tell them that I could no longer play. I did tell them that I couldn't afford to. It was easier for me just to get it over with and, as it happened, a couple of the other guys had the same problem. After my fortunes were revived, I did rejoin the game, but that was a good many years later.

Thirty years later, or sixty years after H.R. had to drop out, my son Matt, married with children, enjoyed playing cards but had the same experience. He, too, completely gave up gambling because it was simply not prudent. I can't begin to tell you how proud I was of him, knowing how difficult it was to do. But then, that's how character is molded.

Three generations faced the same problem, and all of us made the same decision: I'll have to give this up for now, maybe forever. I was very proud of my son because at no time did I counsel him in any way in the matter. As far as I know, my Father never had a role model in this, either. It is the kind of thing you have to learn for yourself and decide for yourself. That is what separates the disciplined from the undisciplined.

Similarly, if you are to be self-employed, there is no one to rattle your cage, get you out of bed in the morning and tell you that you have to go to work, or tell you that you must stay late and do whatever it is that needs to be done. Self-discipline is the key. How many road warriors have someone to answer to on an hour-by-hour basis? In contrast, the person who comes to the office has to be there at a certain hour and others will know if he or she doesn't make it in on time; lunch hours are prescribed — you get the picture. Those who are out on the road calling on accounts or who are otherwise unsupervised have to have the self-discipline to get out and get the job done with no one standing over them. I can tell you from considerable experience, it's not an easy task.

Although few things worth doing are easy, if you are willing to make the sacrifices and accept the tradeoffs, just about anything is possible. Let me give you an example of what I mean.

Not long ago, a gentleman called me from Dallas, Texas. He said he was an accountant, 43 years old and unhappy with his job. That's not an unusual circumstance. I find that professionals who have trained very hard for their disciplines somehow become, disproportionate to the rest of the population, "burned out" in the common parlance or just disenchanted or bored or in some way discontented with their present occupation. He went on to say that one of the things he really wanted to do was to become a lawyer, but he had family, responsibilities, debts, mortgages — in short, the things that the average 43 year old husband and father would have in this great nation of ours. I said I could appreciate all that, having gone back to school a bit younger than he: I was 25 when I started undergraduate work and had youngsters born in my freshman, junior and senior years. I managed to survive, and I mentioned that to him in passing. Then I asked, "Why don't you go to law school?"

"Well," he said, "I told you that I have all these responsibilities, and my wife can't make the kind of money we need."

"I don't recall telling you that your wife should work, although it would certainly help. I'm saying that you should work. Why don't you work full-time and go to law school full-time? Or go to school in the daytime, get yourself a nighttime job and study in between?"

We chatted a moment or two more and ended the conversation. Then came another call: someone disagreeing with what I had just said. (If callers want to take issue with what I say on a substantive or philosophical basis, especially if they have expertise in that area, it's the custom on my program to put them right at the head of the line. It's not important that I am right; what is important is that the information we give is as accurate as we can make it, and I take that part of my job very seriously.)

This caller identified himself as a professor of law, I don't remember where. He wanted to take exception to what I had said, and my producer put him straight through to me. We chatted for a moment; he indicated that he enjoyed the program and as we went through the niceties that generally start a conversation I could already hear the "but" coming... "But I really disagree with you on this law school thing."

"Why so?" I asked.

"I'm a professor and you just simply cannot go to law school and work full-time. It is far more demanding than you can imagine; the discipline of law... it just cannot be done."

"Well, professor, you may be right, but that is going to come as a great shock to my daughter Kelly," I said.

"How so?"

"My daughter worked with me for three years, running three of my companies, all of which were prosperous at the time, and she went to law school full-time and graduated with honors. She is currently a practicing member of the Bar."

"Well, that could be true," he said.

"No, that is true."

Nonetheless, he said, "You just can't work the way you can through the other disciplines."

"Professor, do your colleagues share this point of view?"

"Absolutely, to a man and a woman."

"Well, then, I'm going to offer you guys an opportunity that I don't think you can afford to decline since you are absolutely persuaded that it can't be done. I will wager $1 million, and I can find a million dollars to deposit, and you go to your colleagues and all form a pool to cover my million. I then will apply to law school and get myself admitted and go to school for three years. I will continue to do my program during that period of time, I will continue to write my column thrice weekly, and I will continue whatever activities I am involved with. I will finish law school and graduate in the appropriate three years. The only caveat would be the state of my health: If I were to have a serious health reversal, the wager would go on hold while I regain my health."

I'm still waiting for someone to cover that wager, and let me tell you, I am hoping that someone will; I've repeated it often enough. I figured that it would work out to something like $1,300 a day for going to school — not a bad stipend for something I've always wanted to do. In fairness, I should say that I have audited classes at law school and was appalled at how it took an hour and a half, in some cases, to make a point that could have been made in five minutes and retained by even the less gifted students. It could be that I'm speaking from a slightly different perspective, having been exposed to many things that the students may not have been, but be that as it may, I am convinced that I would have absolutely no difficulty.

Now, I never said that I was going to pick Harvard or Yale, because geographically, they would be out of the picture. All I said was that I would go to an accredited law school and graduate in three years. I never, by the way, said I wouldn't hire a recent graduate as a secretary to take care of my dictated notes, because I would do that, given I have the resources to do so. Actually, I first considered going to law school twenty-five years ago, as an intellectual exercise, having no desire to practice.

The point is this: If you are willing to sacrifice — and as I pointed out to that caller, your social life and much of your family life would have to go on hold for those three years — you can achieve anything. Giving up a social life and some time with your family is a tradeoff for a greater benefit, and it

5

has been my experience that almost everything involves a tradeoff.

The reality is that we have only 24 hours a day, and how we spend those 24 hours makes the difference between success and failure.

If I were to meet you eyeball to eyeball and ask the question, "Are you a bigot?" the likelihood is that you'd say of course not. If I asked you "Do you believe in equality?" I am confident that you would say that you do. If we were talking about social equality that is one thing, but there is absolutely no equality when it comes to us as human beings. Some of us are short, some are tall, some are fat, some are thin, some are males, some are females, some are black, some are white, and some are other skin tones. If we are born in a Third World society we may have a life expectancy of less than forty. Born in another society we might have an easy expectation of seventy-five or eighty and might live into our nineties. Some are smart and some are not so gifted. There is very little equality in this frame of reference, but there is for all the people that I have described one fundamental equality.

It is this: If we live for the next twenty-four hours we will get precisely twenty-four hours or fourteen-hundred and forty minutes or eighty-six thousand four hundred seconds. Everyone, from the wealthiest and most influential among us to the least, will receive the same deposit in their account — no more, no less. The difference will be how that account balance will be spent.

Most people will tell you they work eight or ten hours a day, and I'm here to contradict them. I don't mean that they're lying. They think they're working eight or ten hours a day. In reality they're probably productive only three or four of those hours. The balance of the time is wasted in woolgathering or daydreaming, which have value, but which are not work. The fact remains that those people who learn to focus have the discipline to get the job done without anybody telling them.

6

They use that deposit in the account wisely. They are the people who are destined to succeed.

It is important to plan ahead long term, but you should also plan in the short term as well. Each day I've got twenty-four hours — how shall I make the most of them? I am obliged to make a withdrawal from my account, but it's at my determination on how to spend that withdrawal. (Unlike a regular bank account, you cannot carry a balance; each day goes back to zero.)

Remember, once a minute passes it can never be reclaimed. Once a thought disappears, it seldom reoccurs. Time management must be one of the most critical disciplines exercised. Without this, it's very difficult to see how any success will follow.

2

Hard Work

So many of my callers are looking for the easy way. They want to make a buck — they want a lot of bucks, in fact — but when you ask them if they are willing to work 20 hours a day, or what they are willing to sacrifice for it, that's another program.

Selling Insurance

When I was 22 years old, I went to work for State Farm Insurance as an agent. Why I passed their agency test, given they had so many demanding criteria, I'll never know. But I did pass and was put on some kind of a "draw."

Perhaps I should take a moment to define a draw. The expression is used rather regularly and yet I believe oftentimes carelessly. Under most circumstances, if you go to work for an employer you will be paid a salary that is mutually agreed upon. This is often not true when one is hired to be a commissioned salesperson. Commission is the fairest way to pay someone because they are paid precisely what they are worth, no more or less. On the other hand, it may be very difficult for candidates to support themselves until the commissions start coming in. Visualize a new garden hose. You uncoil it, connect it to the faucet and turn the water on. At the moment you turn the water on, the water doesn't come out the other end. The hose has to fill with water before some comes out at the nozzle end. The same thing may be said for commissions. While you may be earning them, they will not be paid anywhere from a month to three months. The industries recognize that people do need the income at the outset so they have created the "draw." A draw simply put, is a loan. No taxes, Social Security or unemployment insurance is taken out of a draw because the draw is a loan that has to be paid back to the company. The reality is, if someone fails, oftentimes the draw is just forfeited by the company. Then it has to be picked up as income to the person who received the monies and he must pay the appropriate taxes and assessments. When you take a draw in effect you are digging a hole for yourself. Without the draw it might be impossible for many people to accept the challenge of commission sales and possibly sharing in its rewards.

Like all insurance sales endeavors, many are called, but few are chosen. In other words, the attrition rate is incredible, and I was one of those who ultimately went down the tube with attrition, but it was a good experience. One of the things we were required to do was X-dating, "X" standing for expiration date of the insurance policy. We had to come up with, as memory serves me, 25 automobile expiration dates a day, six days a week. You'd have to put out an awful lot of fliers to make that work. How did we do that? We walked up to strangers on the street, in motor vehicle inspection lines, (which were ubiquitous at that time,) car wash lines, construction sites, any place where you could find somebody sitting still for a couple of minutes. I will never forget the pitch, and this is 40 years ago. You'd walk up to somebody in a parking lot of a supermarket and say, "Hello there, I'm Bruce Williams. I represent State Farm, the world's largest insurer of automobiles. Tell me, if you could find a better buy for your insurance dollar, better coverage, and great service at a more favorable rate, you'd want to know about it, wouldn't you? Well, of course you would. Well, here's what I'd like to do. I'd like to jot down your name and your address, your telephone number, and when your present policy expires. I'm going to give you a call about a month before that policy expires and, when I do, I'm going to bring you a road atlas (I would have a Rand McNally atlas under my arm) just like this one, just for the privilege of chatting with you for a few minutes, and I will show you what I have to offer. If I can beat your present rates and give you better service, that's something that's going to interest you, will it not? Fine. When does your present policy expire?"

A lot of people would say, "Get lost," or wouldn't talk to you, but at least 25 a day would give you that information; you put it into your file and eventually had enough leads to call on every single day. That's doing it the hard way. But it worked! And you say, "How could you walk up to people on the street whom you'd never seen before, and start pitching them?" After the first hundred or so, it's easy.

But the easy way is seldom the way that is going to work. Everybody wants to go to heaven, but nobody wants to die. Most people aren't willing to make the effort, but you see, that's good for the hustlers of the world like me, because if everybody were a hustler, can you imagine what kind of a world it would be? The competition would be incredible.

One of the joys of X-dating was that you met all sorts of different people in your endeavors. One day when I was wandering through the Borden milk plant in Newark I ran into a young fellow we will call Marty. Marty was of Greek extraction and had done his time in the Army in the latter part of World War II. He went to Panzer College in New Jersey, which has since been folded into the New Jersey College system. At that time it offered degrees only in Physical Education. To call Marty a "diamond in the rough" would probably be the best description possible. His command of the language was a tad limited as he was first-generation Greek and Greek was the only language spoken at home. Marty was a milkman. He delivered milk door to door and was quite happy with what he did. I got some information out of him about when his insurance expired and we talked about it and I ultimately sold him a policy. At that time he asked me about how he might get a job with the company. That was money from home from my perspective because we got paid a bounty for everybody's name we turned in who became an agent. I took my pieces of silver a la Judas and sold Marty to the company. As it turned out, he was accepted; he went through the training program and did pretty well. He was an interesting guy and he and I became friends.

Hard as it is to believe in today's society, Marty never laid eyes on his wife until his wedding day. The parents arranged the wedding and Patty was brought over from Greece for the wedding. As it turned out, it was a good match and they were together until he passed away some years later.

Time came and went; I left State Farm and went on to other endeavors and finally into college. I lost track of Marty, then ran into him one day and he was as happy as a pig with his snoot in a trough. He was working for a company called Johnson Hall Limited. He was the vice president of the company, doing all manner of traveling back and forth to Europe and in short, having a ball and being quite well paid for it.

I asked him about the company and it turns out that it was an excess lines broker. That is, they wrote insurance policies that companies in this country would not accept at premium rates. U.S. regulatory authorities do not regulate these companies since they operate outside the country. The only thing they have working for them, in terms of regulation, is their own integrity. (One of the better-known excess companies would be Lloyds of London.)

There are many other companies operating out of Zurich, Amsterdam and Bonn. Marty was doing very, very well. One day he came to me when I was a junior in college and told me he was in big trouble. It seems the company had issued a policy on a boat and the boat was scuttled. This would not be a major problem except for the fact that no insurance company was involved. His broker, the boss, was pocketing the money and paying claims as they came along out of these receipts — essentially becoming an insurance company in his own right. I suspect if this had gone on successfully for another four or five years he would have had ample funds to actually start a legitimate insurance company.

As luck would have it, he had taken a large risk on this boat and he lost. The owners and the people who had liens on the boat were looking for their money and that money didn't exist. Desperately, Marty was trying to stall for time and he asked me if I could arrange to have some insurance policies printed for him. As much as I wanted to help him, I was not about to become involved in a felony of that magnitude.

Ultimately the law closed in. He was arrested and indicted. Interestingly, at the end of this whole thing his boss came out smelling like a rose. Every single incriminating document had been signed by Marty, nothing by his boss. Marty's Dad paid his bail and he found other work. Off and on, for a better part of a year, he worked for me at the school doing cleanups. He didn't say a whole lot about the indictment but he did tell me how much he feared going to jail, which seemed to be a certainty.

As it turned out, Marty beat the rap shortly before the final portion of the trial. He had a heart attack and passed away. I often wondered how much I contributed to his fall by getting him into the insurance business. I often think of this guy, he was a simple soul, a hard worker who just got in over his head. The lesson there: Don't be a patsy for somebody else. If you can't think of a decent reason why they're being so good to you, take an extraordinarily close, penetrating view.

That was one kind of hard work I did. There were others.

Summer Job

The summer of my junior year in high school I was thrashing around trying to find a way to make a buck. Of course, I was working at Sam and Joe's Service Drugstore in the afternoons, right through closing time, but I still had time on my hands and had no interest in hanging out in the playgrounds. I have long since forgotten where I heard of it, but it did come to my attention that the Coca-Cola Bottling Company in Newark was hiring helpers for the incredible sum of $12 a day. Twelve bucks a day! I mean nobody made that kind of dough, but naturally I was going to explore it. I mentioned it to my friend John Roberts, and he and I went down to apply.

John was an interesting guy, a scholar, spoke French fluently during his college days, and had one goal in life besides playing basketball - to be a teacher. He wanted to be a teacher for one very important reason. Teachers have the summer off. John and his brother Tom and I were buddies for a number of years. As a matter of fact, John and I purchased our first automobile together, a Model A Ford Station Wagon vintage 1930. You see, John, although old enough to get a driver's license and own an automobile, did not know how to drive. On the other hand, I was a year or two younger, unable to get a driver's license, but I could drive just fine. What a great combination.

We bought the car together from a local police officer for fifty bucks, (would you believe?) and kept it in a garage behind the police officer's apartment. Neither of our parents knew that we owned an automobile. John owned it and I drove it.

We did have a bit of a problem on one occasion when I was trying to show John the intricacies of driving this powerful piece of equipment. Inadvertently, John put it in reverse and sailed through the garage doors of an adjoining garage, shattering them. Imagine trying to put Humpty-Dumpty back together again.

John and I went down to shape up at the local union hall. For the uninitiated, shaping up means that you show up; if you've not been there before, you fill out the appropriate forms that say you will agree to pay whatever money the union demanded of you. You are then "approved." We then had to go over to Coca-Cola, which was some distance away, and hope that there would be a position for us. As it turned out, there were lots of young men coveting this position. After all, twelve bucks a day was a king's ransom. There had to be at least 100 bodies over there waiting to be anointed. For reasons that are totally inexplicable, John (not the most ambitious guy in the world and I say that with affection), of all the applicants was chosen. Several were weeded out because they were under 18, as was I. I took quick note of that deficiency and felt I could correct it in a hurry just with an adjustment of my birth date, but I was not selected. Given that a selection had been made, we were all told to go home; everyone left except John and me. I thought I would wait for him to go home. He was sitting there filling out all sorts of forms that the company required but he got to a stickler: a Social Security number. John had not ever received a Social Security number.

Very candidly, had I faced that circumstance, I'd have very quickly made up a number. What difference would it have made? It would have taken them at least a couple or three months to catch it and by that time summer vacation would be over. Happily from my perspective, John was neither that ingenious or disingenuous but when he told them, "No Social Security number," they said, "Sorry, no job." In the meantime, everybody else had gone home but me. As I remember, I was sixteen at the time or possibly at the most seventeen — certainly under eighteen — and I had noticed the hasty rejections of those of such tender years. Very quickly I added a couple of years to my age by subtracting a couple of years from my birth date and for the balance of the summer I had the highest-paying job among my peers, wrestling cases of Coca-

Cola on and off the truck. That was when I learned details about areas that were adjacent to me.

As an example, not more than a twenty-minute walk from my home was a section of Newark called "Little Italy" where the children literally spoke no English until they went to kindergarten. The kids three or four years old spoke only Italian, which was the language at home and in the streets. Working in that section was an education. It was like being in a foreign country. The markets sold Italian goods, the liquor stores sold Italian wines. Probably the best way I can describe it is that it was like a street out of *The Godfather: Part II,* complete with festivals, gang leaders and the rest. But it was a very cohesive, pleasant neighborhood.

Sometime after I left the area for the Air Force and other adventures, some social scientist decided that people should not be allowed to live in this kind of "poverty." The appropriate public hearings condemnation proceedings were begun to expropriate the brownstone apartments and tenements that dated back to the turn of the century, all of which were eventually razed. Replacing this area was tall apartments; what we have come to know as tall slums or projects. In keeping with the Italian theme, they were christened the "Christopher Columbus" homes, and a bigger disaster could not be imagined.

First of all, an interesting reality quickly took shape. The local population, almost entirely Italian, could not qualify to live in the projects because they made too much money. These were successful people who liked living in their own neighborhood. There has been so much criticism about neighborhoods that do not integrate for whatever reasons. It occurs to me that people have a right to live with folks with whom they are most comfortable. This is why we have Little Italys, Little Havanas and Chinatowns, and I don't find this to be wrong. The social engineers have tried to persuade us that our strength lies in diversity but the facts seem to militate against that position.

This is not to say or imply that we should be allowed or encouraged to discriminate, but why a group of people from one part of the world who choose to live together should not be allowed to, baffles me.

I should say that I object to the speaking of a foreign language as the primary language in those areas, not for any reason of ego, but rather I view this as a huge handicap to the children coming out of that area. Given the fact that English is our social language, it seems to me that the English language is the one that should be insisted upon in schools. I have often spoken out against programs teaching English as a "second language" to immigrants. English should be the required language. In other times immigrants who came here from Italy, Spain, Russia, Germany, etc., all learned English as their primary means of communication. Now to allow groups to come here and have all governmental information, voting records and even driving tests in another language is a travesty. All we do is ensure a perpetuation of second-class citizenship when we don't insist that each person learn the language of commerce and commonality, in our case, English.

A short time ago I had occasion to go into the Miami and Homestead areas of Florida. There is no question that the Cuban population of those areas has grown both in terms of volume and influence. For the most part it has a very positive influence on the economy and growth of Greater Miami.

There is still reluctance on the part of many of the immigrants to learn our language. I stopped at a convenience store and both of the clerks had no ability to converse. They could ring up sales but that was the extent of their ability to communicate. What a shame. They are condemned to have that type of job for the rest of their life and also doomed to live in a relatively modest-sized area where Spanish is spoken. Would it not be more sensible to insist that all who live in this nation learn to speak English? I cannot believe that if I were to live in another nation that I wouldn't make every effort to speak the language. Perhaps not as well as a native-born person but at least I would be able to carry on a reasonable conversation. Is this so much to expect in this age of political correctness? We have gone overboard in some benign effort to accommodate when in reality what we have done is perpetuate a problem.

Having diverted in our little discourse, I would like to point out that had John been a tad quicker on his feet he would have had the job rather than me. There are those who would argue, "But it would have been dishonest to give a false Social Security number, just as it was dishonest for you to move your age forward." My rejoinder would be this: Everything you say is true technically, but where is the hurt? In the first instance, if he applied for a Social Security number after he was working, he could always go in and say, "Gee, I gave you the wrong number," and the records could have been adjusted so that the money was credited to his account.

The second instance, at 6 feet 2 and 200 pounds, whether I was seventeen or eighteen, I don't think mattered very much other than for matters like workers' compensation — then known as workmen's compensation — and even then, the fact that I had misrepresented myself would reflect only on me and not the company. Be that as it may, it is my contention that there are many rules in this life that are made to be bent or broken. Consider all the young men of the World War II generation who added to their age in order to get into the military. Technically wrong? Perhaps.

Air Force

I entered the Air Force on February 26, 1951, a feisty nineteen year old off on a great adventure. I had never been more than 300 miles from home at that time, so the notion of taking a train over a thousand miles to San Antonio was an exciting thought. We traveled from Newark to St. Louis in a sleeper having the run of the train and in the company of two or three female enlistees. Of course, everyone including me was hitting on these girls; to my knowledge it never got any farther than that. We had a ball!

We arrived in St. Louis, had a three-hour layover and then went to meet our train. Things sure changed. From a club car sleeper, we were now on a military train segregated from the ladies and literally strip-searched to make sure there was no alcohol on board. Thus, our introduction to the real military.

The basic training was perhaps a little more difficult then than it is now since there were no rights for the trainees, as I believe should be the case. I did everything from picking up all the pebbles in the parking lot, putting them in a pile, and then putting them back all by hand, to spending an Easter Sunday polishing my canteen cup. It was my contention even then, and certainly now, that the discipline involved will stand you good stead all of your life. Just before we were to be assigned I came down with a viral condition. I was told I was going to Air Force Intelligence and, for whatever reason, I wanted to go, so I went to sick call. I got there determined I was going to be passed on as OK. After the doctor gave me a thermometer, I very carefully shook it back to about the normal range. He put his hand on my head and said, "You feel a lot hotter than that but I guess you're OK." He gave me a couple of the ubiquitous APC pills and sent me on my way.

After spending time at Brooks Air Force Base, I went overseas, did my thing in Korea (I'll talk more about that later), came back and finished out my tour at Kelly Air Force Base in Texas and in Washington, D.C.

I would be eligible, of course, for the American Legion and Veterans of Foreign Wars but I never joined either organization. I just felt this was part of my career that I wanted to put behind me. I certainly have some pleasant memories and one or two that are less than pleasant. I could never see the necessity of becoming a professional veteran. This is in no way criticizing those organizations for those folks who are comfortable with them. For me the military, like many experiences, was just one to enjoy, get over with, then get on with life.

When I joined the Air Force at nineteen, I had to fill out a number of forms acknowledging that no promises were made. I had to laugh. Recently, I determined I'd like to join the Civil Air Patrol, primarily to give young cadets instructional rides according to the Civil Air Patrol syllabus. I contacted the commanding officer of the unit in this area and explained who I was and said I had a very serviceable airplane and I would like to put it to use in the CAP. He was very gracious and came over to talk to me, but let me tell you, my friends, I filled out more papers than I ever filled out to join the real Air Force. On top of that, I got regular communications about having form so-and-so in triplicate.

I really began to question the wisdom of continuing with the CAP. Ultimately, I resigned. With all due respect, I wasn't very military when I was in the military and all I wanted to do here was have the opportunity to use whatever skills I have in aviation to introduce youngsters to those skills. I am active in the Experimental Aircraft Association Young Eagles Program headed by Chuck Yeager. This program gives kids their first ride in sitting in the front of the airplane where they can really see what's going on. I really enjoy that and I believe the program worthwhile.

I envisioned something similar in the Civil Air Patrol. Unhappily, it seems to me that it is bogged down with Air Force-type regulations, some of which are clearly sensible, others not. I believe I am competent to teach the kids and I know I am competent to fly grid search and rescue. I have no desire whatsoever to run around in a uniform and involve myself in other activities. I might mention in passing, I was a cadet in the Civil Air Patrol during my high school days. Upon recollection of what we did then, compared to what the cadets are doing now, I am persuaded the way it was done years ago had far more merit than today. Furthermore, we did not have exposure to airplanes. These kids are fortunate to have volunteer pilots who give them a perspective we never enjoyed.

College

After I was married, it came to me in a blinding revelation (I don't know that any lightning hit a rock, but it was a pretty big revelation to me) that I was not going to get anywhere without a degree. I recognized that what you learned was secondary unless you were going into some kind of a trade, such as law or medicine, but a degree was a very important factor in job selection and, indeed, even in social activities.

I chose Newark State College, now Kean University, because it was cheap. It was a teacher's college and I was enrolled in the education curriculum. That was all there was. I had no problem with that, whether or not I was going to teach was academic. I determined that the first thing to do was get the degree — it didn't matter much what it was in. I've not changed my point of view very much in that regard. I told my children that I didn't care if they got a degree in gum chewing, basket weaving, or whatever. I just wanted them to come back with a legitimate four-year degree. My experience has told me that seldom are you asked what you learned. But you are always asked, "Did you go to college?" and sometimes, "Where?" and "Did you graduate?"

As a consequence, I decided that I would go back to college. Like everything else that I've done in my life, I got into it full time. That was okay, but the problem was that I had to make a living, since my wife was, as they say in the Bible, "with child." Clearly, I would have to give up regular daytime employment.

Driving A Cab

Before my marriage and for a time into it, I had driven a cab in West Orange, New Jersey, on weekends for a young man named Gene Fanning. Gene was a wanna-be television star who, to my knowledge, never made the big time. (I do recall Gene doing one Volvo commercial but after that, I lost track of him.) In any event, it was my introduction to driving a taxicab. Working in West Orange was working with the nice folks. You didn't have to worry about being mugged.

One of the more desirable jobs we used to get was on Sunday afternoon from the Goldman Hotel. If the Catskill Mountains were "the Jewish Alps," then the West Orange Mountains were the poor Jew's foothills. The Goldman was the "primo" hotel in West Orange. Young Jewish folks would come out from New York City, notably Brooklyn, to spend the weekend, singles all. The gals and guys were all looking for a mate; none of them had any money — they saved their lunch money during the week so they could make these weekend trips — and they were all looking to marry well. Buses brought them out on Friday and took them home on Sunday. Invariably, some of them would miss their bus and they would call us. They had to pool their resources to afford the trip, which was $20 or so, a substantial sum in those days. We would pack in four, five and as many as six girls in the back of our cab and drop them off in Brooklyn. In all the two years I drove on weekends, I don't believe I ever got a tip from those kids, not because they were cheap, they had to scrounge like crazy just to come up with the cab fare. It was a lot of money in those days, and the conversations about the near "hits" that they experienced over the weekend were worth the price of admission.

What I always heard was that it had been another failed weekend. The boys they were meeting were as poor as they were. I never said it to them, because I didn't want to screw up the relationship my company had with the hotel, but these kids were working the wrong place to find a wealthy husband or wife. If you want to go duck hunting, the desert is not the place. You have to get out to the swamp where the ducks live. If you are looking for a rich spouse, you have to go where the rich people hang out, not the poor man's Catskills.

That's a lesson that I think can be applied very generously to life. If you have a goal in mind, you really have to figure out not only what you want, but also where the ingredients are to reach that goal.

I drove Saturdays and Sundays and remember vividly that we had a different work ethic than seems to be common today. For my honeymoon, I took off for only Saturday and Sunday of the weekend I was married, and arranged for a replacement to drive my cab. My good friend, then and now, Bob Geyer, had no experience and didn't know the first thing about West Orange, but he picked up the slack. I wonder how today's young people would solve that problem.

When I decided to go back to school, my first thought was I would drive a cab again to support my growing family. It was clear that I couldn't make the kind of living that I wanted to make driving for Gene in West Orange, so I headed for nearby Newark — the big city. Newark was not as rough a town then as it is now, but it was no walk in the park either. It would be difficult for a good many people today to understand the social differences of just a few years ago. The environment that we worked in was a microcosm of the differences.

Let me explain. You can depend on one thing. There was no Equal Employment Opportunity Commission. You got hired or you got fired at the whim of your employer. But when you drove a cab, you were usually not an employee. By today's standards, you were, I guess, an independent contractor. In those days it was called "horse hire." You rented the cab for a period of time, in my case a 12-hour shift, 4 p.m. to 4 a.m.

My owner owned only one cab, #133, known on the street as Brown and White 38. The owner drove the cab in the daytime and let me run it at night. I paid $9 a night for the privilege except on weekends, Friday and Saturday nights, I paid $12. In addition, I had to buy my own gas, and I had to buy it from the "Organization." Gas at that time was probably at 25 or 30 cents a gallon at retail, but we had to buy it from Brown and White at around $1.25. Oil might have been 30 or 40 cents a quart, but it was $2 a quart from the "Organization", and that old tank that I was driving, as I remember a 1950 Plymouth, used about as much oil as it did gas. No matter. You bought your gas and oil from the "Organization."

This is how they supported their activities. Each cab had to buy a certain quantity of gas or the owner had to make up the difference to the "Organization" out of profits. Furthermore, sneaking out and buying some gasoline wasn't really an option; well, in a way it was, but there was a very distinct possibility that if you got caught at it, two or three very ugly and very strong men would teach you a lesson that you'd never forget. Seldom did anybody buy gas twice outside. The exception would be if you were getting a "smart job," which meant an out-of-town job to New York City, northern New Jersey or someplace. If you didn't have much gas in the car, then you could call in and request permission to gas up and they would give it to you, but you'd better get that permission.

It's funny how art imitates life, or is it life imitating art? We had a dispatcher named Mimi, and if Mimi wasn't Danny DeVito from *Taxi*, I'll never see anything more similar. He was a little short Italian guy as pugnacious and loud-mouthed as Danny DeVito was in the show. When I saw *Taxi*, I figured somebody must have had a connection with Brown and White in Newark back in the 1950s. It's too hard to imagine coincidence creating two such similar characters.

I went down to the Brown and White garage and asked if anybody had a cab for rent and made a connection. I don't recall my owner's name and I seldom saw him. I used to leave my envelope with "the end" — the cost of the rent on the cab plus the gas and oil — with the dispatcher, who gave it to the owner when he came in the morning. Some nights you didn't make any money at all. You didn't take enough money in to pay the rent and for your fuel and oil. Other nights you did very well.

In those years, Newark was what was called "a city limit cab." You could go anywhere within the city of Newark, and Newark's a big town, for $1.25. Even if the meter read $5, it didn't matter, $1.25 was all the customer had to pay. It was a 25-cent first drop and a nickel per fifth of a mile. You really had to hustle in order to make a living. But if you hustled you could make a decent living and for all practical purposes, the government wasn't your partner.

The city was whacked up by very, very definable lines. Take Brown and White, the "Organization" that I worked for. These were all independent owners banded together under one label, Brown and White. The cabs were painted brown and white. Some guys owned two or three cabs, but the majority were owned by owner/operators who either leased them on the alternate shift or didn't lease them at all.

There were several such organizations in town. Brown and White were essentially the Italian owners, most of who were just working stiffs, some of whom had organizational ties. We had total monopoly on the public service bus terminal, our "stand" by Military Park, as well as a number of stands throughout the city.

Twentieth Century was strictly owned, operated and driven by Jews. Twentieth Century had Newark Airport, the old terminal, the one that in recent years was operated by People's Express. That was the main terminal until the new terminals were built. (I had occasion to visit there recently, taking my flight physical, and the North Terminal, as it was known, is now once again closed and fenced off. But, like the Phoenix, may rise from the ashes with another airline.)

You could drop passengers off at the airport, but there was no way you would ever pick up a passenger at the airport, except under two specific conditions: if a passenger called your particular company, or if there was too much traffic for Twentieth Century to handle. Back then, conditions made it more likely that planes would be diverted from other airports such as LaGuardia to Newark, and the Twentieth Century's cabs couldn't handle the traffic. On those occasions, a call would go out that "the airport is open," and we would all flock to the airport to grab those great jobs. But aside from that, if you valued your health, and that was not a laughing line, if you wanted to stay healthy, you never took a cab to the airport unless it was painted red and white and bore the markings of Twentieth Century.

Then there were the Yellow Cabs. They were run by Colonel Kelly, who was about as much of a colonel as I was. But, nonetheless, he was addressed as Colonel Kelly and was reputed to be connected with the New Jersey underworld, though I have no way of either substantiating or refuting that. I did drive a Yellow Cab briefly at the end of my college career. Yellow had its own phone clientele, but its claim to fame was Newark's Penn Station. It was a major attraction for the drivers. While any cab could drive up in front of Newark's Penn Station, underneath, where the main traffic was, was restricted to Yellow Cabs. They had a starter inside to steer the passengers out to Yellow.

In back of Penn Station were the Blue and Whites. There were only a few of those, and the Blue and White guys would only take somebody they could "stick." To my knowledge, they would never take an honest job. They would only grab somebody from out of town whom they could hustle in one way or another.

Green Cabs were operated by the people we called "Negroes"

back then. Greens had the "Hill," the black ghetto, pretty well monopolized, although from time to time I used to work up there.

There were times when I really had to go out and scrounge for business. On a rainy weekend, of course, there were more jobs than you could handle, but plenty of times there were no jobs and we had to make "the end." Without the end, working your 12-hour shift ended up costing you. In desperation, what you could do was go up and work on the Hill. I was young and foolish and used to work up there regularly until about 10 or 11 p.m., when, I too, would leave.

Once I pulled up in front of a huge hall. It had been a brewery, but now it was a Hungarian hall. As I was cruising past slowly, looking for work, a man came out wildly waving his arms at me. *Hot dog, got myself a job!*

I pulled up in front of the building and he motioned me to open the back door. He and a friend struggled over what could only be described as a huge cauldron of some type of food, which, before I had a chance to remonstrate, they placed in the back seat of my cab. They didn't speak much English, so they gestured that they would be back and away they went. A few minutes later, they struggled down the steps with yet another pot. They gave more gestures that they were coming back. They returned with a third kettle of golumpki, meatballs wrapped in cabbage leaves stewing in their own gravy.

A lady, not paying too much attention, came up behind my cab and gave it a sharp rap in the rear with her car. In ordinary circumstances, this would have been nothing but an inconvenience, but the sharp hit drove the kettles into the back seat cushion and then, bouncing off that, they tipped over. You had to be there. The meatballs and the cabbage in hot gravy poured out onto the floor, under the seat and up under the front floor. My cab was several inches deep in this goo! When the two guys came out, I thought they were going to have a fit.

They immediately began, with what implements I don't recall, to scoop the stuff up and back into the pots. When they finally had scooped up as much as they could, they squeezed into the cab and directed me to their destination, which turned out to be a physician's home. Would you believe they were catering a dinner?

Into the physician's house went these slightly adulterated goodies. As I remember, I charged them about ten times what the ordinary rate would have been, which was clearly not enough. I went down to the garage and hosed out my cab, but my cab reeked with the smell of this stuff for the better part of a month. People would get in, take a sniff and say, "Thank you, I'll look elsewhere." I hesitate to think of what they thought they smelled. In any event, I often wondered if anybody's digestion was upset with the golumpki from the floor of the cab. *The things you won't do for a buck!*

All of us had to contribute to a fund to provide "gifts" to the Newark Police. There was a set fee for each officer level, right down to the patrolman who worked the areas that concerned the cab fleet operators. I distinctly remember one cop who worked in the middle of a downtown street the first of each month. When you drove past, you had to hand him a very small amount of money like the toll collector he was.

He stood there in the middle of the street with cars stopping as they handed him money. After you paid, you had no problems with parking, double parking or whatever in that area. If you failed to pay, you could depend on being hit with a blizzard of tickets. This system might offend some of my younger readers, but it was an orderly world. You knew your place, you knew what you could do, you knew what you better not do, and it worked. Believe it or not, it worked, and it worked well.

I went to school, usually around 8 in the morning, and finished up sometime around 3 or 3:30 p.m., went over to the garage and picked up my cab at 4 p.m. and drove until 2, sometimes 3 in the morning, and as late as 4 a.m. On weekends, of course, all bets were off. Fortunately, my owner didn't come in early, so I could take the cab out on Friday at 4 p.m. and keep it out until 8 a.m. on Saturday, go back in Saturday afternoon at 4, and keep it out until 8 a.m. Sunday. More often than not, I'd take Sunday night off, though on occasion, I would work seven days. But it was good to have at least one night to myself. Even though, between school and the cab, we had little time together, my wife and I found enough time to get pregnant in the first couple of months of our marriage.

My son, Matthew, was born about the time of freshman exams, first semester. You can imagine that going back to school after a seven-year hiatus was a little difficult, but I managed to adjust. As soon as Matt was safely here, I went out and drove the cab and, as the fates would have it, I got a call to Port Newark, a seaport adjacent to the city. I picked up a couple of out-of-town seamen and, as we rode into town, I gave one of them a cigar and announced the fact that I was a proud Father of a 9-pound baby boy. We talked about it for a while and I wound up with what was, at that time, a huge tip, a few dollars. Well, a big light bulb popped over my head. From that time forward, I carried both boy and girl cigars under the seat of the cab. When I knew I had an out-of-town job, from the port or maybe from the bus station, suddenly I became a proud Father that day. It was amazing how my tips grew geometrically. Dishonest? Probably, but let's face it, I was a kid hustling and I make no apologies, because the only way that you could make a decent living and stay alive, was to be a hustler.

There were many Runyonesque characters in the cab business. When you read about these things, you think that somebody must have made this up. But, as God is my witness, these people did and perhaps still do exist. Almost everyone had a handle of some kind. Some of the guys were known by their given names, but the majority had a nickname of some sort. You notice that seems to be prevalent among certain mobster elements today — Joe "Greasy Thumb" Gusie, that sort of thing. Well, it was true, we had nicknames or, as the CB people say, "handles." It's pretty easy to figure out what mine was, "collich kid," not "college kid."

I remember some of the others. There was one guy who was, I suspect, pretty close to an idiot savant, "Louie the Lug." Louie was not a rocket scientist, but the son of a gun could play multiple games of checkers and usually win. Aside from that, he was not very bright, but boy, could that guy play checkers. They called him "Louie the Lug" because, owing to his small stature, he carried an equalizer, a lug wrench. A lug wrench wasn't a weapon, it was a tool, you couldn't get arrested for that, but you could smack somebody upside the head and get their attention. His son began driving during my tenure with Brown and White, and of course, he had to have a handle. What else? "Louie the Lug's Kid."

Then there was "Turkey Neck." I can see him today driving that huge Dodge with the push-button transmission, with a neck about nine feet long; he moved just like a turkey. "Slicky" was always involved in a three-card Monte game and from time to time, actually drove legitimately (not often). You get the picture.

I used to study while waiting for jobs on the stands. If you were on a stand, you got whatever phone call came in within a prescribed area. One of the stands was opposite a restaurant where my Dad and Mom used to take me as a child: Bibs in the Roseville section of Newark. Across the street was a White Castle knock-off, Red Tower. I used to allow myself two hamburgers and a hot chocolate for supper. If memory serves me, that was something in the order of 30 or 35 cents. That was it. If I got real lucky and got a couple of smart jobs, I might treat myself to a Waldorf Cafeteria down on Broad Street, where I could get meatloaf, mashed potatoes, a vegetable and a roll for about 50 cents. But that was a special treat. Usually it was the two burgers and a hot chocolate, and that was it for the night. I would study and when my turn came to go out and pick up a fare, I would be off and running.

Sometimes I ran into more than I bargained for. While we made a good deal of our living from jobs we picked up at places like the railroad station or on the street, a significant portion of our business came from working the zones. The city was whacked up into, as I recall, 18 or 20 zones. You could call in and say you'd sit in a particular zone until a job came in, but if someone called for a cab in, for example, Zone 15, and no one was sitting there waiting for it and you were the closest to it, you got the job.

One night I answered a routine radio call. I was closest to the address, which was a tavern, and I picked up the fare. The guy who called the cab had a friend with him and they eased into the back of my cab. One man was looking uncomfortable, grimacing with pain, and they told me to get to the Martland Medical Center as quickly as possible. Just as I was turning around, the passenger in pain eased himself sideways and it was clear why he was hurting. He was bleeding profusely with a knife stuck into the side of his back, the handle protruding several inches. There was not much I could do but hurry to the hospital and clean up afterward. Can you imagine? Don't call an ambulance; call a cab!

Another time, I was in the heart of the ghetto making a call from a public phone booth on the street when a young man came up and pounded on the booth. "Are you the driver?" I said I was. "I need your cab." Ordinarily, I might have been a bit reluctant to take anyone in that much of a hurry, but I was young and hungry. So the man came out leading his wife, who was obviously in labor. Once again, Martland Medical Center was our destination. It was nip and tuck between arrival at the hospital and the baby's arrival. In that competition, the baby won. What started out as two passengers ended up as three by the time we got to the emergency room. I called ahead on my radio and, fortunately, the staff was waiting for us. Funny thing though, I never got paid for that job.

I suspect that this experience is one of the reasons why I get impatient with some of my younger callers who complain that they can't afford to go to school and work at the same time.

I am gratified by the number of letters I receive by the people who say I am right and then they go on to recount how I inspired them to go on to college, do something creative at work, etc. While I am pleased at the accolades, these folk did this and they did it on their own. Their letters are testimony to the fact that it can be done. It also must be observed that the beneficiary of this type of persistence and behavior is clearly the person that gets the job done. They are helping themselves and that's as it should be.

Law School

About a quarter of a century ago I decided it might be fun to go to law school and I applied to the State University, Rutgers Law School in New Jersey. I filled out the appropriate forms, got recommendations from various judges and influential folks in the legal communities and submitted my application. I got a call from one of the deans, whose name has long since slipped my mind, asking about my application. He said he had a few questions to ask, first of which was, "Why do you want to go to school at your age? After all, you are older than most." And then he kind of backtracked and tried to say something to pull his foot out of his mouth such as, "Well, you are older, perhaps nontraditional." I acknowledged that there was no question about my age, and there was equally no question that I had five kids and a business and other things to occupy my mind. I did think that going to law school might be a great intellectual exercise. He said, "We do accept 'older' students, but of course we are looking for their life's experiences. For example, we have a student, and I know this is difficult for you to understand, but this gentleman has served on his local planning board. These are the kind of folks we really are very interested in getting into our school because they bring with them a wealth of information." I acknowledged that that might be the case, and if that was a major factor, I think I was in pretty good shape. I had served as a deputy mayor, mayor and member of a planning board of my hometown.

Unhappily, my accountant sat me down and gave me a very objective but strong reality check. He said, "Do you know how much your time is worth, and can you afford to spend it in a critical period in your development? Going to law school, commuting and getting your assignments done will be demanding." Upon very somber reflection the answer was that I really could not afford to spend the time that way. I don't like characterizing it as a regret, but in retrospect, I might have come to another decision.

Class Always Shows

There is in almost any situation the class way to handle it and the classless. We've all seen people standing in front of an airline counter holding their breath, turning purple, and stamping their feet because their plane has been delayed because of a hurricane. "I've got to get to a business meeting. I've got to get home. I've got to, I've got to, I've got to." The fact is that all of the histrionics in the world are not going to change things. Your plane is going to be late. You may as well have another Scotch, open your magazine or novel, or if worst comes to worst, get some work done. The class act will accept what's happened or explore all alternatives. Why not check another routing?

Just the other day I was in Tampa, Florida. I had to make a quick trip and came to find out that everything — and I mean everything — from Tampa to Newark, my destination, was not only booked but overbooked. I started checking other destinations. What about Tampa-Houston-Newark, Tampa-Cleveland-Newark — Tampa-Los Angeles-Newark if it came to that? As it turned out, I did finally manage to get a seat on the Tampa-Cleveland flight and then took the Newark leg, which was no problem. Unless you know how to attack that kind of a problem and what your alternatives are, you are going to be there with the rest of the sheep getting bumped because the planes are overbooked, or at the least being inconvenienced. Once again, I saw so many people screaming at the gate attendants for absolutely no valid reason. Those kids can't change a thing!

An example of real class that I remember so very well concerned my neighbor, Wendell Forbes. Wendell was very wealthy and successful. He had married Lillian, a lady with little formal education but she had panache and was considered the grand dame of the area. Her cocktail parties were something special because the Forbeses knew everybody who was worth knowing. The makers, shakers and the beautiful people would attend their cocktail parties. Of course, it became necessary from time to time for someone to reciprocate. Jack and Ann Joyce, the neighbors across the street, were very favored by "Diamond Lil." Jack was a physicist and a former Navy pilot who, interestingly enough, used to carry his pillow into the cockpit when he was flying a bomber. I have always thought it took more courage to carry the pillow than to leave it home.

Jack became a physicist at David Soronoff Laboratories working on nuclear fusion. Jack and Ann were having a dinner party and we were invited, as well as many of the other neighbors in the area, and of course Wendell and "Diamond Lil." Wendell was chief counsel for Mobil Oil. You can conclude he was effusive and had a great command of the language. Lillian asked him if she could fill a plate for him from a very tastefully set buffet. He thanked her and Lillian went to work and took a piece of ham and covered it with the most potent mustard God ever created. A little dab of that mustard would take care of a whole ham, and here's a guy with his whole portion covered with it. Wendell, the gentlemen that he was, was far more eloquent and loquacious than ever and the reason was obvious. He was nibbling at that ham but to his credit after a couple of hours he neither scraped off the mustard nor acknowledged that there was a problem, even though everyone in the room knew there was and he ate the entire serving of ham. That's class! Classless, at best, might scrape the mustard off, or at the worst reprimand his wife in front of guests for what seemed to be another foolish mistake. As I said earlier, class always shows. Before you lose it in public, before you say things that cannot ever be retracted, consider Mr. Forbes nibbling at the ham.

Delegation

It is my view that no matter how much money you earn, if you are not able to grab a vacation every few weeks, you're a failure and what you have not learned to do is delegate. If you are a one-trick pony, a brain surgeon, and you only do your own surgery with nobody working with you, then you have failed. The fact is that you should be able to take time off.

When I was injured in the airplane crash some years ago, I was not the least bit concerned about my businesses. As a matter of fact, I was unconscious the better part of a month and would you believe, we had the best quarter we ever had. Now that either tells you that I am totally superfluous to our enterprises or alternatively — and I prefer to accept this thesis — I surrounded myself with capable, reliable, dependable folks. I am quite confident in the main that is the case. A clinker or two, sure, but the folks who I work with are really good people and I am very happy to have them with me.

One of the things that you must learn to do is to delegate. As a matter of reality we are involved in many different businesses stretched pretty much from the East into the deep Southwest. There is no way in the world that anyone could visit these sites on a regular basis and have any time left for anything other than going to airports. You must depend upon either your partners or your subordinates to get the job done. Many people will say, yeah, that's all very well but the reality is "nobody can do it as well as I" — and that may be the case. Let's accept that thesis, although I don't necessarily subscribe to it. Hire two people. The job is getting done on an extension basis and you can take that vacation and succeed.

Consider Pizza Hut. It has some 3,700 stores and it is not even a separate corporation. It is a unit of Pepsico. If the CEO of Pizza Hut decided to visit each store, just once, and visit one store a day it would take him 10.13 years to visit every store, and by that time he would probably have moved on to some other enterprise. The point is that there is absolutely no reason for a chief executive officer to visit each unit.

Each unit works essentially the same, and that is true of our concession in hospitals. You visit one; you have been in them all. That is not to say that I don't want to keep in touch with and have close contact with our customers. Our company is a vendor, but I have no reason to visit on a regular basis. Our drivers go there and a specialist drops by once in a while. I'm sure you get the point.

My close associate Steve Belly made a purchase some years ago, and Steven is a guy who can squeeze a dime until Franklin Roosevelt grimaces in agony. Nonetheless, Steven made a purchase of some Christmas tree skirts and told me about it. I opened a catalog and thought, well, Steven's having a bad day but it was only a few pennies and I didn't say very much. Not only could we not sell these stupid things, but we put an ad and said, "free Christmas tree skirts" and guess what? People took one look at them and said, "Not in my house."

Now, did I want to chew Steven out? Of course not! He made an error in judgment but I thought I would kind of pound the lesson home. I took the Christmas tree skirts and put them near the door where he had to walk in every day for the better part of a year. The message was not lost.

I had a caller one day who had succumbed to what is now an ancient scam. He was asked to test a "free" boat with welded compartments. He would get to keep the boat if he would answer all the questions. All he had to do was pay shipping and handling charges and the boat was his. That's a hell of a good deal — or so he thought. He thought he was receiving a compliment — "They respect my ability to rate a boat" — and he went for it.

Well, the boat was a rubber boat that held one person, a little rubber raft, and indeed by definition the rubber glued together was a weld. (**Weld**: to unite by heating or by hammering or compressing with or without previous heating.) Of course, he thought of a metal boat being welded, but rubber, too, is welded or bonded. He said the outboard motor that they put on there was battery operated by two small batteries and went putt, putt, putt, but that was the extent of it.

Well, he thought it was funny, as would I. He then ordered (he doesn't learn, this guy) a home entertainment center for a very low price. It was going to do everything except get him fixed up with a very good-looking movie star. What came was a cheap radio worth about $6 and he paid in the hundreds. His son, a business partner, took the radio, put it into a Plexiglas case and mounted it over our hero's door. Happily, the father had a good sense of humor and he said the rubber boat made a fine backyard pool for his grandchildren.

All of us, no matter how well situated and how experienced, can make bad buys, but if you discourage your employees from making bad buys then they won't make good buys for you either. They have a right to fail, and you have every right to chastise them up to a degree. If you are raising a child, eighteen months or thereabouts, and this little troll is parading around under your jurisdiction, consider this: If each time the kid slipped and every time he skinned a knee you picked him right up and brushed him off, pretty soon this kid is going to walk

37

right off the edge of the Grand Canyon because he knows that God comes out of his heaven and saves him. What you must do is allow the kid to fall down. Chipping a deciduous tooth is not the worst thing in the world. You tell him, "Don't touch the stove" only once, and then let him touch the stove. Burning flesh is a great reminder, after he smells it, that a stove is hot. The same can be said for your employees. You have got to let the employees know that making a mistake from time to time is not a capital crime.

In the investment world we talk about risk and reward. You buy a CD insured by the FDIC, you receive a minimal amount of interest, but $100,000 (more in some cases) is fully guaranteed. You can sleep at night knowing that your money is safe as a prostitute walking down central aisle in church. Now the higher the risk you take, the greater the possible reward. We can stretch that into buying commodity futures, which I don't recommend to amateurs, but that would be one of the highest possible rewards. It also entails the greatest possible risk. The handling of your subordinates is parallel to this. If you encourage them to take some risks on your behalf, then the rewards can increase, not arithmetically, but geometrically.

On the other hand, you are going to have to tolerate some misses. I mean nobody bats a thousand. So many bosses routinely say, "That's his job. Why shouldn't he underwrite it correctly?" But if he makes a mistake then they come down on him like a cloud. The result is the guy doesn't take any risk, he's getting paid anyway, and your bottom line has got to shrink.

Your Customer's Needs And You

It truly amazes me that people will shop for an automobile, go to ten dealers and haggle like crazy. We tell the salesperson to throw in his wife and pension plan — then we might make a deal. Then they will walk into the first bank that is convenient to their home and make a deal for the money. Studies indicate very clearly that the choice of banks for the largest number of our citizenry is not a matter of shopping to see what bank has the appropriate products for your particular situation but rather the following: "It's on my way to work," "They have a big parking lot," "They have a cup of coffee in the lobby," all of which has very little to do with banking.

If you investigate, you will find that almost every bank (and they are becoming fewer and fewer with the mergers) will have specialties. As an example, if you have a bank that is clustered in the middle of three colleges or universities, they very likely will have specials for students to attract that business, such as free checking, minimum balances, that sort of thing.

The same is true in an area in Arizona or Florida where senior citizens are a growth industry. There will be special deals made for the so-called "seasoned citizen." Perhaps a quarter of a point more on the CD's, free checking — you get the picture.

In order to find out these things, you have to go to the different banks involved after you know your situation. If you are twenty-three years old, I don't think a "seasoned citizen" account is going to be of much interest to you. Conversely, if you are pushing seventy, student loans are probably not in your future. There are certain services that are unique to your age and category, i.e. income or service charges, that should be taken into account before the business relationship is established.

Some years ago I spoke to a bankers' association and subsequent to that time, I was asked to come in and talk to a bank about why its loan portfolio was not growing with the alacrity it deserved. The bank in question was located in the Midwest. I walked into the bank. Not a new building, but it was a gracious building: main lobby, tellers' windows and to the left and right, the platform officers, then the senior officers who served from their enclosed offices. If one word would describe the lobby it was "sterile." If one was to describe the help it was "stuffy."

Most of the gentlemen had suits on, one or two with blazers. The women behind the teller's cage and the one woman officer were wearing floppy ties, taupe hose, and looked very businesslike.

You might observe that is the way it should be. Think about this. The average working stiff walking into that bank for an automobile loan was sweating it out down at the factory all day long or in the salmon packing company, he has body odor, he is tired and he probably needs a shave. His female counterpart working at the Quick Check or 7-Eleven, in a factory or hot office, feels the same way. They stop in the bank on the way home or, worse yet, at lunch hour and sit across a mahogany desk big enough for two hockey teams to play on. There is an unsmiling officer giving the fish eye and saying, "I will take your application, Madame."

Now "Slicky Jones" down at the used car lot is wearing checkered pants with a striped shirt, straw hat, also has body odor and he's one of the boys. Who do you think those people are going to borrow money from? You got it. The guy they're more comfortable with.

First thing I told the bank officials was to take off their ties, leave their jackets in their closets and be in their shirtsleeves. I didn't mean sloppily dressed. They could wear Dockers or khaki slacks and a shirt. The ladies could wear slacks or a dark skirt with a light blouse so they would look well groomed but closer to their customer's attire.

Oh yes, in the lobby I suggested that they put in a popcorn machine on a cart, if possible. Popcorn has a very friendly odor.

They put the popcorn cart in, they took off their ties and jackets and loan applications very shortly thereafter increased. Now I'm not suggesting that everybody go to work in jeans as I do. I am lucky in that regard. Unless I am performing, jeans and cowboy boots are the order of the day.

I do think that when you are trying to work with your customers, you don't want to put yourself in a position of what appears to be authority. Why do you suppose in days past all police desks in a police station were several feet higher than the floor? That way the police officer automatically had an aurora of authority because he was looking down at you. The same thing is true here, but that will work against you.

3

Persistence

Upon reflection, I have concluded that those people who were born with a great deal of money have been cheated to some degree. They have never had the opportunity to struggle. I'm not saying that I hope to leave nothing to my children (I have my own views on the confiscatory inheritance taxes) but I'm glad they don't have to do some of the things that I did. On the other hand, in some ways I think they have missed something along the way.

If you've never really lived in a poor neighborhood, you will never have quite the same appreciation of a better one. If you've never had to struggle and never had to worry about what the bill collector was going to say and how you were going to fend him off, you never will completely appreciate the security that comes from a degree of success. We don't get to choose whether or not we will have these experiences. It is just the way the cards are dealt. I have absolutely no regrets about the hands that have been dealt to me.

One thing playing my hand has taught me is how crucial persistence is.

Sometime in 1979 I was invited to participate as a guest on the *Larry King Show.* Larry's show was carried regularly late nights on the station I was then broadcasting on, WMCA in New York. Larry was a frequent visitor to our studios. His was the very first successful long form talk show in the country. One should certainly not forget Herb Jepco who broadcast out of Salt Lake City, but rather than a network, Herb broadcast over individual stations with a myriad of telephone numbers to respond to. Very complicated. King was very straightforward and simple. You called one number and let it ring until he was ready to pick it up. No screening, everybody got on. Larry then, and of course now, had the best interviews: the makers, the shakers, the top authors, and so forth.

He began on January 30, 1978. When I appeared on his program we took questions from all over the country, very similar to the questions I'm taking now. It was clearly a success. We had scads of phone calls, a potpourri of questions, even though there was no screening. It certainly worked out very well. It was my contention that this program could stand on its own.

After several phone calls and letters, I contacted Ruth Ann Meyer who was then a program director at the NBC network. Prior to that time she was the program director at WMCA, one that I assaulted with telephone calls and letters very unsuccessfully. She moved over to NBC and was replaced by Mark Mason, who eventually gave me my shot. As luck would have it, I got in touch with Ms. Meyer on the telephone and told her what I was proposing. She said it sounded interesting and asked if I would put it in writing.

Bear in mind, gentle reader, this was before the days of desktop publishing. Not just anyone could crank out a respectable-looking production in no time at all. In less then three days, I produced a little booklet titled "National Telephone Talk Radio: An Idea Whose Time Has Come." The text is repeated here so there can be no misunderstanding of precisely what I had to say and what I had proposed.

NATIONAL TELEPHONE TALK RADIO

●

An Idea Whose Time Has Come

By Bruce H. Williams

Table of Contents

Forward

As one who has been active as a talk show host for 4 1/2 years and a follower of the phenomenon for many years prior to my entry into the market, the writer concedes some prejudice. This fact, notwithstanding, the success of the telephone talk format has been demonstrated in major and small markets across the country.

There are many hurdles such as the scarcity of affordable top talent, production costs, formats with reasonable universal appeal, lack of enthusiasm for late night radio by local sales force and others, any of which, singularly or in combination, can preclude the adoption of a talk format.

It is the contention of this presentation that these barriers can be over come profitably by a national network talk show. The major points will be discussed with viable (technical and budgetary) solutions to objections frequently raised when this type of proposal is discussed. By its nature, the proposal must be brief. Any given point can and will be addressed in depth upon request.

Need

The need for an alternative to local late night programming is obvious. Essentially, the same sound is heard across the dial. Small outlets are forced by budgetary considerations to hire fledgling broadcasters. With rare exception, they are young people learning their craft. Music predominates. The choice is limited and frequently the quality is poor. We now have a catch-22 situation: poor quality equals low audience, resulting in little sales revenue.

The Alternative

A top quality network program, with ground lines or satellites and dishes in place, enjoys a vast advantage over the local programmer. This advantage properly used can result in superior programming for the public and considerable cash flow for both the network and the local stations it serves. Properly selected, telephone talk provides a creative vehicle to accomplish the ends herein described.

Required Technology

Except for the network feed, the technology required is precisely the same as conducting a local talk show. Exception to this would be broadcasts originating at a subscribing station. (That will be considered later.)

Assuming the flagship station to be New York City based, all incoming calls would come to a 212 area code number in the same manner as they would to a purely local program. Late night telephone rates are very low. Example: Los Angeles to New York-21 cents for first minute. 16 cents for additional minutes. The cost to the caller can be held down by picking up the call just a moment or two before airing (contrasted to putting caller on hold for extended periods). The net result is a listener can participate on a national late night program for less money than many of my listeners currently spend to join me on my New York City program. Technical production costs, as outlined, roughly parallel local program costs so such cost should not be a deterrent to a national production.

From time to time, it is desirable for the program to originate from the studios of major subscribers. I have discussed this aspect with engineers who have set up this type of "remote." This system requires only one additional body, in the person of a producer or director, one cue line (ordinarily in place) telephone with head and mike set patched in for convenience, and one extra loop line for signal. None of these involve significant costs. Program continues as usual with all calls coming from flagship stations numbers.

Personnel

The type of program I am proposing requires a minimum of personnel:

1. Air talent. (See programming section)
2. Producer-screener. Duties include screening calls, noting city of origin and subject to be discussed. Should be bright but no special skills are required.
3. Engineer. Usual duties and under current work rules, as I understand them, only one would be required. If a second engineer is required to accomplish the network feed, the cost factor is not a critical nature.
4. When remotes are undertaken, one additional producer would be needed at the remote site, as well as the producer at the flagship studio.
5. Secretary. The type of program I am proposing develops a large volume of mail that should, at least, receive a form reply.

Profitability

We have demonstrated network costs are reasonable. Direct expense to the subscribing station is limited to one engineer per subscriber. The number of avails to subscribing station is not a matter to be treated here. With a reasonable number of stations on board, there is obvious appeal to the national buyer who would not be interested in each subscribing station individually. In that lines and equipment are in place, it makes good sense to maximize their use.

Programming

There is currently one all night coast-to-coast talk presentation, the Larry King Show on Mutual. This program is presently carried by in excess of 150 local stations. I have been a guest on Larry's show and the response, I am told, was excellent. The questions asked of me then are precisely the same as those asked on my local program, demonstrating the general appeal. I have been with WMCA going on one year. I host a program Monday through Friday afternoons and Saturday morning from 6-10:00 AM. The theme is straightforward and simple. I deal in problems and advice. A large number of my callers' concerns are in the area of real estate, finance, investment and difficulties with merchants and governments. I try to give the caller and the listener, who has or will have a similar problem, reasonable advice and direction or at least help them to see what they must do to resolve the situation. The style is a bit more upbeat than similar presentations I have heard.

General talk has a good deal to recommend. But consider, many individuals like sports and yet many others are turned off. Politics and politicians hold the attention of large numbers of people, but for others, there is nothing less interesting. In short, there is little one can choose to discuss that is of interest and touches the lives of most listeners. Rich or poor, young or old, urban or suburban, all of us at times have problems we need to share and seek guidance in order to arrive at a proper solution. It is the lowest common denominator. In addition, this type of programming can be tuned in at any time. The next call is independent of those proceeding so the listener is not playing catch-up for the first 15 minutes. There is no loss of continuity. Advice at this time is a very hot item, in both print and electronic communication. In my somewhat biased judgement, I contend I could do this format across the country. My mail and sponsor success are testimony to this fact. I am not afraid to say publicly, "I don't know." These three words have enhanced my credibility to my audience.

Hours

I propose a five-day a week, five or five and one-half hour live program, beginning at midnight eastern time. Central, mountain and pacific would be fed the first segments as they are done. They would be taped by the local engineer and aired at the end of the live fed. This gives each local station a full program with as much live time as is possible.

Costs

The type of program I am proposing has much to recommend in terms of low production cost. A general talk show requires, at a minimum, the services of a full time producer to do research, line up guests, as well as the other activity attendant to general broadcasting. In that no guests are used, these costs are not incurred. In that personnel costs are minimized, production costs are reasonable.

Conclusion

Mutual Broadcasting has done the spadework and has a commanding lead: commanding but not one that cannot be overcome with a quality offering. As a practical matter, there is certainly room in the market for two or more national programs. There is little question that there will be more network late night talk. The only question to be resolved is who will take the initiative and next enter the market. I am confident that together we can make it work. I welcome the opportunity to discuss this proposal in depth, at your earliest convenience.

Bruce H. Williams

A short time afterward, on December 5, 1979, (December the 5th seems to be a big day in my life. Precisely three years later is when I whacked up my airplane.) I received a note, which is also reproduced here. Essentially she said, "No deal but we'll keep it in our file."

National Broadcasting Company, Inc.

Thirty Rockefeller Plaza
New York, N.Y. 10020

212-664-2045

Ruth A. Meyer
Director
Program Development
Radio Network

December 5, 1979

Mr. Bruce Williams
Franklin Park, NJ 08823

Dear Mr. Williams,

Please forgive my elusiveness…it's been a rather frantic several weeks!

I'm afraid that we aren't any closer to firming up plans for the kind of show you outlined in your very impressive presentation but, if you don't mind, I'd like to keep your material in my active file in case we find we're able to start moving in that direction.

Again, thanks for your patience and good luck.

Sincerely,

Ruth Meyer

Some six weeks later in Louisville, Kentucky, NBC tested my idea, using as talent, Bernard Meltzer, a successful talk show host of WOR. To say that I was fit to be tied, ticked off, or whatever, is a gross understatement. I did my very best to get into see Ms. Meyer; however, NBC at Rockefeller Plaza had then and still does have in place, a rather formidable security system, one that I was unable to crack! I remember clearly standing out in the rear of the building just adjacent to the ice rink and in my very mature manner gave the building the middle-finger salute and said, "Someday this will cost you." Some years later when I was renewing a contract, I reminded the management team of this little incident and indeed that debt was paid.

In the radio business, I have heard so many "wanna-be" talk show hosts say, "I sent the program director a tape. What more can I do?" You've got to be kidding. When I first aspired to get into the radio business, I literally attacked Tony Morano, who was eventually my mentor in this business. Tony was the general manager of WCTC and WQMR, in New Brunswick, New Jersey, a Greater Media outlet. I knew Tony reasonably well socially and his locker was next to mine at the YMCA. But the health club was no place to try to do business, particularly with not-quite-middle-aged guys running around buck-naked. It took me well over a year and a half of constantly haranguing Tony before he was amenable to sitting down and seriously talking to me.

A little further on in my career, I had ambitions of working in New York City. Doesn't everyone in broadcasting? At that time, there were only two talk stations in New York, WOR and WMCA. WOR had a program very similar to the one I wanted to do, hosted by Bernard Meltzer. The advice I dispensed was very similar. Given that set of circumstances, the chances of employment at WOR were slim to none. There were two executives at WOR, whom I contacted even though I had a small shot. Both of these worthies I would get to know in future years, and both are very capable executives.

The first was the general manager of WOR at the time. And while he had no hope for me to get employed, there were at least two occasions when I called that he did make an appointment to see me. The other was Rick Develon. Rick has gone on to be very successful in station ownership, as well as working with some of the major companies. I must have called Rick on fifteen or twenty occasions but simply could not get through to him or make an appointment to see him. Some years later when my NBC contract was up for renewal, I got a call from ABC asking me to meet with them and talk over the possibility of making a connection with them.

We met in a restaurant called the Italian Pavilion with Rick, me, the president of ABC and one or two other executives. We talked for a while about whether or not we could come to an accommodation. I commented to the president of ABC Radio, "I wondered if things would have been different if Rick had spoken to me some years before." He asked, "What's that all about?" and I recounted the story that I had applied to WOR on numerous occasions for a position but never saw Rick. The executive turned to Rick and said, "You #!*#*, you had a chance to hire him and you didn't?" It was a sweet moment for me, as you could understand.

This enterprise is fiercely competitive and it is frequently very difficult to get to the makers and the shakers. It is difficult to tell you how disappointing this can be. But then if it were easy, everybody would be doing it. I certainly bear Rick no malice. He has been extremely successful in his career and we have exchanged pleasantries on many occasions, but on this particular occasion on that particular afternoon, I could say to Rick, "Gotcha."

So I attacked WMCA. I worked through two program directors, the second Mark Mason, who is still a program director in New York City. I sent Mark and his boss, the late Ellen Strauss, in excess of 500 letters over a two to three year period. I called the program director's office more than 3,000 times. No matter where I was, each business day I would call WMCA at least two or three times. More often than not, I would be told that Mr. Mason or his predecessor was not available, but I would leave a message. Some of my friends asked, "Aren't you afraid of ticking them off?" My rejoinder was simple and direct: "What do I have to lose? I don't have a job there now, they're not talking to me now, and they're not considering me now. So, if I tick them off, I'm no worse off than I am today."

I recall very vividly being in New York City for the Christmas season of 1978, buying some Christmas merchandise at the Toy Center at 200th Avenue. I even remember the gal whom I was dealing with because she mentioned that she was being divorced. She said, "You probably wouldn't know my husband, but he is in the clothing business. His name is Calvin Klein." In any event, during the course of the day I called WMCA my obligatory two or three times. When I returned to my office in New Jersey, Steve Belly, then a very young lad, now my business partner, said, "Mark Mason has called." I figured he was calling to return one of my calls and say, get off my back. When I called him, he asked me if I would like to come in and see him. Would I be interested in doing a show on Sunday?

You gotta be kidding? I would have killed four sacrificial lambs and eaten a snake to do a show on Sunday. As it happened, the Barry Farber show was not doing as well as it might on Sunday afternoon (Sunday being the toilet of radio), so I was offered a show from 2 p.m. to 6 p.m. I didn't have any idea what it paid — and I didn't care.

In those days, one of the things used in talk radio was called a "busy counter." After the incoming lines were filled (however many there were, usually ten or twelve), the busy counter would take over. The way it worked was simple. Every time someone called, a little meter clicked and it was recorded — one, two, three. After my four-hour show, which went reasonably well and had decent calls, we went into the studio where the "busy counter" was located. The producer assigned to me for the day was ecstatic. We had 260 busies, as memory serves me.

"Well, that's pretty good, I guess," I said.

"That's very good," she said.

"Only 200?" I asked.

"I've made a huge mistake, it's 2,260," she replied.

Let me tell you, that was no accident. I had enlisted the aid of all of my friends. I had them on the telephone for the entire four hours, dialing, getting a busy signal, and re-dialing. There was no way in the world I was going to have anything but a high busy count — this in the days of no automatic redial.

On Monday morning, when Ellen Strauss came in and saw the high busy count, a career was born. Mrs. Strauss could be extremely difficult to deal with. She was the "Mrs. Pynchon" of the radio business. If you remember the *Lou Grant* TV show, you will remember the character played by Nancy Marchand and know precisely what I'm talking about.

She was born to the purple, a member of the *New York Times* family and married into the Macy family. We certainly had our differences, but I was, and continue to be very grateful to Mrs. Strauss. While we often disagreed, I can never say I was treated unfairly. Clearly, my three years at WMCA contributed to my experience and my marketability, and ultimately to my winding up on the network.

In the early '90s it was determined that Ellen was suffering from cancer. I'd met her son Eric Strauss at one of the conventions and he confided in me that his mom was quite ill. I wrote Ellen a letter expressing my concern about her condition but more important I wanted to thank her for those things that she did for me during my career that helped me move in the appropriate direction. Like all of us, I believe, she made some poor judgments and some very good ones, but on balance, I think she made the right decisions for the family radio station.

With all deference to her husband, Peter, I think she was the more competent of the two in terms of their executive ability. We all have different strengths and weaknesses. The son, Eric, a very talented young man, is now managing some of the family radio stations. If my information is accurate, the fact that Eric was the son of the owners didn't cut him much slack. He learned the business from the ground up.

Sometimes having prominent parents can be a handicap. His sister, Jean, is happily married and not active in the business. Ellen Strauss passed away on February 24, 1995, and her funeral was attended by Who's Who in Broadcasting — a silent endorsement of the industry's opinion of Ellen Sulzberger Strauss. I take some considerable comfort in the fact I told her how much I appreciated her while she was alive, not at her funeral. A good lesson to remember.

After that came a number of bumps on the road. A good many years ago, when we first began thinking about doing personal appearances across the country, we had a little different approach, one that has been certainly refined over the years. My then-manager, Bill Lally, made arrangements with a couple of radio stations that would promote my appearance. We would pick up the expenses for the auditorium, travel and all that sort of good stuff, and when all the expenses had been paid, the revenue would be divided by some formula.

The first of these arrangements was in New Orleans, Louisiana, and it left a vivid memory. The year was 1984. It was during the New Orleans World's Fair, so I took my family with me, thinking I might as well take them to the World's Fair and make a lot of money at the same time. Well, we accomplished the first goal — we took in the World's Fair — but we most certainly did not accomplish the second. The station (which was relatively small and is no longer an affiliate) did promote the affair to the best of its ability — I have no quarrel with that. However, for whatever reason, and we were new in the business, we did not get the response that we had hoped. As a matter of fact, we had a huge auditorium in a hotel and about 125 people showed up. I cannot tell you how difficult it can be to perform in a large room with a few people. You can get all the funny lines off like: "Boy, you guys must be rich, because you each bought five seats apiece," but nonetheless, it is tough.

I remember with some fondness my son, Matthew, who came with me (I didn't want the rest with me because this was embarrassing), saying, "Pop, I was never so proud of you, because you just spoke like you had a full house." The old line, "You can only impress those who come, not the thousands who stay away," has to apply. I had to give it my best shot because they did pay and they were entitled to the best that I had. They got the best that I had.

The following week I was scheduled to do the same thing in Norfolk, Virginia. When I was in New Orleans, I couldn't draw flies. I went to Norfolk and not only did we fill the house, but we had to do two performances the same night. How do you explain that? Because of the success in Norfolk, we continued with the venture and it has worked out very well over the years for me, for our stations, and for our public. I enjoy getting to meet the public.

The point is, failing once should not dissuade you from trying again.

I am pleased that I am the beneficiary of a very forgiving system we have in this country. One can fail, and fail repeatedly, and still come back and try again and succeed. I have read somewhere that as an academic exercise Winston Churchill's school records were given to several schools that were asked if they would admit this person. On every occasion they said, no, this guy is going no place. Mr. Churchill fooled them, didn't he! Well, it may not be to that magnitude, but the same thing might be said of me.

My Mother, God bless her, kept many of my report cards starting with kindergarten and going right through high school. In the earlier grades it was clear that I was not going to be the conventional student, in more ways than one. I chuckle when I read the report cards, given the fact that I suspect those teachers, having long since gone to their reward, were pretty much on point. Of course, in other areas I might tend to disagree. Would you believe in kindergarten I flunked skipping and galloping? I like to think I have a fair degree of coordination.

Be that as it may, there is a common thread running through my early school report cards. I say "God bless my Mother." Had I received report cards like this from my children, I would have either been arrested as a child abuser or at the very least, had some very serious conversations with the offender. The common thread in my report card was this: I asked too many questions, talked out of turn, did not do well in subjects such as spelling but did exceptionally well when it came to contributing knowledge because I read so much more than my peers.

It seems to me a teacher would encourage kids to ask questions, however, I realize one or two students can dominate the classroom and that can't be allowed. If I had any success in this life, part of that success has been because I kept asking questions, kept reading and would not accept precisely what the establishment was willing to tell me.

In high school, for the first couple of years, for all intents and purposes, I failed completely. It wasn't that I couldn't handle the academic rigors of freshman or sophomore years of high school. It was simply that I had a different agenda. Nobody in the academic community at that time seemed to recognize that.

65

I worked every day after school. I was interested in starting little businesses. I had so much on my mind that worrying about algebra was of absolutely no consequence to me.

Once again my Mom and Dad must have had wings tucked away someplace under their clothing. If I was forced to sign a report card such as I brought home (on a couple of occasions I didn't bring them home – I managed to have the signature forged) I think I would have killed the kid.

I remember quite well when I turned sixteen years old, the principal of the high school was giving me a lecture and he suggested it might be better for me to leave (they had to keep you 'til you turned sixteen). I didn't want to go home with that story. As little as my Dad was home, I still believe he would have been able to take my quarter if I was chucked out of school. The windup was, I took the courses for all four years in the remaining two years and, while I didn't ace each course, I did get my share of A's and B's. I managed to cram them all in and graduate with my class.

All the dire predictions of my teachers in those years, fortuitously, have not come to pass. Eventually, I earned my bachelor's degree and did attend graduate school. The education process culminated in June of 1992, when my alma mater conferred an honorary doctorate of human letters on me.

The point of this discourse is: just because one fails or does not show great inclination towards academics, this does in no way diminish the possibility this individual has a good deal to offer and should be encouraged. I was lucky. With all of these failures, I still managed to put together a pretty good life. I encourage my readers to be a bit generous with those who march to a different drummer.

I have yet to meet anybody who has done anything worthwhile who hasn't failed many times. Consider a major league batter. If he hits .333, which is a phenomenal batting average, it means two out of three times he has failed. As long as the sum of the successes exceeds the debit of the failures, you are in tall cotton. If you are afraid to fail, don't play. If you don't have the intestinal fortitude to get up and try again if you fail, don't play.

Here is an example of what I mean.

On September 18, 1961, my wife and I opened a nursery school, which over the course of time, was expanded into a summer camp and the early elementary grades. Before opening the school, I had purchased a house on the G.I. Bill with no money down for around $10,000 — a princely sum at the time. I sold it for perhaps $12,000, giving us $2,000 to invest in this embryonic enterprise. To say that money was in short supply would be the understatement of the decade. I rented, with an option to purchase, a 16-room farmhouse situated on 26 acres of farmland. The farmland was lying fallow and debris was everywhere. In addition, on the property there were several outbuildings that had to go, as well as a building some 200 feet long and 50 feet wide that was used at one time for a commercial chicken operation.

In the course of straightening out the property, I took more than 200 two-ton truckloads of manure out of the building. The manure was literally from floor to ceiling. The chickens were allowed to live in there and continued to do their thing. In addition, there were huge piles of manure in front of the building that ultimately became known as the "long house." Today, it is air-conditioned and contains several classrooms.

The interesting thing, from my perspective today, is how difficult it would be to get rid of that stuff in this era. I'm sure we would have EPA considerations, toxic problems, etc. None of these things were an issue in those days. I remember hiring a backhoe to dig a hole where I threw all of the combustible debris from the property. For some six weeks, a fire raged in that hole, often burning asphalt, tiles, tar paper rolls and, of course, dozens and dozens of old tires. I had a smoke column going to several thousand feet. Can you imagine pulling a stunt like that today?

The non-combustible, non-metallic debris was buried, and I suspect is still there several decades later. The things that you don't realize when you are young and ambitious and want to get things done.

One of the sheds was jam-packed with Nineteenth Century pornography. I can attest that there is not very much new other than the type of clothing. The activities portrayed in the literature were very similar to what one would find in a modern pornographic magazine. Having no use for this material, I pitched it into the pit where we were burning everything. I came to find out later that material would likely have sold for more than the $52,500 I paid for the farm and building. Oh well, another missed opportunity.

I also destroyed thousands and thousands of postcards from the turn of the century, having no idea that they had any value. And, to add insult to injury, I had to pay someone to open up the packages of cards, because they wouldn't burn unless they were opened and fluffed up. I became aware of their value on a Saturday afternoon when I was cooking hot dogs at a Jaycee fund-raiser. It was a type of flea market where vendors would come in to sell their wares.

On a break from my hot dog duties, I was wandering through the vendors and I saw a guy selling antique postcards. I took a closer look. They were precisely the same kind of cards that, at that very instant, I was paying a teenager to throw into a fire, and the vendor was asking anywhere from $1 to $5 apiece. I threw down my apron, ran home and managed to salvage a few hundred cards. But once again, I suspect I burned more than the cost of the property. Oh yes, I did save hundreds of 1920s magazines. I thought they would have some value and indeed they did: waste paper value. So much for understanding what has value and what does not.

The clean up was slow and arduous in that the only labor that was available was my own. Adjacent to the main building were half a dozen rather stately, albeit neglected, shade trees. It took more than two years of intense effort to get rid of the debris around the building and cut down the weeds and scrub material before I touched those trees. Another challenge was to get rid of hundreds of bales of fence wire that had been allowed to lie neglected so that the vegetation had grown in, on, around and through them — a worthy project just to get the wire free from the vegetation that bound it to the ground.

— I took possession of the school on September 15, 1961, and opened for business on September 18, 1961 — a total of three days to get ready for action.

Before that, I had visited one Mr. Wolfson in Philadelphia. Mr. Wolfson was a vendor of preschool material. I had my wife and three children and everything I owned in a station wagon when I called on Mr. Wolfson at his place of business. I walked in with all the authority I could muster and announced that I was opening a new preschool and would, of course, want the very best of materials. Immediately, dollar signs clicked in Mr. Wolfson's eyes. That was what I intended. We wandered through his display area saying, well; we'll have three of those and four of these. We picked out unit blocks, refrigerators, children's chairs, cots, and a number of things. As a matter of fact, a very substantial number of things. The bigger the pile got, the happier Mr. Wolfson became.

After I made my selections — and I should tell you now that they were made very, very carefully with every nickel added up in my mind, but nothing committed to paper, because I was trying to show that I was nonchalant about this transaction, that money was not a factor — Mr. Wolfson asked, "Now, how will you be paying for this?" And I said, "Well, of course I'd like for them to be net 30 days." He was taken back and said, "I would like some kind of a down payment." He looked a bit perplexed because he could see the biggest sale of the week going out the door. And I said, "Suppose I give you my check

69

for 10 percent now." He thought about that, and agreed that would be satisfactory.

Now, you should know that I had done my calculations each item at a time, and I knew precisely how much 10 percent of the total would be, which was my entire bankroll. He said that he would have it delivered in a week or so. I said that wouldn't be necessary, that I appreciated the accommodation, but I was sure we could load it in, on and up to the roof of the station wagon. Everything went with me. I wasn't giving the mark a chance to change his mind. I had no intention of screwing him out of his money, but on the other hand, I knew doggone well I wouldn't be able to pay him in 30 days, not unless there was a huge rush for enrollment, and I didn't anticipate that happening. I might have been naive, but not stupid.

A month or so after we opened, when I couldn't pay the bill, I received an angry call from Mr. Wolfson. I told him I was sorry, but I just didn't have the money, and I would get it to him just as soon as I could. Well, one angry call followed another and I'd send him $50 here and $20 there. Finally, after about a year, we became "friends." "Hi, this is Mr. Wolfson down at the Play-Art Company. Do you think you could send me twenty bucks?" Well, he got paid off. As I recall, it took about two years, but he did get every dime. I am certain he changed his credit-granting policies as a result of this experience. I do hope so for his sake. Once again, this was a case of doing what was necessary to survive and to make the business work. I didn't have anybody to run to for money.

A couple of months into the business, I was desperate. The phone company was ready to disconnect my service, the utilities were screaming for their payment and, although for an embryonic enterprise we were doing okay, cash was at a premium. The rent had to be paid, the few employees I had wanted their money. Priorities had to be established. The chance of borrowing any money seemed slim to none; certainly no legitimate lender such as a bank was going to go near me for understandable reasons.

We were renting this building from Minnie Coronas, the owner of the building. She was a lot slower in moving out than she'd agreed to, but there was little we could do about that. The side effect of that was that she did give us a rent concession, which was welcomed. We were occupying the front of the building for the school and living quarters. My wife and I were sleeping on the floor, my children were sleeping on the nursery school nap cots and Mrs. Coronas was ensconced in the back part of the building. She was moving to a development house several miles away. Bear in mind, she had 16 rooms of furniture here and moving into perhaps a seven-room home. This was quite an accommodation and one she was having difficulty in making.

In any event, I saw a notice in the *New Brunswick Home News* mentioning that Beneficial Finance was opening a new branch in a Kendall Park, New Jersey, shopping center the following Monday. The notice gave the address adjacent to the National Bank of New Jersey, my bank at the time. Monday morning bright and early found me walking up and down the sidewalk in the shopping center in front of the newly opened Beneficial Finance office. I had deliberately set my watch back about seven or eight minutes. As I walked up and down, glancing at my watch, the manager of the new branch walked out and said hello, as I anticipated he would. He's opening up at 9 a.m. and looking for his first fish. Anybody who is opening a new business can appreciate that emotion. In any case, we exchanged pleasantries and he asked what I was doing.

"I'm waiting for the bank to open," I said.

"Well, the bank is open."

"No, not yet. It's only four minutes to 9."

"No, no, no, it's a couple minutes after 9."

"Oh, son of a gun, how did that happen? I guess my watch

must be slow. Better set it," which I did.

We talked for a moment, and he asked, "Do you need any money?"

"Money? Not really, but what are you talking about?" I asked.

"Well, I'm the manager of this new office here so let's go in and talk." Hmm, which fish had the hook in his mouth? In we went. Well, the windup was, the maximum that the New Jersey small loan laws would allow any one customer was $500, and very quickly I got the conversation around to how much $500 would cost me. It turns out it was $26.77 a month. I said, "You know, maybe I could use that $500."

"Maybe?" I was salivating.

The next question was, "Do you have any collateral?" I asked, "What's collateral?" knowing full well that I could have defined it better than he. He said "Something that we could kind of look to in case you don't pay us, like, do you have any furniture?"

"Well, yeah, I've got some furniture, of course, doesn't everybody have furniture?"

"Could I see it?" he asked.

"Sure you could," I said.

I called my wife and said Mr. so-and-so from Beneficial Finance would be coming down in a few minutes. Would she show him through the house? Now, I never said, "Show him our furniture," because our furniture consisted of a 30 year old refrigerator and a beat-up grand piano — that was it. What I did say was, "Show him through the house." Mrs. Coronas had not removed her possessions, items such as valuable antiques, Oriental rugs, a big freezer and refrigerators. He went down, saw all this stuff and assumed that it belonged to me. He was never told that it belonged to me, just that he could take a look through the house. I then proceeded to give him a mortgage on all of my furniture at R.D. 3, Box 365. Had he known his mortgage was on an old refrigerator and a piano it might have made him a little bit nervous, but in any event, I got the $500. It kept me afloat for another couple of months, and Beneficial Finance got every nickel to which it was entitled.

The fact is, had I gone to an existing office and requested a loan, the loan officer wouldn't have thrown me out — he would have probably had me executed. I knew that the new guy would be hungry. I also knew that I had to find some way to get him to come to me. Even a new guy would get nervous with somebody like me walking through the door.

This is an illustration of doing what had to be done to keep things going. My critics could clearly, and with some justification, say what I did was, at the very least, skirting on dishonesty, and I would have to agree with that. But unfortunately — or perhaps fortunately — I had nobody to go to. I had to work it out myself and I couldn't give up.

Not giving up was equally important. Some years ago, when I first went into the wholesale flower business, I determined that I would like to be the vendor in as many hospitals as possible in my part of the world. Happily, after sputtering somewhat, the business took off. There were a couple of hospitals, however, that I was unable to crack. At one of them was a lady who was particularly miserable and difficult to speak to. On top of all that, to add insult to injury, I had to park in the parking lot and pay 50 cents for the privilege. Every Monday morning my first stop was at that hospital. I paid the half of a buck, went inside, seldom got to see the lady and when I did, got abused, and went on about my business. I did that for the better part of three years. First of all, I figured I'd do it on Monday morning first thing, get it out of the way — the rest of the week had to get better. Second, as a practical matter, I was convinced that the competition, also trying to get in there, would call once or twice and give up, and I wasn't about to do that.

73

Well, one bright Monday morning, I was very much surprised to have her ask me to come in and make a full presentation, which I did. The windup was, that for whatever reason, I caught her on the right day, in the right humor and we opened what was to be one of my largest accounts for several years.

On another occasion I got on my car phone and called in to see what was going on and I thought, "Well, I feel like being abused, so I think I'll go see Mrs. Hurley."

Lillian Hurley was the buyer for Elizabeth General Hospital in Elizabeth, New Jersey. Getting to see Mrs. Hurley was a bit of an accomplishment. Her office was behind the food service area. In order to get into that food service area it was necessary to get past security. In the dead of winter (in New Jersey winters can be a bit on the raw side) I would park my car and walk to the hospital without a coat on. I'd go in with my tie loosened and my sleeves turned up a couple of turns. I'd walk briskly past the security guard saying, "Hello, Henry, how are you doing?" By the time he figured out his name was George, I would be 30 feet down the hall and he couldn't find me.

That's how I used to crash Mrs. Hurley on a regular basis. Once I got to her office, she would usually have something less than kind to say, and throw me the heck out. But, once again, nobody else was getting past Lillian Hurley either. She was a tough gal. She was also a very astute businesswoman. Very astute. She ran the hospital gift shop and snack bar in as efficient a manner as anyone I have ever seen. She even ran a beauty parlor in the hospital for the employees.

When I approached her office, cardiac arrest was near. Thank goodness I was in the hospital because I was told, "Come on in, Bruce, let's talk." It seems that she had just been reviewing her overall gross numbers, which were down, and she thought maybe we could help.

That was many years ago, and Mrs. Hurley has long since retired. But in the meantime, she became one of our biggest boosters and helped us get into other hospitals. We established

74

a relationship and years later she said, "The only thing I regret is that I didn't let you in many years before." The fact is, though, the only reason we got there was because I was persistent. I wasn't about to give up.

Now, not everything you try is going to work out. Oftentimes you get a germ of an idea, pursue it as far as you are able, and still it doesn't result in anything. Have you failed? Well, if that is a definition of failure, then how in the world would you characterize pure research?

Some years ago, it occurred to me that if an idea was a good idea, it ought to have a certain amount of, for lack of a better way of putting it, staying power. It seemed to me that rather than try to reinvent the wheel, why not do some research for the past 75 or 100 years and see if there's not some notion that we can retool and rework? I went to the public library in New York City and I dragged out all of the old Sears Roebuck catalogs.

I had a misconception of what Sears Roebuck was many years ago. Yes, it was a mail order house, but no, it was nothing like a general mail order house at the very beginning. Essentially, it was mail order for jewelry, watches, rings, necklaces, and that sort of thing. Moving ahead a few years, I was interested to watch the metamorphosis from a very specific endeavor, i.e., jewelry, into the general merchandise business. My idea was that maybe there were some toys that kids played with a million years ago that could be remanufactured and introduced to the current market, albeit with safety concerns, etc., in mind.

I spent a great deal of time in the library with a microfiche — most of the original catalogs are not available, at least in the New York Public Library, but the microfiche was. I spent a good deal of time going through the records to find the toy sections of those catalogs. Regrettably, unlike the more modern catalogs, there was very little devoted to the kids. There were farm implements and that sort of thing, and clothing, but few children's toys.

The point of this little revelation is that I spent a good many days going through these catalogs with absolutely no bottom-line profitability. I did not find anything but I haven't given up on that endeavor. I still believe there were things that interested our great-grandparents and amused them as children and adults that we could replicate today, and one day, I intend to pursue this with renewed vigor, time permitting.

I don't feel this was a waste. First, it was entertaining. Second, I learned a lot about how merchandising was done, what claims were made — and clearly, the claims that were made in those days would not be allowed under today's rules. One interesting note is that in the earlier Sears catalogs the writers told readers that only a fool would shop at a retail store with all of the attendant overhead. The smart people would order by mail and reap the savings. Wouldn't it be fun to post those same notices in the stores of one of our nation's largest retailers? But then that also underscores another truism: Times change and you have to change with them.

A business practice that you eschew and, indeed, ridicule one day, may be your own the next.

Many years ago, I had an acquaintance, Ed Burns, who was the depot manager for a regional dairy company. He had about 80 milk routes working out of his warehouse. The drivers would pull in, fill up their trucks in the morning and deliver milk door-to-door to the ubiquitous milk box many of us remember from childhood. Again, here's another idea that has gone full circle. I am told that in many parts of the country, the milk truck is back. For a great many years, however, it disappeared from the scene. I remember vividly, when my firstborn arrived, (Matthew was born when I was a freshman in college) as poor as we were, and we were on the short line, we nonetheless had milk and eggs delivered to our door.

I remember discussing with Ed the stores that then were known as jug stores. These stores, in essence, sold only milk and dairy products. They were the forerunners of today's convenience stores. Ed had nothing but unkind words to say about the jug stores and how people were crazy to buy their milk there. It was not too many months later when it was clear that the dairy stores were the wave of the future. The first thing you know, his company was operating a couple of dozen stores. When I asked Ed about it, since he was managing them, he just shrugged his shoulders and said, "Well, some days you wear brown shoes, some days you wear black." It was his way of saying that you've got to go with the flow.

For most to be successful, you simply have to run with your ideas. Try them out. Test new theories. The crude expression is "You throw enough stuff against the wall, and no matter how slick the wall, sooner or later some is going to stick."

That is true. Don't be afraid to explore areas where someone else tells you you're crazy. Don't be afraid to fail.

And if you do fail, don't give up! I have a propensity for getting very impatient with people who say, "Well, I asked them and they said, 'No,'" or words to that effect. You see, there is always a way to get things done if you put your mind to it. Now, sometimes things are important and sometimes they are less important. Here is an example of the latter.

Some years ago, I was scheduled to do a pilot for a television program in St. Louis, Missouri, on, as I remember, a Monday morning. I spent the weekend in Norfolk, Virginia, got tied up with some very bad weather and, as a result, got into St. Louis very late. I was staying at a Marriott Hotel, which was at that time noted for shutting down room service and everything else at 10 p.m. (That was one of the reasons I avoided Marriott Hotels whenever possible.) I like to be able to get something to eat when I check in, no matter what the hour.

I had to do a flight miracle around a storm to get out of Virginia, so I got into St. Louis in the wee hours of the morning. I got into the cab and asked the cabdriver if there was someplace where I could grab something to eat, and he said, "Well, most everything is closed." I said, "Wait a minute. Isn't St. Louis a White Castle town?" He said, "Yeah, they're open," because White Castles are open 24 hours a day. Now, those greasy little sliders are a real weakness of mine. Some years ago I used to do a commercial for White Castle, telling people they could order those great hamburgers they had grown up on by dialing 1-800-W-CASTLE. In the commercial I used to say, "My kids will swear that I know every White Castle within 25 miles of my home," and that was absolutely true. So down we went to a White Castle before I checked into the hotel.

Those of you who remember, a significant number of White Castles were located in neighborhoods where you needed two armed guards and an Uzi for safety, particularly at 1 or 2 o'clock in the morning. This has changed some. We got to the White Castle and I was comforted to see an armed police officer at the door. I went in and ordered my greasy little hamburgers.

I went to the hotel content with the idea that I was going to dine in luxury. When I was firmly ensconced in the room, I was acquainted with a brutal fact of life. A White Castle created on the East Coast was quite different from one made in the Midwest. The difference was that on the East Coast, they put ketchup on your hamburger without asking, but in the Midwest you had to ask, otherwise you got the thing naked. What a pathetic sight! What to do? I called the bell desk and asked if they could provide me with some ketchup. The bellman was very polite and said, "I'm sorry, sir, the restaurant closes at 10 p.m. It will be open again tomorrow at 6 a.m." That was information I already knew and didn't want to hear again.

But this is where a little extra creative thought comes into play. I said to the young fellow who answered the phone, "I'll tell you what. In my right hand, right now, I have a $20 bill, and if someone were to put a bottle of ketchup in that right hand in the next 90 seconds, I'd be very happy to give them that $20 bill — but 90 seconds, and 90 seconds only." And I hung up the phone. A little over a minute later there was a pounding on the door, and here was a kid in a hot sweat with a bottle of Heinz Tomato Ketchup in his hand.

You see, lots of folks speak English, some speak French, some speak Chinese, but almost everybody speaks "Green." He just needed a little stimulation to make things happen. Sometimes you grease the skids with a little extra money, sometimes you grease them with kindness, sometimes it's a combination. But the fact is that ordinarily, if you think it out, there are ways to get the job done. Just because somebody says "No" the first time is no reason to fail to pursue it from some other angle.

Oh yes, we did shoot the TV pilot the next morning and, by mutual agreement, the project was dropped. I could not see myself running around in what amounted to a chicken pit, five days a week, sticking a microphone into people's faces and asking if they had slept with their minister or worn women's underwear to the office. I never could understand how guys could do that for a living, year in and year out. Amazing what we'll do for money, isn't it?

During the years I have been on a network we have gone through a number of ownership changes. In the formative years, from 1981 through 1986, we were owned by NBC, which was in turn owned by RCA. Down on the third floor was Howard Stern, the sixth floor Dave Letterman, and we were doing our thing from the fifth floor. Along about the end of that five-year period, Westwood One came in and bought the NBC network. From there we eventually became part of the CBS family.

Back in our NBC Radio days, I had a constant parade of producer-screeners. This is the norm for the enterprise and not something to be concerned about. One of the fellows who passed through was Mike Thompson. Mike and I have kept in touch. I still see Mike from time to time and regard him with a great deal of affection. Michael knows my show as well as anyone. He has a grasp of talk radio not shared by many. Anyone he works with will come away the better for it, if they pay attention.

One day, along about 7:30 Eastern Time when Mike was working the show, I was telling a story about a time when I was a junior in college. I was asked to try to find a stunt to promote the 100th anniversary of the township of East Brunswick, where I was living. As it happened, that day I read a small article about the George Washington Bridge. It said in essence, "Every toll contingency had been met except one." They had three-wheel bikes, four-wheel bikes, carts and whatever, but never had anybody taken any sheep across the George Washington Bridge.

Now bear in mind, this is 1960, so not too many herds of sheep are finding their way through the canyons of Manhattan. In any event, that seemed a natural to me. The following weekend, which coincidentally was Labor Day, we showed up on the New York side of the bridge with a truckload of sheep, a dozen or fifteen and, of course, we had our Judas goat. Everybody knows sheep follow goats right into the slaughterhouse. Right? Only problem was, our sheep had never heard of a goat! That wasn't too much of a problem given the fact that we had members of the Chamber of Commerce with a choke collar around each sheep, something like a dog's leash.

Well, clearly to get the publicity, we had to let the media know what was going on! We notified every television and radio station that we could think of to let them know about this colossal event coming off on Saturday morning. Interestingly enough, a whole bunch of folks showed up, including the late Dorothy Kilgallen, who at that time was a major celebrity on television. The bridge commissioner from the Port Authority was flown down from Connecticut by helicopter because of the

80

uproar we were causing. The ASPCA showed up and insisted that the joints across the bridge be covered with plywood so that the sheep wouldn't hurt their tootsies. All in all, it was a very interesting event. We walked our sheep, who seemed bent on suicide by trying to jump off the bridge about halfway across, and the goat was paying no attention to anybody.

Finally, the police said, "Okay, this is enough! Put your sheep on your truck and get them on the other side." I still don't recall if we ever paid the tolls for the sheep or just the truck. I can attest for one thing, however. Sheep, when excited, have a propensity for one physical activity. You can imagine what the back of that truck looked like!

I told this story, perhaps in a little more detail, and Michael was sitting behind the glass mouthing, "No way, you're lying." I assured him I was not. A little while later, on a break, he walked into the studio and said, "Son-of-a-bitch, you weren't lying." I asked, "How do you know that, Mike? What convinced you?" He said he called the Los Angles Public Library (three hours earlier by time zone) and had them look up the *New York Times* that week, "and there you were on the front page with a crewcut holding onto a sheep."

I made a believer out of Mike! It was fun to do that sort of thing. It was harmless. But, I'm not at all sure the publicity had one bit of impact on East Brunswick, New Jersey. Nonetheless, the idea was fun.

Prior to that, and more importantly subsequent to that, I have done many stunts to make my job easier, or in fact, to get attention so I can do a job. The blurb in the paper, that was the genesis of the stunt, was there for all to see the potential for exploiting. I must conclude the picture was seen by very few. This is how I see the world. How can a picture or event be viewed and used to my advantage? Think out of the box.

4

Curiosity

Some years ago, I was taking my youngest son, Michael, from school to school, trying to get him placed in college. One of the schools was the American University in Washington, D.C., and adjacent to American University was the studio for NBC Radio. At that time, it was owned by RCA. Radio station WRC, which carried my program at that time, was one of our "owned and operated" stations. The manager of that station was a gentleman named Jerry Nachman, whom I've come to respect for many reasons. Jerry has been, among other things, the general manager of a San Francisco station and WRC in Washington, a vice president of NBC, a vice president of CBS and the editor of the *New York Post*. Obviously, a man of no mean accomplishment, and one of the brightest individuals I have ever met.

In any event, he and I had just met for the first time and I told him why I was there, and he said, "Let me talk to your boy." Michael at that time was probably eighteen years old. Jerry brought Mike into his office and paid little attention to Michael's Mother or to me, and he said, "Michael, I've had some successes and I want to tell you some of the reasons I've been successful. I never paid attention to what my teachers told me." Michael just stared at him, as he expanded. "All of the things that they told me to do, such as stop asking questions, don't be so curious, I ignored. I was curious. There has been many a stupid answer, but never a stupid question. Keep talking, find out, never take the establishment's word for anything."

Think about that. How many teachers' say, "Sit down, Charles, you talk too much"? Well, Charles, not the kid who just sits there very quietly and docilely, is probably the guy who will be the winner in that class — the kid who asks the questions.

One of my favorite talk show hosts, Barry Farber, always ended his programs by saying, "Keep asking questions." I'm really sorry he did that because if he hadn't, I would have used it for my signature.

If I asked, how many of you are curious, I suspect that the overwhelming majority would say, "I am curious," and yet I am prepared to demonstrate that only a select few have the curiosity that I believe is essential to becoming successful — not to mention having a more interesting life! This addresses those of you who have flown commercially. If an aircraft is a smaller one such as a DC9, M80, or a 737, a flight attendant will lead you through a safety demonstration.

On the wide bodies now, the safety demonstration is on video. If you were to listen to the safety demonstration, someplace in the middle of it, it would say, "In the unlikely event of a sudden cabin depressurization a mask will fall from the ceiling above you or from the seat in front." The video shows the mask falling, and everybody is smiling and looking for their masks.

Now, you can bet in real life, they would have panic and terror in those faces! The video goes on to say, "In the event the mask is deployed, place the mask over yourself first," as the cabin attendant is demonstrating. (Notice the rubber band never touches that person's hair. That's the first thing they teach them in flight attendant school, never let the band touch your hair.) "If you're traveling with someone who needs attention, take care of yourself first, then see to their needs. Sharply tug the line; even though the oxygen is flowing the plastic bag may not inflate. Continue to wear the mask until such time you are told to remove it by a uniformed crew member." Now, we've all heard that pitch, however many times you have flown — a hundred, a thousand. I am prepared to gamble not one of you ever said to the flight attendant, "Why doesn't the plastic bag inflate?" Now, you'd be wasting your time, because the likelihood is, she wouldn't know. I have never found a flight attendant who did, and unless the crew — meaning the guys up front — was military trained, they probably wouldn't know either! Why the bag does or doesn't inflate is not an issue here. The issue is, how can you hear what is apparently a contradiction, time after time, without once questioning it and asking for an explanation?

Some years ago when I was working at 30 Rockefeller Plaza, the RCA Building, now the General Electric Building, I received a note that read, "Please excuse me for writing on company stationery, but I am on my lunch hour," and she went on to ask me a question, as many listeners do. At the end of the letter she closed with, "I only wish we had someone like you here at NBC."

Hmm, seems to me I'm working for NBC. Well, 30 Rockefeller Plaza is a very large building, seventy stories high, but then I looked at the address. Lo and behold, she is on the fifth floor; I'm on the fifth floor. I did meet her and she was a very pleasant woman, a very intelligent woman, and an executive working in the operations center for NBC Television. If you left my office, about forty feet to the left was her office, and she worked evenings. In short, she would walk past the door where I was doing my program live, certainly twenty-five to fifty times every night, five nights a week, and yet she wasn't curious enough to ask what was going on behind that door. Amazing?

Well, the folks at NBC wanted to use this story in their promos but I would not allow her to be embarrassed, I am sure she has long since retired — I am out of Rockefeller Center, something in the order of 15 years, so I am confident we cannot trace this story back to her now — but the point is, how could you walk past a closed door twenty-five times a night and not ask what's in there? It used to say Edit Room B on the door. How in the world could you do that? How could you walk past something like that without opening the door or knocking? What's going on in there? I could never do that.

— My former boss, Maurice Tunic at NBC, who is now the executive producer of the Sally Jessie Raphael television program, was once assigned to go to a leadership conference. This is one of those deals that management cooks up where they take all of the executives to a motel or hotel in the middle of nowhere so there are no distractions, and they can talk management for a week or ten days. The benefit of these adventures is something that I think a lot of folks would question, but then that's another subject.

During one of the free periods, perhaps at the bar, Maurice met a fellow who had said that they both were doing essentially the same kind of work, although Maurice did his in radio and this guy did it in television.

The other fellow asked, "What floor do you work on?"

"Five," Maurice replied.

And the guy said, "Wow, I work on the fifth floor too. Where do you work?"

Maurice asked, "Well, do you know the radio studios?"

The guy had a blank expression.

Now, let me explain how the fifth floor was laid out. Inside a U on that floor were elevators on three walls, and everyone — no matter which elevator he exited from, whether turning left or right or going straight ahead — had to exit through the opening in the U. Directly in front of that opening was the quintessential, albeit antiquated, radio broadcast room with two studios enclosed in glass. In front of that was a huge desk with clocks for all of the major cities of the world proudly displayed and at least a dozen stations where reporters would be preparing their stories.

The system was set up so that you moved from position to position so that anyone could tell who the next on-air person would be in the event of an emergency. Signs saying "NBC Radio" were evident and anybody who has seen a movie from the 1930s or '40s surely would have recognized what this was.

In any event, this fellow went on to say, "Wow, that's a radio studio? I've always wondered what that was." Bear in mind that the fellow had worked at NBC and gotten off that elevator for more than 10 years and still didn't know what was inside this big glass enclosure. It boggles my mind to think that anybody could get off the same elevator for ten years and not inquire as to what it was. But you can believe this, our guy was not an executive who was going very far.

The fact that he couldn't figure out that it was a broadcast studio didn't say much for him, but if you couldn't figure it out, wouldn't you go over and knock on the door sometime during that ten years and ask, "What do you guys do in here?"

Curious? Not by a long shot.

A while ago I was touring the oil platforms off Santa Barbara, California. They all had these great macho names — "Platform Hondo," for example — and I was running around in a helicopter driven by this guy with about a size 22 neck. I was wearing my orange jumpsuit and going from place to place, the VIP trip — you know how that works. Well, when I got off the helicopter on Platform Hondo, I was met by a very young fellow who was my guide. You do a tremendous amount of walking up hill, down dale, on these oil platforms. I went to dinner and saw how it worked. You can get tired doing this. At the end, we were down in the bowels of this thing, in the command center, and it was time for me to go and get my helicopter, which was up on top. We walked up together and when we got there I was more out of breath than he, and I said,

"I've got $100 here." He said, "$100?" I said, "Yeah, just tell me how many steps we just climbed." He looked at me and I asked him, "How many times a day do you walk up those steps?"

He answered, "Four or five times."

"How long have you been here?"

"Two years," he replied.

"Two years, four or five times a day, how many steps?"

He said, "I never counted."

Well, I ask, why would you not? I counted them, and there were 102 steps. By the way, I can't walk up a flight of stairs more than two or three times without counting them.

Is that information going to make me rich? I don't know. Is it going to hurt me to have it at my disposal? Clearly not.

Some years ago, I was doing a personal appearance in Omaha, Nebraska. General Benjamin O. Davis Jr. had invited me out for a VIP tour. General Davis, commander of the Strategic Air Command at that time, was a West Point graduate, a player for the Army football team, and all together a really regular guy. In World War II, he was the commander of the Army Air Forces' black fighter pilots, the "Fighting 99th," whose story was told in the 1995 HBO movie, *The Tuskegee Airmen.* He went on to become the Air Force's first black three-star general.

After our VIP orientation, which was to my way of thinking, largely a propaganda exercise, I was taken to the underground command center. Bear in mind that I survived almost four years of what we laughingly called "Air Force Intelligence," albeit in an extremely minor role. I was told this was a highly classified area and, indeed, it was something out of a James Bond movie. We went into a hallway, up and down stairs, around corners, through security checkpoints. At each one of the checkpoints we had to be identified as to where we were going and the like. Finally, we arrived at our destination, well under the ground at Offutt Air Force Base. It was, in fact, a very impressive sight.

They had a big command board made up of a million lights, and on it was "Welcome, Bruce Williams," which impressed me, of course. There was a map of the world showing all of the military sites under their command, and they sent out an alert, (a practice alert obviously) and all of the little lights flickered on, meaning that each command post had checked in appropriately. They let me sit in the chair where the ultimate commander would be in case the United States was attacked — all very impressive. With all the lights and the people, it looked like something out of a war movie, a very expensive war movie. As a former corporal I was really impressed by having a full "bull" colonel carrying my raincoat. After we went upstairs, I commented to the colonel, "That's pretty interesting, that command center."

He replied, "Yes, it is."

I asked — and here I forget the number I used, so I'll just say "50." "Is 50 feet below the ground deep enough to keep it from any kind of nuclear penetration?"

His eyes widened, and he asked, "How did you learn that number? It's a classified number! Who told you? That is a very serious breach of security. Who told you how deep it is? You have to tell me, Mr. Williams, because we have to plug the leak."

I said, "Colonel, no one told me."

"Then how do you know how deep it is?"

"Well, it wasn't hard to figure. I just counted the stairs, plus and minus, up and down, and measured the height of the stair tread, and did the arithmetic."

That didn't seem like rocket science to me. I was curious as to how many stairs it would be down into this place, and I

counted them going down and I re-counted them coming out —
same number — and I estimated the height of the stair tread.
Curious? Yeah! Now, did that do me any good? Probably not,
but the fact is that I am always doing these kinds of
calculations in my head. Counting stairs, estimating how high a
building is, estimating the diameter of a pipe, asking why a
particular building was built the way it is.

Now, all of this may do you no good, but I promise you, over a
period of time, if you ask enough questions, some of the
answers will put you a cut above the rest, and that little bit of
an extra edge may mean you'll get the job or get the task
accomplished best. And hey, even if it never helps you, it
makes life more interesting, doesn't it?

I am willing to take anyone to the Holland or Lincoln Tunnel in
New York City. I ask only that they bring a huge pillowcase of
$10 bills, and I will bring a pillowcase full of $100 bills. We
will stop at the tollgate before the tunnel. We will approach the
drivers — only the people with New York and New Jersey
license plates, no out-of-towners — and ask, "How long is this
tunnel?" For everyone who can give me a correct answer, I will
give you $100. For everyone who gives me no answer or an
incorrect answer, you hand me $10. I will have my pillowcase
jammed full with your $10 bills in no time.

How anybody can drive through the tunnels on a regular basis
— and the people we would be talking to are, for the most part
commuters — without looking at the odometer, at least once, is
beyond my understanding. And yet, people will go through
those tunnels thousands of times, twice a day, five days a week,
fifty weeks a year for years, and never look at the odometer.
And the real tragedy is that at the Holland Tunnel there are
mile markers that will tell you how long the tunnels are. By the
way, they are both the same length. I'll let you look at your
odometer to figure just how long they are.

Curiosity is what makes it work. There has never been a stupid
question — though there are a lot of stupid answers. If you

don't understand, or if someone hasn't explained something thoroughly enough, or if you are just driving past an event or an object that you don't understand, stop and ask. It's amazing how much people can tell you, and oftentimes those in the know are flattered that you would inquire about their activity.

What I have come to find out is that all the bits and snippets of information that I have inquired about have left me in good stead. While I certainly can't tell you that a great deal of this information has ever done me any good, you never know when someone will ask you a question about something you've inquired about, and having the answer when no one else in the room does can help you in many environments, social as well as business.

5

Ingenuity

When you don't have a lot of money, you are obliged to make do with what you've got or be innovative. When I was starting and operating some of my first businesses, innovation was the name of the game. Sometimes, I have to think that my kids were a little cheated because they seldom have been forced to do that kind of innovative thinking.

On second thought, this is not altogether true. While my conniving and working things out, generally speaking, had a basis in dollars (even though I didn't have any!) my kids are forced to do it under other conditions.

When we were getting ready to open our nightclub on the Boardwalk in Walt Disney World some problems popped up that were quite unusual and clearly unexpected. Our deal with Disney was that we would put up a sum of money and they would furnish the club. The building belonged to the Disney organization. One of the things they were responsible for providing us with was the furniture.

We clearly dropped the ball by not monitoring this process closely. You could imagine our consternation when tables and chairs that arrived just a few days before opening were totally inappropriate. These tables might have been great for a Bennigan's Tavern, but they were far too cumbersome and large for a nightclub. Could you imagine a nightclub with 30-inch tables and heavy wooden furniture? I think not!

The windup was that my daughter, Robbins, had to make deals with different companies to purchase tables and chairs and pick them up at the factory with a three-day window. She also had to hand-decorate the otherwise drab tables in time for the opening. How she got it done I'll never know. But she got the task done. At the same time, some beer coolers were installed that had doors so big they couldn't be opened without touching the front of the bar. Through regular channels the suppliers told the folks at Disney it would take six to eight weeks to replace these coolers. My son, Michael, rented a U-Haul truck, drove to Atlanta, Georgia, and returned within twenty-four hours with the appropriate coolers ready to be installed.

In both of these instances, it wasn't because of the shortage of dollars, it was simply because mistakes had been made that had to be corrected. Oftentimes going through traditional channels will produce nothing but frustration. Both Robbins and Michael got the job done by working way outside the box.

Ingenuity was a lesson I learned young, and one of the best schools for that was a little place called the Service Drug Company.

I've had few regrets in my life, but one regret has always been that my children never had the opportunity of meeting Sam Laffer and Joe Shaffman, and that Sam and Joe never met my kids. Both of these worthy gentlemen passed away before my kids were old enough to be introduced to them.

Sam and Joe were the proprietors of the Service Drug Company on the corner of Park Avenue and Grove Street in East Orange, New Jersey. Two more different individuals would be difficult to imagine; perhaps that was the reason for their success. They complemented each other. What one could and would do, the other could not. Where one had strengths in a given area, the other complemented it with strengths of his own. Sam and Joe had been partners since the 1920s, running the drugstore. They had a profound effect on my life. They taught me more than I had ever learned in any formal educational setting.

Previously, I had worked in a drugstore, Remley's Pharmacy in the Ampere section of East Orange for Everett Price. After I was discharged from the Air Force, Bob Geyer and I wound up buying the place and turning it into a luncheonette, but more about that at another time.

I learned something about making do at Remley's, where we served sandwiches behind the soda fountain as well as confections. When I was 13, there was a shortage of mayonnaise, so we made our own mayonnaise out of mineral oil and eggs. We whipped it up in the back room and then put it into our tuna fish, which was really not tuna but bonito. In any case, it didn't taste bad, but I can imagine what this concoction of mineral oil might have done to the digestive tract of some of our patrons.

Mr. Price became ill. I was no longer working there. I applied for a job with Sam and Joe because it was known that they hired lots of young guys to work in their store.

During the interview with Joe, we talked about the hours and what I would be expected to do: jerk sodas, make deliveries, put stock on the shelves and, in short, do whatever had to be done. Then we came to salary. Joe asked me how much I thought I should be paid. With my heart in my throat, I said, "I think I'm worth at least 35 cents an hour." Joe looked at me solemnly and agreed that was a good number. I was as happy as a pig with his snoot in the trough, because they would give me all the hours I wanted. In those days, we weren't quite as protective of our youth. I used to work after school from 3 p.m. to usually 10 in the evening, later on Saturdays and frequently, a half to a full day on Sunday.

It was behind that soda fountain that I was to meet a 14 year old young woman who later became my wife of 28 years and the mother of our five children. That young woman was a lady when we married and was a lady when we decided to separate and divorce.

Working with Sam and Joe was an adventure. Joe was Phi Beta Kappa, Rutgers University, a philosopher by nature and a registered pharmacist. Sam, on the other hand, to my knowledge never completed high school. In fact I'm not even certain that he ever saw the inside of a high school. But a more astute businessman you would never meet. Sam also compounded prescriptions with the best of them. Happily, from his perspective, the drugstore had a phone, and if the Board of Pharmacy was going to make an inspection, the phone would ring, Sam would go home and Joe would take over. In the five or six years that I worked in the drugstore, never was Sam there during an inspection — what an amazing coincidence. Of course, in those days being a druggist was quite different from being a druggist today.

While today there are many more complex remedies, the difference is that today's pharmacist will take tablets, capsules and other medications from a large bottle and put them into a small bottle, put a label on it and put it on the racks.

In those days, prescriptions were actually mixed in a mortar with a pestle, and I remember many a time watching them make tablets. It was done in the following fashion: They would mix whatever the ingredients would be with a mortar and pestle and add a small quantity of water for a binder. Then they laid a glass plate on the counter. On top of the plate was put a metal plate with holes in it the appropriate size and depth for the medication prescribed. Then they would take a spatula and fill up all the holes in the plate, scrape off the excess with the spatula, put the material back in the mortar and put another glass plate on top and allow the tablets to dry. When they were dry, they pushed out the tablets and put them into a bottle. I spent many an hour filling prescriptions in that fashion at the tender age of 15 and older.

It would be difficult to go into the Service Drug Company in those days and ask for something they did not have. There was a Post Office substation, every type of hardware you could think of and, of course, the prescription department. And don't forget other items that one associates with a drugstore, including the soda fountain with perhaps eight stools. In the corner was a large cigar case with enticing aromas coming forth. The cigarettes and candy bars were appropriately displayed.

Newspapers were an important part of the neighborhood. I remember the *Newark Evening News* had four or five editions a day, starting with the State and ending with the Sports Final. People would stand waiting for the latest edition of the newspaper. There were many more New York newspapers in those days; the list included, but was not limited to, the *New York Times*, the *New York Daily News*, the *New York Mirror*, the *New York Sun*, the *Telegram,* the *Journal American*, and the *Herald Tribune*, and each had to be sorted and displayed.

Putting together the Sunday newspaper was an adventure which I still think is shared by many a young man or woman today — though more often in a convenience store than a drugstore. The drugstore was a meeting place and on Sunday morning after church, it was an obligatory stop to pick up the paper and enjoy a chocolate Coke. Of course, your Coke at Sam and Joe's wasn't, necessarily, Coca-Cola.

During the period after World War II, but before the Korean War, often there was a shortage of Coca-Cola syrup. The Coca-Cola Company says that because of sugar rationing, its product may not have been readily available in all markets after the end of the war and may even have been rationed in certain places. That did not slow Sam and Joe down. We used to go into the back room and shut the door. We would melt down sugar and water and concoct something with different ingredients that they would conjure up from the drugstore and make our own cola syrup. It didn't taste too swell, but when you mixed chocolate syrup or cherry in it, for a chocolate coke or a cherry coke, it got us by.

The name of the drugstore was Service Drug, and did I learn about service! Sam and Joe gave service. If you wanted a half pint of ice cream delivered, they would deliver it — "they" meaning kids like me and, for a number of years, it was me. Have a prescription? They would go pick it up, fill it and then deliver it. And, everything could be charged, though there were no credit cards at that time, only "house charges." Something as small as a pack of cigarettes could be delivered in a pinch.

One of the infrequent visitors to our drugstore was a very young fellow, younger than I, with his famous father. When his father showed up, all the kids in the neighborhood would hear that the Colonel was there, and they would race in for an autograph or at least a glimpse. The Colonel was the former head of the New Jersey State Police and the host of a radio program called *Gang Busters,* a very popular shoot-'em-up thriller of the day. The Colonel's mother lived across the street at 262 N. Grove Street, and he would come to visit his mom and bring his son along. The son grew up with a good deal of fame; you will remember him as "Stormin'" Norman Schwarzkopf of Gulf War fame. The General's dad, Colonel Schwarzkopf, was the first commander of the New Jersey State Police.   He became famous with the arrest of Bruno Hauptmann, the kidnapper of the Lindberg baby. "Old lady Schwarzkopf" was one of our regular customers to whom I delivered various small items during my tenure with Sam and Joe.

Sam and Joe were the masters of gerry-rigging. It is difficult for the current generation to imagine, but there were acute shortages of just about everything during World War II. Filling all those pent-up needs took years. As a consequence, building materials and the like were in very short supply during the late 1940s and early '50s, but that didn't stop things from wearing out. I remember spending many an hour in the basement of the drugstore taping up pipes that had just completely rotted out. I would cover them with oil-based paint in layers, allow the paint to dry, then apply more tape, more paint, more tape, more paint. I often wonder what was the final disposition of that plumbing system.

Finding ways to make things work under severe constraints — shortages of supplies or, more often today, money — was a lesson that stood me in good stead when I struck out on my own.

A small business, unlike a big one, absolutely demands ingenuity. Big business, I am persuaded, succeeds many times in spite of itself, rather than because of itself. It does so by spending enormous sums of money, or to put it another way, throwing money at its problems.

The budding entrepreneur simply does not enjoy that luxury. You have to make do with what you have. Let me give you two examples of that in terms of my building the nursery school, a time to which I continue to return because it illustrates so clearly the pressures on the brand-new, undercapitalized businessperson — and that was the period in my life when I was both new and undercapitalized. It doesn't matter whether this happened three weeks ago or thirty years ago, because the same conditions, whatever your stage of life or whatever your enterprise, must be dealt with.

My first problem, and I had to deal with it quickly, was drainage. I had a big field next to the main school building. For many years this had been a farmer's field growing various crops. When I first took over the school I, like the former owner, rented the field to a local guy to grow soybeans and such. Then the time came when I chose to make this into a playing field for my expanding enterprise. Although as a youngster of thirteen I had driven a tractor on a farm, I didn't have a clue how to properly operate one. But I did borrow a tractor, a plow and a disk from a friend and proceeded to plow and disk the field. With the knowledge I have today, I could have done a far better job, but this is the way you learn. I don't think I had ever driven a tractor with a plow and disk before that week I graded the field.

As a consequence, the grading was not pool-table smooth. There were some swales out there that did not cause any difficulty in terms of a large playing field but did cause severe problems in terms of drainage. The field by this time was seeded, well sodded and kept as a lawn, but when rains came these swales would fill up with water in substantial quantities, many thousands of gallons. And that wasn't the worst part! For whatever reason, when that water went into the ground in the field, it would find its way into the basement of the school, causing me industrial strength problems. During the rain, my basement was dry as a bone, but four days later, when the fields would finally give up the moisture, allowing it to seep into the ground, it would find its way through the shale right into the basement. I sometimes had as much as a foot of water. Clearly, this had to change.

I talked to my late friend Bob Pierry about this problem. Bob, an engineer, figured fixing the problem would cost as much as $10,000, which might as well have been $10 million. No way.

After some thought, I figured I could get the job done for a little bit less money — "a little bit" meaning a total less than $500. With one of my employees, I dug a rather large hole at the very lowest point near the school building. It was strategically located so that the various low water points were not too terribly far away. I lined the hole with cinder blocks. At the bottom I put in several wheelbarrows full of crushed rock. I then put a grate over the top surrounded by concrete with several Orangeburg pipes going into the drain, each one on a slight incline from our low spots. Now, when the water collected in the swales, it would immediately go into the drains that I built and into this pit. In the bottom of the pit was a very simple and inexpensive Sears Roebuck submersible pump, which would kick on when enough pressure was built up by the water above it. The pump was connected to a plastic pipe that led to a ditch that was about 50 feet away and that was pitched in the right direction to carry the water off. For the next dozen or so years, I had a perfectly dry basement and a dry field. The only difficulty was that from time to time debris had to be cleaned out of my catch basin. Sometimes the pump would clog up. The biggest problem was that the kids kept running softballs down the pipe, which sometimes had to be cleaned out.

The pump had to have a breathing tube, and in order to camouflage it; I built a little bench around a nearby tree where I had the electric outlet for the pump. The bench let people sit, but more importantly, it kept the breathing tube out of sight and out of little people's clammy paws. They probably would have filled it up with dirt, disabling the system.

The point is, if I'd had plenty of money, I'd probably have let Bob do his thing, which was arguably the proper way to get it done. There was no way in the world that I could have spent all that money engineering and installing appropriate drain systems by gravity. My little pump under the ground in the drain worked for at least the dozen years that I continued to operate the school, and I have no way of knowing for how long afterward, perhaps to this very day.

At the same operation, we had a septic tank close to the building and not terribly far from our well. The septic tank was built for a home, not for hundreds of children, and as a consequence, it simply could not handle the volume of wastewater. The soil in that area was not the best for percolation. There are a lot of things you are supposed to do in a situation like that, but I could not afford any of them. So this is what I did. I dug a ditch about 200 yards toward the rear of the property, but still a half-mile from my rear yard line so I was not offending anybody. I took a backhoe, dug a hole the size of a small swimming pool, filled it with debris and put a pipe into the hole. I bought a fairly large electric pump and put it into the garage, then pumped the water from the septic tank out to this huge pit, which could take water forever. In order to monitor the water in the pipe, I bought some Louisiana Hot Sauce. It came in a long thin bottle. With a glass saw I purchased at the hardware store, I cut the top and bottom off the bottle and inserted it into the pipe so I had a viewing window to check the progress of my twice-daily pumping. I'm confident the Board of Health would have had apoplectic fits, but the thing worked. It was sanitary and it got the job done for relatively little money.

The same principle applies to many other situations. When I had my first swimming pool, I built my own filter out of a 55-gallon drum, some sand, gravel, charcoal and an old washing machine motor. It worked! Now, in today's world, I suspect that my kids, who do things far more efficiently than I, would call the filter company. "Hello, filter company? Send us the Rolls Royce of your filters. Oh, on second thought, better make that two — we may need a backup." I didn't have the luxury for that kind of order, so I had to make do with what I could.

Now, I believe in using experts, particularly in legal, accounting and medical matters. But in other areas, especially when you are a budding entrepreneur, you may have to disregard the experts' advice, simply as a matter of survival.

Many years ago, I had an old barn that was leaning at about 15 degrees. Clearly, something had to be done pretty quickly, or one night I would come out and the barn would be lying flat on its back, something I couldn't afford, as I needed that pool barn for dressing rooms and storage. I talked to several engineers who told me there was no way to salvage this barn without a major renovation and guy wires and all sorts of things I could not afford.

I rigged my own solution. I found a large boulder, dug a hole and dropped the boulder in. That gave me a solid footing. Then I nailed 2-by-10 boards across the front of the barn to spread the load and rented a huge hydraulic jack, connecting the jack with a 4-by-4 post to the 2-by-10's on the side of the barn. I braced the jack against my rock in the ground. With a few turns of the jack the barn was up, straight as a string. Then it was simply a matter of going inside and nailing boards at an angle across the supporting members. I gently took the jack away and the barn stood for some 20 years in a perfectly upright position — all at a very modest cost. It probably violated every rule of engineering, building codes, etc., but it got the job done.

Innovative thinking is an absolute prerequisite to success, particularly when you are riding the short line — in other words, when you are short of money.

In a similar vein, long before Judge Green made what I ended up doing legal, I built my own telephone system at the school. I had a number of reasons. For one thing, I couldn't afford to have the phone company put in a lot of extensions. For another, they wouldn't do it the way I wanted it done. All of my utilities, water lines and communication lines were underground. I was ahead of my time in that regard.

This is how I did it. Whenever I was going to put a line in, let's say electricity to an out-building, I would dig a ditch, lay a plastic pipe of perhaps 2 inches in diameter, and bury it. Before putting the pipe into the ground, I had run two or three fishing lines through so I could drag the electrical line through. We would use one fishing line to drag a second through and drag that one backward so we always had the same number of available lines to pull new material through the pipe.

In any event, from the main electrical source in back of the building I could pull through not only electrical lines but also a small water line and have all of my services underground. They were under the frost line and, more importantly, not available for the kids to get into.

I wanted to do the same thing with telephone extensions. The telephone company refused, saying the lines had to be above ground where they could be serviced, unless I wanted the company to install underground conduits at some exorbitant price. I wasn't going to do that and, furthermore, I didn't want to pay for all of these telephones. Consequently, I acquired — I don't remember where, probably through some less than proper means — enough telephones to do the job. I had several phone lines coming in. These were single-line phones so I bought small switches at a supply company and hooked the phones up so that by turning a little switch I could go from line to line. I also put in what amounted to a paging system through these same conduits. After that, I had phones in the barns and the outbuildings, a couple on trees inside secure boxes — all over the school.

The telephone company took a very narrow view of this activity. By using some kind of resistance system, it could detect the fact that instead of having the appropriate two or three instruments on my system, I had perhaps a dozen.

One day, two guys showed up at the door, both wearing green jackets. "We're from the telephone company," one said. "My name is Walter Duff." I have forgotten the other guy's name, but Walter Duff I came to know. About the same time I was mayor of my community, he was mayor of a neighboring community. I said, "Yeah, what are you here for, gentlemen?"

"We've got to inspect your phone system." I knew exactly where that was going. I was also aware of the law, which said that they had to come at a reasonable time, and the middle of the day was a reasonable time, and that they had to give reasonable notice. Aha, they hadn't given me any notice! I said I would be very happy to let them inspect my phone system. "Would an hour and a half from now be convenient?"

"We'd rather do it now."

"No, that doesn't work for me, I'm kind of busy, and you know you have to give me notice."

They raised an eyebrow, but they left and I went downstairs. It took me no more than five or ten minutes to remove the alligator clips tapping into the phone system, roll those wires up, and put them out of the way. When they came back, I said, "Gentlemen, take a look at the board." Well, they looked at it and knew exactly what was going on, but there was nothing they could do about it.

A week or so later, they came back — same caper: Come back an hour from now. I undid the wires. When they finished their inspection, I said, "Fellows, we've got to sit down and talk."

I said, "I think you are the same Walter Duff who is the mayor of Metuchen."

"Yes."

"Well, I'm involved in Franklin Township politics. Guys, you know what I'm doing and I know what I'm doing. I'm doing it for a purpose. It doesn't hurt you, it doesn't deprive you of any revenue, and all of the phones that I have installed, albeit somewhat clandestinely, are compatible with your phone system. As a matter of fact, they are all AT&T phones made by Western Electric. Now, we can go on and play this game for the rest of the time that I am in business, which I hope is a long time."

Finally, Mr. Duff said, "Off the record, show me what you have done, and it will strictly be off the record." I said sure, why not, and I took them out to the barns and the various outbuildings to show them the phone system I had built. It was a bit crude by today's standards but it worked just fine. Duff said, "You know, I think you built a better system than we could build for you." I was complimented. He said, "Well, we've got to get around this some way. Tell you what; would you mind paying a bill like $150 for equipment installation? That way, this will legitimize your system and we'll be off your back and we don't have to worry about this anymore." I think we negotiated it down to about $100. The next month there was a $100 charge on my phone bill for phone installation, and that was the end of it.

When I did my first building renovation, I didn't know a piece of drywall from volcanic ash — never heard of the stuff. But you learn how to do things by looking around, just seeing what other people are doing and, most of all, making tons of mistakes. When we first opened the school there was no question about who was going to do the maintenance repairs, additions or whatever. Me! I worked cheap! You also should understand I was essentially a city guy, although I did live in a suburban setting for a couple of years prior to finishing my undergraduate work. I didn't have a clue about what some of the relatively common materials used today were. As an example there was drywall. I didn't know the first thing about the stuff, but I was having a new bathroom put into the school. I was very proud. Now I had boys and girls bathrooms, not unisex.

I was watching the mechanic whom I hired to put the thing together and he was cutting the stuff up like a jigsaw puzzle and slapping it up on the walls, using all the scraps. I thought, what in the world is he doing? It's going to look terrible! Well, of course he spackled the joints of the scraps very carefully, sanded it down and when it was painted you couldn't tell the scraps were used. You could bet this; from that time forward I knew how to put up drywall. This is the way you learn, from someone else or experimenting. Never be afraid to experiment. All you could do is foul something up. There's no reason in the world to worry about that! I have never met anyone, who has done anything, that has not at one time or another failed.

Never stop asking questions. I didn't have a clue about the telephone until I took one apart to figure out how it was wired and what I would do. I had never had a random thought about a swimming pool filter until my lack of money forced me to build one. If you just ask people what they know about things, it's amazing how readily agreeable they are to sharing that knowledge. A little bit here and a little bit there, the first thing you know, you get the job done and at a price you can deal with.

There is an old expression, "If you get a bag full of lemons, make some lemonade." I'm not certain that's always possible, but I am certain that it is possible to turn what is an apparent negative into at least a neutral and, sometimes, a positive.

When we opened our first nightclub in Pittsburgh, Pennsylvania, at Station Square, we took over a restaurant. A bar was in place. We subsequently added a second, along with the doors and the bathrooms. This was a major advantage over going into a vanilla box and putting in all these things. The restaurant was an Italian restaurant that served pizza not only inside, but also through a walk-up window that opened into the mall and was covered only by a folding canvas door. While that was appropriate for the restaurant, it was inappropriate for us.

Our lease arrangement with the mall required anything of ours facing into the mall to blend in architecturally with what was already there — an understandable and not unreasonable requirement, but difficult to deal with. Most of the windows in our section were of smoked glass that would be extremely difficult to duplicate. Furthermore, since the orifice that we had to fill up was of an odd size, even if we squared it out it would still be very costly, somewhere in the area of $10,000. This was more than we could afford. I sat and looked at that hole for the better part of half an hour one day, trying to figure out what to do with it. Suddenly, I had a notion. I called my good friend Kenny Langdon, gave him the dimensions of the hole and had him build a piano keyboard in perfect scale with that hole. My daughter, Robbins, set the keyboard in place with some molding, filled the rest of the hole with wood and painted in a huge upright piano in scale with "Jellyrolls" written across the top. That piano is there to this day.

The keyboard is about 9 feet long, with pedals and all. It's amazing to watch people walk up and, when they think no one is looking, push on one of the keys to see if it works. The point is that we now had a great piece of advertising material at about 20 percent of the cost of replacing it with glass that, at best, would have looked very pedestrian.

We took what was a heavy-duty liability and turned it into, at worst, a neutral. And, in my opinion we made it an asset, since almost no one walks down that mall without noticing that piano. I wish we had something in all of our locations equally eye-catching at that kind of a price. It is not unusual to spend $15,000 to $20,000 for a neon sign to attract some attention, and while the signs are great, that piano is better than any sign we have ever purchased.

When you don't have the bread, you have to have the ingenuity.

Ingenuity doesn't come in handy just in making an existing enterprise go. You need it when deciding what to do in the first place.

I believe that there are many ways to make a buck if you are sufficiently motivated to discover what they are. And because of that belief, when I am doing personal appearances and someone laments, "That's all very well, Bruce, you were lucky to be born at the right time; there are no opportunities like that today," I always offer the following proposition — which, by the way, no one has ever accepted.

I am prepared to wager $1 million (and I would expect the person accepting the wager to match that amount, depositing it in some type of escrow account) that I could go to any U.S. community of decent size with only three things — a valid driver's license, an old truck and a couple of thousand dollars in cash — at a season of my choosing, and I would earn $40,000 inside one year. I would keep records, not use any influence, my name or any educational credentials, but nonetheless, with the sweat of my brow and the use of my wits, I would make at least $40,000 that first year. (And let me tell you, I think I could do it in a couple or three months; I give myself a year because I always like an edge.)

You might ask, what would I do? The answer is, I don't know. I really don't. I do know that I would look in the poorer sections of the community for opportunity, because that's where I know it will be.

The first thing I would do would be to buy the local newspaper and read the classifieds which, if properly read, can tell you more about a community than a front page or the sports page. It is my contention that there is opportunity everywhere. All you have got to do is open your eyes. It's true that you may be a little frailer in your older years, so you may have to make some adjustments. As a child, I could shovel snow for 16 hours during a blizzard; I clearly could not do that today. I hope that I have accumulated enough knowledge along the way to offset the decline in my physical abilities.

With a little ingenuity, anyone can find opportunities to profit just about anywhere. Let me give you an example.

I commute regularly between my offices in New Jersey and my offices in Florida, on a weekly basis, sometimes even twice a week. I take the occasion on the New Jersey end to have my former employee and now business partner, Steven Belly, drive me to and from the airport. I'm not trying to make him a gopher, but the drive gives us a private opportunity to talk about our business endeavors without interruption.

I have mentioned Steve before, but let me say a little more about him here. Something on the order of a quarter of a century ago, I was advertising for a florist to work in our Franklin Park shop. A lady applied and as it turned out the schedule or something was incompatible with her hours. She suggested we might want to speak with her son. Her son was seventeen years old and just finished florist school, although he had never held a job in the industry.

"Why not? We are looking for a warm body and maybe this is the answer." Well that is when Steve Belly and I became acquainted. Steven has worked with me for the past twenty-three years. He has been the manager of our New Jersey enterprises for a very substantial portion of that time. Steve is far more than an employee to me. He is a confidant and a very capable young fellow. He has done just about everything in our New Jersey operation from driving a truck, unloading Christmas trees, managing the stores, to bringing in new accounts. Steven is now my partner in those enterprises and upon my leaving this vale of tears; he will be the owner of these operations in their entirety.

How do you characterize someone who is far more then a co-worker, partner and employee? At the risk of sounding corny, I think of Steve as my fourth son. I cannot think of a higher compliment that I can pay him.

One day, on the way to the airport right after Christmas, we passed a cemetery. Steve and I had been making grave blankets — Steve more than I — for a good many years. (For the uninitiated, grave blankets are decorations for graves that are used at Christmastime, primarily in areas of European ethnicity. They seem to be unknown in many parts of the country, but making them is a very big activity in New York, New Jersey, Pennsylvania and other areas where many European immigrants have chosen to reside.) A grave blanket is simply a Styrofoam block lashed to a wooden block for strength. Greens (ordinarily balsam) are inserted into the Styrofoam, which is then decorated with plastic poinsettias, feathers, pinecones and a big ribbon. Go past a Christian cemetery on the East Coast and you will find thousands of these covers decorating graves. We sell them at our stores in New Jersey. I commented to Steve on the way, "I wonder what happens to that stuff now? Tell you what, Steve, on the way home, instead of going back to the office after dropping me off at the airport, go to a dozen cemeteries and see how they handle it."

The windup is, not only did we receive contracts for cleaning cemeteries, but we are also salvaging the pinecones, the boards, the poinsettias and the feathers from the grave blankets. We are salvaging thousands and thousands of dollars worth of material. Almost no one can tell that they have been used before, not that it makes a difference, and we can deliver a far finer product because our costs have been reduced significantly.

This is an opportunity that has been out there for years. It is hard for me to believe that very few people have taken advantage of it. Most of that material is going into the dump, at a cost to the cemetery. If push came to shove, I could make a living, a full-time living, in cleaning cemeteries during January, February and March and then reassemble the materials to sell either wholesale or in grave blanket form for the following Christmas. I wouldn't make a princely living, but I could certainly earn $50,000 a year or more doing that. Now, if that kind of opportunity can be seen at a glance, imagine what would happen if you really went out there and looked.

Here is another example that came up during several excursions to the Caribbean.

Like many people, I really enjoy my newspaper in the morning, and the *Island Gleaner* just does not do it for me. I want to read a major metropolitan paper, *USA Today* or something similar.

When visiting the Caribbean, I always had to wait either until late in the day or, more often than not, until the following day to a get a newspaper, and then I would pay $2.50 or $3, for a 50-cent item. I realize that economies of scale simply would not allow anyone to put up a print shop to print *USA Today* on a small island, even though it is done by satellite. Yet, there are certainly at least a hundred people, including tourists, who would pay a premium for a current newspaper. The problem is, where do you get one?

Let us explore the alternatives. You could have them air-freighted down on the morning flight from wherever, but the costs would be prohibitive. And, we know that we cannot afford to have them printed on-site. How then can we acquire newspapers at an affordable price and get them out to people the same morning they were printed?

Every day there are early-morning and midmorning flights arriving from the major metropolitan centers, and you can bet your life that hundreds of those passengers brought on board newspapers to read during the flight. It's equally true that the majority of those folks will leave the newspapers on the plane to be discarded when the flight arrives in St. Maarten or St. Thomas or wherever.

If I were living on one of those islands, I would make a deal with the airplane cleaners. All they have got to do is pick them up, not try to assemble them. Sure, there will be coffee stains, and maybe some of the crossword puzzles have been attacked. There may even be something torn out of a page here and there, but I guarantee you that someone like me would gladly pay $2 or $3 for a used newspaper on the day of publication, considering it a bargain over a virgin paper the following day.

The point is that you could take trash that is now being thrown away and turn it over for, I would bet, a couple or three hundred dollars a day in profit. Everybody wins: the reader, the cleaner, the vendor and you. What is wrong with that? Why it hasn't been done is something I'll never understand.

There are literally thousands of ways to make money that people just seem to overlook. Every time you suffer the frustration of an unmet need, there is a possibility of business. You should always think, "If I need this and can't get it, how many others are in the same boat?"

Speaking of boats, each time I have visited the island of Oahu in Hawaii I have made it my business to visit the Arizona Memorial, located in Pearl Harbor. As I'm sure you know this is the resting place of the battleship *Arizona,* and on the top of it is a very striking memorial operated by the Navy.

There is no cost to visit the *Arizona,* but one must wait one's turn for the boat that shuttles people out to the sunken battleship. The last time I was there you would walk up to a stand and take a number, which might be four or five boats down range. When they ultimately call your number an hour to two hours later, you go into a theater, see a film and then go out and board the boat. Immediately it occurred to me that some young entrepreneur in Hawaii might want to consider getting out there when it opened and get a number (which is free to the public and I don't believe they could restrict you and why should they, really?). When his number is about ready to be called he could walk up to someone who just got a number and say, "For $5 or $10 a ticket I will give you one ready to go in, and you won't have to sit here for an hour or an hour and a half." I can tell you I would have responded affirmatively in a heartbeat. Most people who are in Hawaii on vacation are spending a considerable amount of money per hour for the privilege of being there and resent sitting around waiting for their number to be called. Any shortcut must be applauded and most would gladly accept the offer.

In the meantime, the kid would take your number and do the same thing when your number came up again, and of course it can be worked out so you had one for every boat. At fifteen or twenty bucks a boat, he could make himself a decent living. I'm sure there are those people who would say, "But he's taking advantage of others." Not at all! If you want to wait for the hour or hour and a half, you have the privilege to do so, but if you want to trade your dollars for the time involved you also have that privilege, and he makes himself a buck or two. The example doesn't have to be taken literally, although I think it will work. The fact is, you have to look around with open eyes, not peering down a very narrow perspective. Get out of the box.

So let's say you've shown some curiosity and gotten an idea for making money. You're self-disciplined and willing to work persistently and hard. What are the pitfalls? What can help you succeed?

Read on.

Murphy's Law

W e've all heard of "Murphy's Law." What can go wrong will. I've traveled all over these United States for the last fifteen years and have tried to anticipate all of the problems that could develop. In the main, I've been very fortunate in that regard. Once burned, twice shy. Repetitive or single screw-ups are the spice of living, of course, after the fact.

Consider some years ago. I was doing a television appearance in Cleveland, Ohio. I had to do a live bit, (something on the order of 8 o'clock in the morning, on a program called *The Morning Exchange*) then a couple of tape shows, lunch and a personal appearance with the sponsors, then back to Newark Airport.

In those days when I made a quick trip like that I'd show up with nothing except my airplane ticket and whoever was traveling with me. I've come to learn that is a major mistake. I arrived at the ABC studios and inquired where the makeup rooms were. Ordinarily, in the bigger cities there is a makeup artist who will apply the stuff to your face and get your hair looking the way it's supposed to look. If you are not made up, television tends to make you look washed out. In any event, the people in the studio just pointed to the room with M-E-N on the door. I asked if there was makeup in there. The response was "No, you are supposed to bring your own." I had not heard of that custom before, nor have I since. I know I had to get something done to cut down the glare on my face; otherwise I was not going to make a very good impression. I should tell you when I am made up appropriately; I wear more makeup than Tammy Faye Bakker. When you get to be my age and have a face like mine, which is a great face for radio, these are things that you have to do in order to put your best face forward.

Now, I have an interesting challenge for you males. Walk up to a woman whom you have never laid eyes on and ask her if you can borrow her makeup! You are sure to get some very strange responses. One lady was very gracious and loaned me a bottle of what she termed "base." I didn't know what base was, but I was told if I put this on with a brush it would dry and accomplish what I was trying to make happen with respect to the glare. For those of you who are not familiar with base it's a brownish liquid with the viscosity of about forty-weight motor oil. I went into the men's room ready to do my thing, and I was spreading the base on my face when, somehow or other, the bottle got away from me. It slipped out of my fingers. The men's room floor was a good solid tile, so the bottle shattered when it hit. I had this stuff on my pants, on my shirt, on my tie, on my jacket, and a little bit on my face. If Cook & Dunn could make their paint go half this far, you could paint a three-bedroom home with a quart. I was covered with this goo and it was now five minutes to the hour. It quickly became obvious that I was not going to get this makeup off my clothing. I took off my jacket. The tie miraculously didn't show the stuff too much, and my pants could be cut out of the shot. I gave strict instructions to the camera crew that it was only to be headshots. We got through that live program pretty well and we very quickly did some taping.

However, I was still perplexed. There was no way I was going to go back to New Jersey on an airplane looking like this. My limousine driver said, "Not to worry." He had already called a cleaner in Cleveland (the cleaner was a fan of mine). I was to go over there in the limo and they would do an express job on my suit and clean me all up.

After we left the studio, it became clear that time was an important element. Given the fact that I was in a white limousine with gray windows and if you couldn't see out, you couldn't see in either, I figured I would get a jump on the cleaners. I took off my jacket, took off my shirt, took off my pants and sat there in a tan raincoat. (We all know what kind of people run around in tan raincoats undressed like that.) We pulled up to the cleaners, and the driver had no idea that I had disrobed. He flung open the door and there must have been two hundred women standing around there on the sidewalk. The cleaner had called all of his friends and said, "Guess who's coming to my store this morning?" There I was in a raincoat in my underwear signing autographs. This is the kind of screw-up that happens. They get worse, but most times they allow me to grin after the fact.

A couple of years ago we had one of our self-induced screw-ups. We scheduled one of our trips to Alaska, accompanied by a lot of our listeners. Unknowingly, my office scheduled me to be in Alaska on the ship and at a Spokane, Washington, convention at the same time. Since this was a convention and couldn't be rescheduled and the ship commitment was firm, it was up to me to do a lot of fancy footwork to be in both places at one time. Obviously the most reasonable approach, should everything work, would be to get off the ship at one of the ports of call, which worked out to be either Ketchikan or Juneau. I could then fly down to Washington state, do my thing on a Saturday evening and fly back and meet the ship the following day. Easy to say, very difficult to accomplish.

As it turned out, the ship arrived in Juneau an hour or so after the final flight of the day left for Seattle. This connection would have taken me to where I wanted to go. There were no other connections. As many of you may know, Juneau is completely surrounded by water and mountains. It's on the edge of the coastline, and can only be reached by water or air. (Those politicians up in Alaska know how to work things. Put the capital where the average guy can never get to without considerable expense.)

To solve my problem, it seemed to me if we could charter a water taxi out from Juneau, thirty or forty miles, I could board the taxi and be taken into Juneau to catch the last flight of the day. Everything would have worked out and I would have reconnected with the cruise ship in Skagway the next day. Problem was, the cruise line said that was illegal. Now why would this be illegal?

Some eighty years ago, a congressman or senator — I'm not certain which — named Jones introduced and had adopted legislation appropriately named the Jones Act. The Jones Act stipulates that a foreign flag carrier may not carry passengers between two U.S. ports unless they are intermediate stops and the passenger is booked to the far end. This was to protect shipping interests out of Washington state, where for all intents and purposes, Alaska was controlled.

Remember, we had recently acquired the territory from Russia. The purchase was dubbed "Seward's Folly," named after Secretary of State William H. Seward, who signed the agreement. The cruise line officially said, "Sorry, we'll get fined $10,000." We then called to the appropriate authorities and I spoke with a couple of them and they said, "Sorry, we can't let passengers off." I thought about that and called them back and asked, "How about crew members?" "Oh yes, they can come and go with no problem." I said, "I'm a crew member. I'm entertaining on this ship." "Are you being paid to be on this ship and are not a paying passenger?" "That's correct." "Oh, not to worry, Mr. Williams." Bing, bing, bing and it's done. The lesson there - if you ask the wrong question, you don't get the right answer.

All the cruise ship guys did was ask if I could get off the ship. They didn't qualify it. What they should have asked is what are provisions for people, not just passengers, to leave the ship. I got myself an exit visa off the ship. Next problem was to physically get off. I mentioned the neat place to do it would be Juneau, but the only problem was, the ship got there an hour after the last plane connecting with Seattle left. I really had no desire to get off at Ketchikan, where I would be off a day early. Let's face it; we had a couple of hundred people on that ship that had come because of me. I didn't feel that was the way to go. I did discuss this with the captain at some length, as well as the then-president of the line, who happened to be on board. I said, "Why can't we send a little tender out from Juneau to pick me up? I'll pay for it. How about a helicopter?" No, they couldn't do that. "How about a dry suit? I'll jump overboard." "Oh my God, we can't allow that."

The result was, the only way I could meet my obligation in Spokane was to get off the ship with the exchange of pilots. Now, each cruise ship going through the Inside Passage requires a pilot from the host country. So when you are in U.S. waters, the pilot is from the United States, and conversely the Canadian pilot is in charge in Canadian water. We were entering U.S. waters again so that the American pilot came on board and the Canadian pilot left. They allowed me to jump on to the little tender, no big deal.

On the other hand, here I am with nothing but a briefcase and I look up and there's a ton of people leaning over the railing waving handkerchiefs goodbye. The word got around very quickly. The fellows on the pilot boat were as nice as they possibly could have been. They got on the horn, started calling about airplanes. What are my options?

My options, as it turned out, were very limited. Toward the end of our journey, which had to have been forty-five minutes to an hour, to someplace I never heard of in Canada, the captain said, "There is a plane out of here with one stop, winding up in Vancouver. The only problem is, we can't make it." I looked at the map and I said, "How about you let me off here," pointing to a dock, "we can call ahead and have a car waiting?" "That might work," and that's exactly what we did. I went jumping off the dock, saying goodbye to my shipmates, running into a car that was waiting and by a whisker made the Air Canada flight.

The airplane was a 737, made by Boeing, a very reliable aircraft. My friends know I fly a great deal. I was working on the airplane, as I tend to do. I looked out the window and son-of-a-gun, we were flying well below terrain level, mountains on both sides at four and a half hundred miles an hour. That might be great for a military hot-dogger, but I don't think that's appropriate for an airline.

When we landed in our intermediate stop — once again, a very nondescript airport in the middle of nowhere — I went up and had a chat with the guy in the left seat. I said, "I think I understand why you're doing it, but I will tell you this. I am extremely uncomfortable flying along a couple of thousand feet below terrain." "Oh, the customers love this," said he. "I'm one customer that doesn't," I responded. I don't know what the Canadian rules are, but I'm confident that the crew would be breaking some rules in the U.S., given the relatively close proximity to the terrain. He assured me we were going to 28,000 feet on the way down to Vancouver. I sat back far more relaxed.

As it turned out, I was going down to this little assignation on July 1st. Now July 1st means not much to you guys, but July 1st is Canada Day, followed by U.S. Independence Day, July 4th, a very heavy travel weekend. I never thought I'd have any difficulties finding a place to lay my body down for a few hours that night, but nothing was further from the truth. I made a dozen phone calls or more and there was no room at the inn.

Finally, I did get an accommodation in the Roach Motel. As you may know in Canada, they have limited gambling. The hotel I was "privileged" to stay at had a casino, largely if not completely, patronized by local Asians, all of who had a huge smoking habit. The smoke literally poured out of the casino into the halls of the hotel. When I inquired about what kind of groceries I might be able to find in the hotel, I was directed into the smoke-filled room where greasy sandwiches were available. Thank you very much.

I wandered across the street and found a very good Chinese restaurant. I ordered my meal and went back to the hotel room. I specifically told them I was staying in a hotel and they accommodated me by completely forgetting to put any kind of utensils into my take-out. The windup was, there I was in a dirty hotel room, at midnight in a strange city without a fork. You think this is a glamorous life?

The next morning, bright and early, I flashed on down to Seattle and then over to Spokane. The folks at the convention at Spokane were very accommodating. We went to an outdoor luncheon, a very pleasant buffet, and otherwise had a great afternoon. As it is my custom, I did not carry a bag but rather had my clothing shipped Federal Express to Spokane where one of our hosts picked it up as I requested and hung it in her closet. When she returned my suit to me, unhappily upon examination, I determined there were no trousers. **Here we go again.** I looked; I called home, no trousers there.

It's now about 3:30 in the afternoon. I have to do an appearance and all I have is a good blue suit jacket and no pants. I called a couple of the custom tailors in town, told them my problem and said the price was absolutely no object. I simply had to have a pair of trousers. A couple of fellows would call back.

In the meantime, I ran into my hostess in the lobby. She and her son who had taken me around the town were going someplace. They asked where I was going. I started to explain the situation. She said, "Oh my gosh, let me check." Well, happily my pants were in her bedroom closet — now there is something for her to explain to her husband. They fell off the hanger in a bunch.

121

The hotel staff assured me there would be no problem getting them pressed. Well that assurance fell through. Apparently in Spokane, Washington, everybody shuts down about noon on Saturday. The performance went on, wrinkled pants and all.

The following morning I flipped over to Seattle and back up to Juneau. Funny thing, though, the computer would not give me a seat from Juneau to Skagway. All it said was that I had a ticket. That question was answered very quickly when we went out to the airplane. There were only six seats in the airplane, including the guy driving. I asked if anybody else was a pilot and they said no. So I asked, "With your permission, may I sit in the right seat?" If something happens to this fellow I'm a pretty decent backup.

I have not flown a great deal in Alaska. I have ridden in seaplanes, helicopters and the like, but not in the left-hand seat. I said to this young fellow — and "young" is the operative word, he was probably no more than twenty — "I don't want to be pushy or forward but it seems to me you might want to set the compass and the altimeter." His response was, "We don't have to do that, we never get above eight hundred feet and it's under the clouds all the way. I don't need either one of those." Somehow or another that was more cavalier than I felt was warranted. In any case, Sunday morning, after leaving late Friday night, I rejoined the ship in Skagway, which by the way is a neat little town, one that you should put on your hit list.

The balance of the voyage was mercifully uneventful. It seems to me this cruise might have had a jinx on it from the very beginning. We boarded the ship with pickets from the ships' union surrounding the ship. Although they made no effort to interfere with us once we were aboard, it became obvious that no services were available. The president of the cruise line then announced we had a couple of options. We could eat off the ship, at their expense, with an extra bottle of wine. The other was to go to a restaurant of our choice. The baggage arrived at the wharf, but there were no crews to take the baggage on board. Each of the passengers were asked to get in line, select his own baggage and carry it on board or wait till late that night or the next morning. It was a real sight to watch some less than well-conditioned folks struggle with their bags to get them on the ship.

The sailing was in danger for some time. The ship had to go with the tide and in order to make its ports of call they had to do a certain amount of acceleration. Had this adventure begun properly on time, the foregoing wouldn't have happened since we would have made port in Juneau in time for me to make my airplane connection. Happily, the strike was settled, and the sailing took place, but that was just the beginning of our difficulties.

As I have repeated many times, Murphy has a habit of enforcing his law, "What can go wrong, will."

A short time ago I was doing a presentation in Harrisburg, Pennsylvania. Because that is relatively close to my home in New Jersey, I drove to Harrisburg, an uneventful pleasant drive. I met with the folks from Dame Media, who were most gracious, and then retired to my suite for a little rest before doing the show. Now I have learned the hard way, always check to see if the tuxedo is in good shape, if the slacks are appropriately hung and unwrinkled, that the red handkerchief is available, my signature black boots, black onyx and diamond cufflinks and studs are in place and, of course, the most important shirt stud is the one that belonged to my Father a half a century ago. Double check everything before we go: evening watch, the right suspenders, extra collar stays. I check these things because every one of them has gone astray at one time or another. Well, I believe that I have this getting dressed thing beat. I slipped on my dinner shirt at about five past 7. Come to find out the cleaner substituted a top button for me from a reasonably large button to one that was very small. The very small button had two qualities that I had to deal with.

One, it was extremely difficult to get through a starched shirt which has very little give to it. Two, it was so small the pressure would not be absorbed by my finger. The button would sink into the soft part of the finger and I simply couldn't get it buttoned. On the one occasion that I did, it pulled right out. It was too small to hold.

Well, we have choices here and I tried most of them. It's only five past seven; they're picking me up at twenty minutes after, no problem. Well, it was a heck of a problem. At twenty after, I was no closer to getting my shirt buttoned than I was at five after. I tried sewing the hole shut, which is an interesting exercise when you're running that needle through tough material adjacent to your Adam's apple, but that plan didn't work. It was 7:30 when I came across putting something into the buttonhole to spread it. Now I am racing down stairs, pocket-handkerchief in hand, all because of a lousy button change that I'm sure the cleaner did to please me not to frustrate me. It's just another item on my checklist. Check the buttonholes all the way down. My ritual now is putting the shirt on to make sure that it's perfect and then put it back in the dry cleaner bag for its next voyage.

Another lesson in these Murphyisms is this, "Never believe what somebody tells you. Back it up." Sometime ago I was going to Grand Rapids, Michigan, and for reasons that totally escape me at this point, I was traveling from Chicago to Detroit to Grand Rapids. I was on the road someplace prior to this, but I have no recollection of where it might have been. I walked into the airline club in Chicago and asked if my flight was on time. The young lady was very pleasant. She wrote down the time the plane was leaving, the gate and the rest. I had over an hour to kill. I sat in the club, read a magazine, and had a couple of Diet Cokes and snacks.

When I arrived at the gate, there was nobody there. The gate attendant said, "Mr. Williams, we've been looking for you." I said, "Oh?" She said, "The flight left half an hour ago." I showed her the paper that the lady wrote the information down on, and her reply was, "I think she goofed." "You bet your butt she goofed." I'm sitting in Chicago, when I should be on an airplane to Detroit. They did get me to Detroit. By that time, Detroit was having heavy snow. I had an obligation to be in Grand Rapids. I wound up renting a car and driving much faster than might seem prudent to get to my gig in Grand Rapids.

The thing is, I went by only this one woman's word. Now when I go into the same club or its counterpart anywhere in the country, I look at the monitor. I have her check, and then I go and look at the monitor again. Gates change and times change. In this instance she just misread the times. Not a capital crime! But it sure did louse up my day. Once burned their fault, twice burned my fault. I have no reservation about asking people to repeat themselves a second time. Mistakes like this are costly and very inconvenient.

I have done countless stage presentations around the country, perhaps in your part of the world. Hopefully, most folks enjoy these encounters. I have also learned that Mr. Murphy is right there.

I was doing a program in Providence, Rhode Island. It was held in a hotel, in a room that was a little difficult to work in given the fact there were pillars in the room itself. With a decent riser we could make it work. One of the conditions that I request is a hand-held cordless microphone. The reason for this is simple. I like moving around the stage and occasionally jumping off and going into the audience. I don't want the restrictions of a hard line.

I talked to the engineers involved and made it very clear that I needed three cordless microphones: two for the audience and one for me. Our people handle the microphones in the audience. It is imperative that the technicians change the batteries in the cordless microphones so there is absolutely no possibility of the mikes dying in the middle of the show. That had happened to me sometime previously and I wasn't going to let it happen again. I looked the guy right in his face and said, "Now you can assure me there are brand-new, virgin, never-before-used batteries in these microphones?" "Absolutely, Mr. Williams, we just installed them a short time ago." I said, "I don't want to hear about a short time ago, I want to know they are in there for me, first time." "Yes sir, that is the condition," was his response. I am sure you could finish this story.

Right in the middle of the performance the batteries went dead! I'm standing there talking to a dead microphone, shouting, "Stand by a minute." It took a while to find some new batteries. I made fun of him. If I came down on him hard people would be sympathetic to him. I just talked about, "It's easy to see that this guy is definitely a company man. He saved his boss at least two bucks for batteries and whether it went dead in the middle of a performance or not, I'm sure they'll get paid the entire bill."

The point is you do your best to be certain that things don't go wrong and still they will continue to. I always check every venue that I speak in. I don't for the most part like a lectern on the stage and I really don't like a lot of things sitting around, potted palms, flowers and that sort of thing. I've walked into speaking engagements where I thought I died. It looked like I was the guest of honor at a funeral. I prefer to have nothing other than a little table with a Diet Coke, and a barstool I can sit on from time to time. It doesn't matter how often or how hard we stress this, somebody frequently tries to second-guess us. I always insist, perhaps as a matter of superstition, to come in from stage right. Every so often, for no apparent reason, someone tries to change the system. Why? I'll never know.

We were doing the show in the Midwest. No further identification to protect the guilty. It was in a gorgeous older theater. I enjoy these places, sixty, seventy years old with the elaborate ceilings and wall hangings. I often think it would be great to have my kids with me. It might be instructive to show them something over fifty they could all respect. One of the accouterments was an elevator that let the orchestra either drop out of sight, or be pushed up in front of the stage.

My host had a neat idea. I would stand on that stage and rise out of the ground and make my entrance that way. I suggested that I would rather have had it up in place and come in from the right-hand side as I always do, but his judgment prevailed. The result was, I stood down there and the announcer said, "Ladies and gentlemen, here is Bruce Williams," as the stage majestically rose in the air.

Difficulties began when the stage stalled. So there I stood, looking at the audience with a live microphone in hand, with only my head and shoulders coming out of this hole in the floor. I finally said to the audience, "Forget this ever happened. We are going to get this thing in place. Please hold your applause, because we are going to start this show off on the right foot." I had a sinking feeling I was going to have a serious problem delivering! I didn't know how to climb out of this thing. If I climbed up on the stage I was afraid I'm going to rip something. I finally had to bail out of the door that I came in through, then jump down three or four feet. Murphy, you did it again!

"Time to spare, go by air." This may sound like fiction, but it's absolutely true. I was vacationing in the Virgin Islands. It was a very pleasant vacation, but it was time to leave because I had to do a speaking engagement in Salt Lake City, Utah.

The plan was to fly from the Virgin Islands to Chicago then over to Salt Lake. There was only one problem. The day I was supposed to leave there was a huge ice storm in the southern U.S. One of the cities that was completely iced in was Atlanta. Those of you who fly fairly regularly know, if you lose Atlanta or any major hub, the entire system is disrupted.

The airplane that we were to go out on was on the tarmac. The crew was stranded elsewhere. All day long at Harry S. Truman Airport, (now known as King Airport) we waited in a very small and uncomfortable waiting area, with no food or drink. I had to be in Salt Lake City the next day. I finally said to the young fellow who seemed to be in charge, "What's going on?" He said, "You are all going to hotels and spend the night." They were going to put us on buses and bring us to the hotel.

I told him that I wasn't going to a hotel; I'm out of here one way or another. He said, "Well sir, your flight has been canceled." I said, "Tell me every flight going out of here, lets start with London." He looked at me kind of funny and asked, "London?" I said, "That's right, I want to know every flight out of here." He said, "We do have an American Eagle going from here over to San Juan. The problem is the plane from San Juan to Chicago is overbooked, as is the flight to New York." I replied, "I'll go to San Juan and settle this matter."

I got onto the American Eagle flight at 8:44, and boarded the plane with everybody onboard except the crew. Finally, two guys got on, not with the snappy black suits with the yellow stripes on the sleeves, but rather sweat suits! I raised an eyebrow. This is a commuter plane. It should come with uniformed crewmembers. What's going on? These two guys said, "Not to worry, we were called to fly you folks into San Juan, because the regular crew is not available. We are here going to flight school." The lady in back of me muttered, "I hoped they passed."

What they meant to say was that they were being trained on bigger equipment. They were fully qualified to fly this aircraft back to San Juan, which they did.

At the airport I inquired as to space and I was told it was fully booked. However, there was always a possibility of a cancellation. Possibility? A certainty. The plane was so late; there couldn't have been more than a dozen of us on the airplane. Everyone else went home for another day. The reason was the storm that screwed up Atlanta was now over New York. JFK was on the iffy side. There was also a plane out of Newark an hour after the JFK arrival that would get me out to Denver and then into Salt Lake City. But how do you get from Kennedy to Newark in less than an hour in a blizzard?

The problem was solved when I got hold of two of my sons, Matthew and Michael, who took the family Jeep, put it in four-wheel drive and raced over in the snow and picked me up at JFK and then on to Newark where I made the connection to Denver. In Denver, the station chief met the airplane and said, "I've got good news and I've got bad news. The bad news is, your flight to Salt Lake has been canceled. The good news is, I got you on with United." More bad news. "You won't have time to change." I quickly went into the airline club and had a fast wash-off, and on to Salt Lake. As you could imagine I was pretty beat, but I think the show went well.

I had been invited previously to a fundraiser in Park City, Utah. The chairman of the event was Steve Garvey. This was before his unfortunate notoriety for things other than baseball. The fundraiser was for a very good cause. After doing my show I went out to a waiting limousine and inside the limo was not only a driver, but also a very attractive blond. She said, "So and so (somebody whose name I will not disclose here) thought you would enjoy my company." I took one look at her and told her, "You are welcome to come to dinner, but I'll be coming right back here, because in my condition, there is no way I can spend any more time with you." We both knew what that meant! I did go up to Park City, literally fell asleep in my soup, and in the middle of dinner, after introductions were out of the way, I made my way alone back to the hotel. The only thing that didn't happen was that in the snowstorm going back to the hotel we did not leave the road. Frankly, I thought the possibility a very real one.

How To Do It

Starting your own business can be the most satisfying and rewarding work you can do, for a number of reasons. Your own business lets you call the shots. You are your own boss, and the responsibility for success or failure rests squarely on your own shoulders.

Not everyone is cut out for it. Some people seem perfectly content to let others make the decisions and take the responsibility. But anyone with a streak of independence will eventually flirt with the notion of striking out on his own.

Success in small business — and the new entrepreneur almost invariably will start out small — takes a combination of qualities and characteristics that I am trying to illustrate in this book. Toward the end of this chapter, I will offer some tips for getting started and becoming profitable. A more detailed treatment will be found in my book, *In Business for Yourself* (Scarborough House, 1991). This book, however, is intended more to lay the foundation for becoming the kind of person you need to be to make it in a venture of your own, and I do that by showing you how I went about it.

Paradoxically, one of the best ways to prepare for success is to be prepared to fail. It is not that you should plan to fail, but you should be prepared for the possibility of failure. If your plans collapse around your head, you should be able to pick yourself up, dust yourself off and look for a way to turn that rubble around you into gold.

In addition to the qualities I mentioned in the first section of this book, one of the prime characteristics of a successful businessperson is resilience, the ability to bounce back from defeat and turn it into triumph. That, in fact, is the theme of much of the next chapter, which recounts a bit of my history in small enterprise.

7
Making It

I have been buying and selling, and wheeling and dealing, all of my life. I was about to say adult life, but it really started out well before adulthood.

When I was a youngster in Glens Falls, New York, ten or eleven years old, one of the ways we would manage to get a little spending money was sucking nickels. The meters in those days had a slot that faced the sidewalk. A nickel was dropped into the slot and fell down in the meter, and then a handle was turned to crank up the one hour the nickel paid for. Happily for kids like me, oftentimes a nickel, for whatever reason, got inside the meter but didn't fall down. There was one obvious way to retract the nickel.

I would walk up and down the streets after school, Glen Street, South Street, side streets, and keep my head constantly cocked to the left. Whenever I saw a nickel in such a position, I'd walk over, put my mouth over the hole and suck the nickel out. You'd be surprised how many nickels one can make in the course of an afternoon. Was this honest? I suppose not. On the other hand, as a kid it seemed to me perfectly logical. The nickels were in the meter not doing anybody any good and we just cleared the way for another guy to put one in that might go down.

Then when I was 14, I had my appendix removed, shortly before Thanksgiving. Even at that age, I was out hustling, but having the surgery slowed me down for a bit.

I persuaded my Mother to take me out to the "woods." What I

wanted to do was cut down several white birch trees, bring them back to the house and transform them, as I will describe in a moment. What my Mother didn't know was that the "woods" I was taking her to were really part of the Essex County park system, and I suspect the local constabulary would have frowned on my chopping down trees in the park, had they known I was at work. I managed to purloin a significant number of these trees, cut the branches off, get them into bite-size chunks and load them into my Mother's 1937 Cadillac.

I sawed the logs into sections approximately 12 to 14 inches long, then took a small branch, split it in half, nailed the curved side to the bottom for feet and drilled three holes into the log for candles. I inserted candles, two red and one white, and on occasion dripped white wax on the red candles to make it look like snow, and then stapled balsam branches between the candles, and glued on pinecones facing in opposite directions. They made a respectable Yule Log. After manufacturing about a dozen or so, I'd take them out door-to-door and peddle them. I have no recollection as to what I charged for them, but my expenses clearly were limited to the cost of the candles and the staples. Everything else, the greens and, of course, the main ingredient, the birch log, were acquired at no cost.

The following year was my first adventure into Christmas trees, with my close friend, Bob Geyer. Bob and I were introduced by our parents when we were about six and five years old, respectively, and I never let him forget that he is a year or so older than I. We hated each other instantly. We fought and that was the end of that. About seven years later we were reintroduced at church, and we hit it off right away. It was kind of a tentative relationship, but we decided to go downtown to Newark. We were walking down Market Street in Newark and passed a marquee with a picture of a very comely movie star with a rose situated just off her hip near a sensitive area of her anatomy. Bob looked at that and said, "My objective is about four inches to the right." We hit it off very well after that. That established the ground rules.

We sold Christmas trees on the corner of Park Avenue and Grove Street, in East Orange, in front of Sam and Joe's. I had a friend lug the trees from the rail yards where we purchased them. While we made a little money with Christmas trees, we made a lot more money with mistletoe and corsages. At that time, mistletoe was sold by the branch, most of it grown in Texas. We bought ours from the Muller brothers in Newark. Half a century later, I have a business still doing business with Fritzie Muller, who still runs his very successful wholesale florist. At the time, I thought Fritzie was an elderly gentleman. He was probably in his early thirties, but then the perspective of a teenager is quite different from the one I currently enjoy.

In any case, the mistletoe came in bulk and oftentimes, due to rough handling; the berries would fall off completely. Fritzie, taking advantage of youngsters, would offer us the mistletoe at a heavily discounted price because florists would never buy the stuff without the berries. You must understand that at that time, plastics were not ubiquitous as they are today.

As a matter of fact, the only thing I can remember that came in plastic bags was nuts, meaning loose nuts that were sold in most stores, including the drug store, the Service Drug Company, where I was employed. The Double K nut machine had several trays of nuts and a rotating center tray, and in the back were plastic bags into which the clerk would place the nuts. I bought a lot of these bags from Sam and Joe. We would put a sprig of mistletoe into the bag and a handful of berries and then tape it up with red Scotch Tape. We would tell the customers, "Never take the mistletoe out of the bag, because the berries may fall off the branch and, of course, they are poisonous and you wouldn't want your children or pets to get into them. Just hang it up in the bag and then dispose of it after Christmas." In this way, we took damaged merchandise and sold a ton of it. We were limited, however, to the number of people who would come by, and we were looking for a way around that.

I harkened back to my very early childhood. When I was six or seven years old, people from the Curtis Publishing Company used to hover around schools after school to persuade youngsters of my age to sell the *Saturday Evening Post* and the *Ladies Home Journal*. You got a bag that went over your shoulder and you were rewarded with all sorts of prizes, such as a catcher's mitt. Well, it worked for them, why not for me?

Bob and I worked out a deal. We would work with the kids at the local elementary school. And, of course, the word got around very quickly that you could make some money with these guys on the corner. We eventually rented a store. We would buy Christmas corsages from Fritzie Muller for 18 cents a pop, and have the kids sell them door-to-door for a half-dollar. The kids kept 10 cents for themselves. They would sell the mistletoe for a quarter a bag, keeping a nickel for themselves. Imagine hundreds of kids fanning out over a neighborhood going door-to-door peddling this stuff. People would actually buy it and tack it on the door as defense against another Lilliputian salesman rapping on their door.

The kids never were asked their names. We just gave them a number. I can still hear these little whippersnappers coming in, piping, "I'm Number 211, sir," in their high-pitched voices and turning in their money. A few of them didn't show up, but, on balance, we sold hundreds of corsages and literally thousands and thousands of bags of mistletoe, at then, outrageous prices.

That experience taught me a valuable lesson: packaging and merchandising is everything. You can have the best product in the world, but unless you get it out there and in a package that people can identify with, no sale.

During our teen years, you must remember, if we didn't earn it, we didn't have it. It wasn't a question of our families' willingness to give us money; it was simply that they didn't have it. My Dad traveled for Saks Fifth Avenue and was away about nine months a year, leaving the raising of me to my Mom, who was a strong woman, but not necessarily up to the

Me at age two. A ham in the making.

Florence E. Williams
1897 - 1992

Harold R. Williams
1894 - 1969

Bruce seated on an ANGR-26, commonly known as an "angry 26". It housed radio transmitters and cryptographic equipment.

Twenty year old hotshot in Korea.
Really thought I was tough.
How wrong I was.

My mentors: partners Sam Laffer (L),
Joe Shaffman (R), and Sam's daughter Jean.
Circa 1952.

It Really Happened!
Refer to pg. 81.

Things that really happened.

NEW JERSEY
STATE TEACHERS COLLEGE
NEWARK 4

Memorandum

To: Bruce Williams
From: Dr. Vaughn-Eames
Date: August 19, 1958
Dictated August 18

Subject

The turkey seems to me to be a ver...
You will get the entire amount for...
expect any percentage to be turned...
would like to have the boxes lett...
that it is dedication lunch.

I am sorry I was so tied up today...
in September.

Pg. 162

ORIGINAL INVOICE   MARKET 7-5341

Play-Art Educational Equipment Co.

437-439 ARCH ST., PHILADELPHIA 6, PA.

No. 28003

SOLD TO: Mr. B.H. Williams
Lane Robbins School
Box 365, Cortelyou Lane, FranklinPark
off Rt.27, Somerset, N.J.

SHIP TO:

TERMS 15 DAYS NET 90 DAYS	DATE OF INVOICE 9/28/61	YOUR ORDER NO.	DATE SHIPPED	OUR ORDER NO.	SHIPPED BY	YOUR REQ. NO.

NOTE BACKORDER COLUMN: ☐ WILL FOLLOW   ☐ DISCONTINUED AND/OR CANCELLED

ITEM NO.	QUANTITY ORDERED	SHIPPED	BACK ORDER	CATALOG NO.	DESCRIPTION	UNIT PRICE	EXTENSION	TOTAL AMOUNT
1					Glazed Paper	.75	.75	
1	set			E	Unit Blocks	53.00	53.00	
2					P.Phones	.98	1.96	
6					Saran Cots	14.25net		85.50net
6	Pts				Poster Paint	1.00	6.00	
1					Lincoln Logs	5.00	5.00	
1	Dz			A26	Brushes	2.75	2.75	
1					Milk Carrier	2.00	2.00	

Paper

	3.00	3.00
	3.60	3.60
	.45	2.70
	2.00	2.00
	.50	.50
	2.25	2.25
	6.00	6.00
	1.50	9.00
	5.95	5.95

...nt Sp. 16.00 16.00
...g Set   3.00 3.00
	2.00	2.00
	6.00	6.00
	2.50	2.50
	3.95	3.95
...eight Train 3.95 3.95
...age   2.50 2.50
| | 9.95 | 9.95 |
| | 1.00 | 1.00 |

...MAGES MUST BE MADE WITHIN 5 DAYS
...UMN—"DROP SHIPMENT"

Pg. 69

Name and Address

BRUCE WILLIAMS
R.D. #3, BOX 365, CORTELYOU LANE
SOMERSET, NEW JERSEY

INDIVIDUAL RECEIPT

Payment received from the above named on this date (which
is the date of entry shown hereon) has been applied to Note No.
____ as specified hereon.

Please bring your Receipt Book next time with this receipt and we will
give you proper credit in for this payment. This will avoid error.

THANK YOU

Pg. 71

CASH RECEIPT VOUCHER

NEW JERSEY STATE TEACHERS COLLEGE
AT NEWARK

9162

Date Jan 28 1958

Received From Williams, Bruce

TUITION - FULL TIME	$	75	00
SERVICE AND LABORATORY FEES - 02		10	00
STUDENT TEACHING FEE		7	50
CAFETERIA SALES			
MISC. RECEIPTS APPROPRIATED - 01			
" RECEIPTS UNAPPROPRIATED			
PRIOR YEARS' ACCOUNT			
TOTAL - FOR STATE TREAS. ACCOUNT	$	92	50
STUDENT ORGANIZATION FEE	$	12	50
TOTAL COLLECTED		105	00

ENTERED BY   RECEIVED BY
Autographic Business Forms, Inc., Hoboken, N.J.   PAT'D. NO. 2.231.105

Pg. 21

FOOD HANDLER'S CERTIFICATE
DEPARTMENT OF HEALTH, EAST ORANGE, N.J.

No. 995

Issued to Bruce H. Williams   Age 24
Street Address 83 No. Walnut St.
City East Orange, N.J.
Type of Establishment Brubob's   114 Fourth Avenue
Date of last Blood Test 1956   Date of last Smallpox Vaccination 1956
Date of last X Ray   Date of Diphtheria Immunization

Signature of Food Handler
Fee $1.00

The above person, having complied with the ordinance and no disease in a com-
municable stage being found, is herewith issued a certificate as a Food Handler in
East Orange for one year from Nov. 27, 1956
This Certificate must be presented at time of renewal.

Health Officer

FOOD HANDLER'S CERTIFICATE
DEPARTMENT OF HEALTH
EAST ORANGE, N.J.

Pg. 157

Documents that support some of my wild youthful exploits.

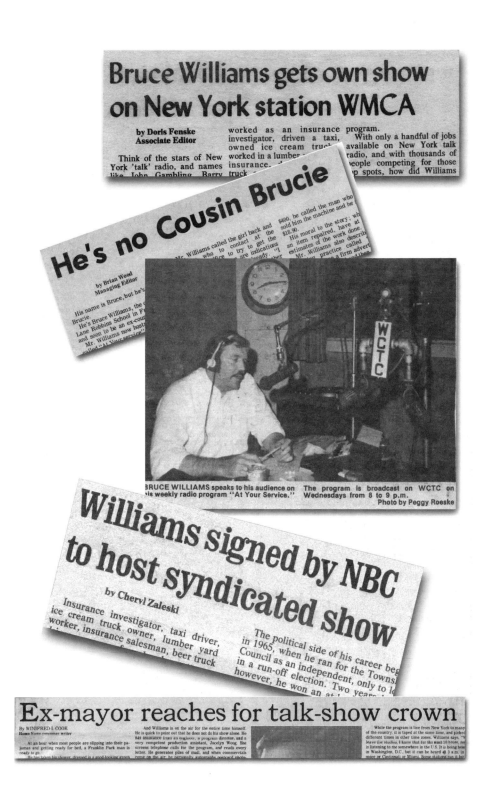

Bruce Williams gets own show on New York station WMCA

by Doris Fenske
Associate Editor

Think of the stars of New York 'talk' radio, and names like John Gambling, Barry

worked as an insurance investigator, driven a taxi, owned ice cream truck, worked in a lumber insurance. truck

program.
With only a handful of jobs available on New York talk radio, and with thousands of people competing for those top spots, how did Williams

He's no Cousin Brucie

by Brian Wood
Managing Editor

His name is Bruce, but he's Brucie.
He's Bruce Williams, the Lane Robbins School in F and soon to be an ex-cour Mr. Williams now host

Mr. Williams called the girl back and who to contact at the office to try to get the are indications

$400, he called the man who sold him the machine and he $18.90.
His moral to the story; wh an item repaired. have at estimates of the work done.
Mr. Williams also describ practice called a firm adver

BRUCE WILLIAMS speaks to his audience on his weekly radio program "At Your Service." The program is broadcast on WCTC on Wednesdays from 8 to 9 p.m.
Photo by Peggy Roeske

Williams signed by NBC to host syndicated show

by Cheryl Zaleski

Insurance investigator, taxi driver, ice cream truck owner, lumber yard worker, insurance salesman, beer truck

The political side of his career beg in 1965, when he ran for the Towns Council as an independent, only to l in a run-off election. Two years however, he won an at

Ex-mayor reaches for talk-show crown

By WINIFRED I. COOK
Home News consumer writer

At an hour when most people are slipping into their pajamas and getting ready for bed, a Franklin Park man is ready to go.

And Williams is on the air for the entire time himself.
He is quick to point out that he does not do his show alone. He has assistance from an engineer, a program director, and a very competent production assistant, Jocelyn Woog. She screens telephone calls for the program, and reads every letter. He generates piles of mail, and when commercials come on the air, he personally autographs postcard photos.

While the program is live from New York to many of the country, it is taped at the same time, and picked different times in other time zones. Williams says, "leave the studio, I know that for the next 10 hours, som is listening to me somewhere in the U.S. It is being bro in Washington, D.C., bet it can be heard at 3 a.m. in more or Cincinnati or Miami. Some stations run it be

3 hurt in Princeton plane crash

THE TRENTONIAN, TUESDAY MORNING, DECEMBER 7, 1982   .7

Radio Personality Williams Still Critical

By PAULA SCHNORBUS
Staff Writer

PRINCETON — The condition of NBC radio personality Bruce Williams remained critical yesterday following the crash of a small single-engine plane he was piloting Sunday in Montgomery Township.

Williams, 50, of Franklin Park, hosts a financial program. The Bruce Williams Show,'' locally aired on radio station WHWH. The show is part of a group of nationally syndicated programs entitled ''Talknet,'' aired live in more than 100 markets across the country. He also served as a councilman in Franklin before being named mayor in 1968.

Williams and two other passengers, Ralph Blasingame, 62, of East Brunswick, and Jay Panter, 51, of Edison, were treated for multiple injuries at the Medical Center at Princeton.

A hospital spokeswoman said Blasingame and Panter were in stable condition and out of the intensive care unit yesterday. Williams' son, Matthew, said that his father underwent major surgery and had ''stabilized somewhat.'' Hospital officials said he was suffering from a broken leg and intestinal lacerations.

Blasingame said Sunday that Williams had twice tried to land his 1964 Cessna 182 Skylane at Princeton Airport while returning from a recreational flight to Monmouth County Airport. As the plane began climbing again, the ''stall warning'' device'' activated.

The craft's nose was high in the air when the plane struck some trees about 300 yards beyond the end of the runway. An onlooker said the plane stalled and crashed. Both wings were almost lost on impact in the swampy area.

RADIO ROUNDUP By VAL ADAMS

Williams taking house calls in hospital

BRUCE WILLLIAMS, WHO DOES a call-in show on personal finance for NBC's Talknet affiliates, resumed broadcasting Thursday night from his hospital bed in Princeton (N.J.) Medical Center, where he has been since Dec. 5, when the airplane he was piloting crash-landed.

To facilitate the hospital hookup, telephone lines were connected in Williams' room. Calls were directed to Talknet's regular toll-free number at the NBC studios in New York and then relayed to Williams.

There is no indication of when Williams will be released from the hospital, but after that he'll be recuperating at home. He plans to continue broadcasting from his home in Franklin, N.J.

Photo by Steve Klaver

NBC radio talk show host Bruce Williams relaxes in his bed at Princeton Medical Center

Full Circle. Thrilled to receive an Honorary Doctorate from my Alma Mater with all of my children and grandchildren in attendance. Refer to pg. 66.

Bruce Williams entertaining at the "Bruce Williams 'Eats Crow' Party". Refer to pg. 240.

Re-elect a Proven Leader . . .

Councilman BRUCE WILLIAMS

the Williams family — wife Ruthann, Matt,
Robbins, Kelly, Michael, Mark, & "Suckey."

The family man in action.
Campaign post card, 1971.

Pool area at Lane Robbins. A good place to raise
kids. The barn in the background is mentioned in
the book on pg. 102.

Ice Cream truck.
Refer to pg. 168.

The Partners in 1954.

Robert E. (Bob) Geyer (r.)
&
Bruce H. Williams (l.)

The homemade ice cream
truck in background.

Forty plus
years and
still partners.

Here's my baby.

Here is the machine that was our 'Pigeon' referred to on pg.138. Not fully restored but we are getting there.

Thats me (in red jacket) counting Christmas trees as they are unloaded.

My son Mark and me just before my epic first parachute jump from 13,500 feet.

Our first Jellyrolls in Pittsburg, Pennsylvania
Paul Elliot seated on the "Piano". Pg 107.

Pistol Williams,
6 months old.

Pool and Gym area in our home. See the Piano lounge in the upper level. This is my favorite place in the house. Note the carousel horse on the second level and to the right in the picture, it's genuine.

Studio in my home in Florida. This is where it happens.

Susan and me on our very special day.
The wedding was performed by
Rev. "Shorty" Brown in 1998.

task of handling someone like me. I was out early and came home late, and as long as no serious trouble developed, I guess my Mother learned to live with it.

Bob and I established a window-washing route in Newark along Seventh Avenue. In those days, there were many four-story walk-ups occupied by middle-class working families and a smattering of retirees. One of the things that posed a problem for those folks in the upper floors was washing their windows. Most of these buildings came with either a part or a full-time janitor called the "super," but either they were ill-equipped to do this, or they would charge so much that the residents either could not afford it or were unwilling to pay so much. In any case, having a couple of kids coming to the door offering to wash the windows at a reasonable price was attractive.

Upon reflection, I think my friend Bob took advantage of his younger colleague, because it seems to me I was always the outside man. In other words, I would have to climb out on a little ledge, two or three inches wide, perhaps as much as five inches. Bob would close the window and I would hang on by my fingernails and wash the window with water, vinegar and newspapers. Happily, I never took a fall — though I came pretty close on several occasions. I can't image today climbing out of a third or fourth story window and hanging on the ledge with the window closed washing it. But then, we do a lot of things when we are younger, don't we?

That was one of our more upright endeavors. But we had others.

For a time, Bob was employed by Englehard Industries. Charlie Englehard was the proprietor of a much smaller enterprise then, a company that made thermal metals. Bob did some kind of blueprint reading or reproduction, I'm not sure which, but he was — and continues to be — a pretty smooth character. He persuaded one of the men in the machine shop to produce a steel die that would cut metal in small disc forms —

coincidentally? — a fraction under the size of a nickel. We then would cast sheets of metal out of soft lead just under the thickness of a nickel. Presto, instant slugs.

In those days, almost every merchant would have one or two pinball machines in his store or luncheonette. The machines were run by the local racketeers and paid off in money. The cost of a game was a nickel, for which you got five balls and, after achieving a certain score (if memory serves me, it was 48,000), the machine started to rack up "free" games. If you won five games you could call the owner of the store over, he would look, give you 25 cents, and then hit a button under the machine. The games would disappear from the meter and you walked out with your quarter. Obviously, this was illegal, but it was ubiquitous and I never heard of an occasion when the law frowned.

One machine that came out during World War II was called "Victory," starting with a V in the top left-hand corner, I, C, then T on the bottom, and O R Y, with the Y at the top of the machine at the end of the chute that carries the ball up and onto the machine for play. At the top of the machine on the chute there were three brads that were to prevent the ball from going in the back way behind the Y. If you took the machine and put it up on your toes so that it was slanted from right to left, the left being the low side, and very carefully just eased a ball up the chute, the ball would sit upon the brads. The next ball was "thumbed," or sent up with a great deal of speed. The brad would bend over and you could hop the ball in behind the Y, where it was trapped. It was simply a matter then of putting the machine back on its four legs, inserting a coin, and very gently rocking the machine. The ball was trapped, it would run up the score, and the first thing you knew, you had 30, 40 games — $2, a lot of money in those days. You would hop the ball back out again and call the proprietor over, collect your $2 and leave, then come back again a day or two later.

There were several of these machines, but the one that stands out in my mind was the one in a luncheonette on Seventh Avenue in the Roseville section of Newark. That machine became our pigeon. Then we became even greedier. We started producing our own slugs out of the metal that we would pour between two sheets of asbestos and then punch out with the die that Bob had made at Englehard. We would make rolls of slugs. The slugs, being of a soft metal, would work, but they would also frequently jam up the machine. So now, we were not only cheating the owners out of their games by gimmicking the machines, we weren't even putting in the first nickel.

A variation of that was cutting a nickel in half and having it welded onto a hacksaw blade, which would go down the chute and prevent the pin from dropping through the hole. The machine would operate but it wouldn't go in far enough so as to be collected. In that way, once again, we could operate the machines without benefit of coins. This, by the way, is why they have glass on top of the machines: so you can see the last coin. That way on these and others, such as the manual slot machines, a worker could stroll past and determine if coins were being fed into the machine in the appropriate way, or if the management was being cheated.

Bob and I had a good thing going there for a long time, by beating the Victory machine and by the other variations, such as drilling holes in the side of the machine, inserting a small wire and once again, hitting a bumper and running up the score. The operators soon learned how that was done and even to this day, there is a band of steel around the top of the pinball machines to prevent players from drilling in and using a wire to run up a score. (I wonder now, with the invention of cordless drills, how they are dealing with that? With a power drill, I suspect, you could go right through any metal, given sufficient time.)

One night, Bob and I were on Seventh Avenue working our deal, when two, decidedly old, rough-looking characters came up (old is defined as twenty-something). One of them said, "Boys, we want to talk to you." We knew immediately who they were! He said, "Boys, not only are you stealing our money, but you're screwing up our machines with your slugs, and it's going to stop, and if it doesn't stop, you've got a problem. Now, you guys probably have a future with us, and when you're a year or two older, you ought to come down and see us." Then he mentioned Thom's, a famous restaurant in Newark where everyone who, had any knowledge at all of what was going on, knew the "wise guys" hung out. He said, "In the meantime, if this happens again, we know who you are and you got no future." We got the message in a hurry, and that was the end of our pinball adventures. These were not people to be trifled with.

Over the years I have thought about our enterprise with the pinball machines with some degree of affection. After all, these are the things that kids remember. I've always wondered whether or not the Victory machine was actually as I recollected. Now that I have moved into a fairly spacious home I've taken to collecting things such as that machine. Where do you find a Victory machine from World War II? Would you believe after about two years of looking I found it on the Internet? That's right, the Internet! In San Diego, California, the fellow who was selling it swore it was in good condition and was operable. We agreed upon a price and had it shipped to Florida. I found out that that was an exaggeration. The machine was inoperable. Nonetheless, I was very happy to have the machine.

I've come to learn that the glass back plate on the machine is the most important part, since they are considered objects of art. Many were taken out and framed. The back piece on my machine is original. The Gotleib Manufacturing Company manufactured the machine in 1933 in Chicago. It is currently being rebuilt and since all the parts have to be custom-made this may take some time. I have already staked out a location in my home where the Victory machine goes when it finally arrives.

Bob and I jumped in and out of many businesses, starting with the Christmas trees and the mistletoe. Eventually, though, it came time to go into the Service. Bob wanted to go into the Navy and I wanted to go into the Air Force. We were going to compromise and go into the Airborne because they got an extra $30 or $40 a month to jump out of airplanes. Happily, sanity prevailed at the last minute. Bob went into the Navy and I went into the Air Force, and we went our separate ways for four years.

To my recollection, we never saw each other during that period. Bob decided to get married and asked me to be his best man, but I was in Texas and he was in New Jersey. At that time one never even considered flying home for a weekend. Today you can just jump on a jet and show up, but it was the early 1950s and I never had a random thought in that direction. There were no commercial jets and, more importantly, you just didn't think about flying across the country for something as trivial as a wedding. How times have changed.

If I had to characterize my military career with one word, it would have to be "undistinguished." What an admission, this late in life, but that's what it was. I enlisted, did my thing, did what I was told to do, and survived with no serious injuries, and got on with my life. But, upon reflection, the story may be worth recounting.

The war, or more properly, the police action in Korea, began days after I graduated from high school. I went down to the New Jersey shore to work behind a soda fountain. I inquired as to whether I could have a job the following year operating a Ferris wheel, a much more prestigious and better-paying job. The operator said, "Sure, come on back if you are not in the Army. We will be glad to have you." I laughed and asked, "What do you mean in the Army?" America was convinced that the Korean episode would be over in a heartbeat. Those little suckers from North Korea would be kicked out and that would be the end of it. We were in for a nasty surprise when the Chinese intervened and the war got serious.

As a consequence, while I was a part-time student in college and working nights in a factory to support that habit, I determined that if they were going to have a party, they could at least invite me. I went down to enlist in the Air Force in December 1950, at the tender age of eighteen. There were no more than four or five would-be recruits the day that I went to present myself. I was told to go home and enjoy Christmas and New Year's Eve and come back the first of January. When I returned to the recruiting office, there were literally thousands of young men trying to enlist in the Navy and the Air Force.

The majority of these guys were around twenty-two or twenty-three, draft bait, and they were doing everything they could to avoid getting into the Army. I, however, was eighteen and had no such concerns, but I did want to get into things. Because of the death of a recruit at Lackland Air Force Base in San Antonio, Texas, Air Force enlistments were frozen, so I was not permitted to go when I was supposed to. I had already quit my job, and although I immediately found a job working in a supermarket and making hamburgers, never having been unemployed for more than a couple of days, I nonetheless was eager to get on with my military adventure.

I went to see a local politician in Orange, New Jersey, Armand Cassini Sr.. Mr. Cassini was an attorney who was deeply involved in the dominant Democratic politics of the time. Mr. Cassini was a friend of the family and when I told him I was coming in to see him about the military, he assumed I was looking for a deferment. He was incredulous when he discovered that, not only was I not looking for a deferment, I was looking for influence to get into the military. He said that in all his years I was the first one who ever came to use juice to get in, not to stay out. Juice notwithstanding, I was required to wait until the latter part of February before a slot opened up for me in basic training.

I received my basic training at Lackland and then received advanced training in various intelligence disciplines at Brooks Air Force Base. Before I enlisted I had no clue what OCS was. I decided that it might be to my advantage to apply for Army Officers Candidate School. With only a high school education, there was no way I would get into the Air Force OCS, but the Army was clamoring for cannon fodder and you were allowed to transfer from the Air Force to the Army if you were accepted to Officers Candidate School. You had to apply for Infantry, Armored or Artillery, all combat areas. I applied for and was accepted into Army OCS and immediately the Air Force assigned me overseas. They weren't about to lose a warm, trained body.

I arrived in Japan in December 1951, and ultimately was assigned to Ashiya, Japan, near Fukuoka. Imagine my surprise to find out that the tour in Japan was two and a half years and the tour in Korea only one year. You earned credits or points to go home. 1.2 points a month for service in Japan, 3 points a month in Korea. It was clear where I wanted to be. First, Korea was where the action was, and second, you got to go home a lot quicker. The idea of being safely in Japan or less safe in Korea never crossed this nineteen year old's mind.

Our arrival on December the 7th, 1951, ten years to the day of the anniversary of the Pearl Harbor attack, could not have been more memorable for this teenager. Imagine this. We arrived about midnight and were off-loaded from very uncomfortable train cars, perhaps 200 "men," the oldest of whom might have reached twenty. It was cold and there was one light bulb burning in the mist, giving the halo effect. The only thing we could see was huge piles of coal in every direction and this little shack masquerading as a place for headquarters.

After we were welcomed appropriately, we were told to listen for our name and fall out in a different area. All but perhaps a dozen names were called, mine was one of them. The enlisted man in charge then said, addressing the larger group, "You airmen will have breakfast tonight. First thing tomorrow morning you will be airlifted to Korea and you'll be home for Christmas in twelve months." Those guys were very happy with that. They then turned to us and said, "You gentleman are permanently assigned to Ashiya Air Force Base, and you will be here for two and a half years." I cannot tell you how far down my heart dropped. Here I am in a damp, cold-infested camp, and I'm going to be here two and a half years. They might have just as well said twenty-five years.

We were escorted to a tent-like affair. The frame was wooden with canvas stretched across the top with a potbelly stove in the middle. We were given a couple of blankets and a see you in the morning! What a depressing evening that was. Things did look a little better the next morning. The sun came up and they did have a good chow hall and the start of a decent facility, but I wanted absolutely no part of this place.

I came to find out very quickly that many other youngsters like me coveted the Korean assignment. It was difficult to come by, but the senior non-commissioned officers, the career types, did not quite understand why many of us wanted to go to Korea. I found out in a hurry that the only way to get there was to screw up. It was something like the TV show, *Black Sheep Squadron.*

I had taken a distinct dislike to one of our sergeants and, as a consequence, picked a fight with him on February 16th. While I won the fight, on February 17th I was processed and on February 18th, my birthday, I was sent to Korea. The sergeant thought he was getting even.

For the first six months in Korea, I was assigned to various tasks that had to be performed in this very small intelligence community. Nothing very exciting. I did have a significant amount of time to myself.

One of the things that I was quick to note was that there was no place close by to purchase a Coke or a candy bar. While they did give out candy, gum and cigarettes at breakfast, courtesy of patriotic organizations of the United States, during the day it would have been nice to have something to drink. The other problem was lack of refrigeration and clean ice. Most of the ice that was available was cut out of the Han River in the wintertime. The Han River was one of the most polluted bodies of water that one can imagine, not only with ordinary industrial pollutants, but unhappily, with human body parts from time to time since the river flowed through the area our forces and the Chinese were constantly bickering over.

In any event, a friend, Harry Bruns, and I did as follows. We found a source for clean ice in Seoul, or perhaps I should say relatively clean ice. We didn't know of anybody who ever got really sick eating it. We made a deal in Inchon, site of the famous landing, to pick up Coca-Cola by the truckload at a nickel a bottle. We would grab a truck out of the motor pool, front the money, bring a truckload of Coke over, and stack it behind what amounted to a very small Quonset hut, called a "Jamesway Half," made out of fabric. We then took a 55-gallon drum, half filled it with sand and brick and then water and then threw the ice in. We sold cold Cokes for a dime a smack, or a thousand won. This turned into a very viable venture.

Our little Jamesway became the hangout for most of the squadron. Unhappily, many of our guys rotated back to the States. Harry had to go to work so he had to leave our little venture. I had it set up in back of a building that was part of EWAH Christian University where a substantial portion of my military activity took place. I then expanded my activities to buying cases of peanuts, packages of crackers and other snack items, working on a profit of a straight nickel an item no matter what it cost me.

It became obvious even to a neophyte entrepreneur that there were other ways to make a buck.

For example, the legitimate exchange rate for won was 6,000 to a dollar, but on the black market, it was something on the order of 11,000 to 12,000 to a dollar, ultimately going to some 50,000 before devaluation. In other words, if you changed your money from military payment certificates to won at the finance office, you took a tremendous beating, so I set up my own little money exchange.

When the old man greeted a new arrival to the squadron, he would say that you can go down to finance and get 6,000 won to a buck but you're better off going to see Willie, who will give you the legitimate exchange rate. And, of course, I took the spread coming and going. I also got involved in speculating in Hong Kong dollars and other currencies. Not a bad sideline for a corporal.

One of the problems for my business was that more often than not, the guys were broke by the middle of the month. No problem. I came out with what I believe to be one of the first credit cards. On a Teletype machine, I printed cards with little numbers on the outside, rather like the old-fashioned "meal ticket," with a place for the name to be written and signed in the middle.

That would have been very simple to counterfeit, so I went into Seoul, purchased a very unusual coin, mutilated it, then heated it with an acetylene torch and burned it into my credit cards so that no one could counterfeit them. Everybody got credit. I would loan money at some usurious rate — six for five per month stands out in my mind — and then on the first of the month when the troops were paid, you walked inside the orderly room, saluted the old man, got your money and walked to the next table, mine, where you paid me off. You couldn't get out of the room without paying Willie.

Inside my Jamesway, I had another little deal cooking that treated my very well. I had a house poker game going usually twenty-four hours a day. Anybody could sit in and as long as you were in the game, you had unlimited amounts of liquor, beer and snacks. I had my houseboy, Mike, sitting in the game and simply taking twenty-five cents from each pot at the beginning of a hand. Boy did those quarters add up! It was a very profitable venture and everybody had a good time. You should understand that I was paying no more than a dollar or a dollar and a half a bottle for hard liquor. I forgot what beer cost but it was not expensive and was more then covered by those quarters that we cut, sometimes twenty-four hours a day.

This little arrangement was working out so well that I extended my tour of duty three times. Unfortunately, toward the end of the second tour, people started rotating back to the States with no replacements. Suddenly I went from being superfluous, to being one of the two or three people trained to do a particular task and, as a consequence, eventually I was forced to fold my little business, but not before I learned a good deal about business and, on the side, made a few bucks.

One of the amazing military institutions that I became acquainted with while I was in Korea was a thing called "Direct Exchange." It worked like this. The Direct Exchange depot dealt with automobile parts, everything from small parts to engines to gasoline. If you went in with a half of dozen spark plugs you just turned them in, signed the name of the squadron, not your own name, and they gave you six new spark plugs: Direct Exchange. But the really amazing thing was that if you signed for six items and took five spark plugs and one engine, it was the same thing, six items.

Oftentimes, I would go down to Direct Exchange for the squadron and take a load of things in to be exchanged. I'm going to tell you now, some forty years later, that on no occasion did I take advantage of this to sell military items. It always amazed me that this was the way they operated. The thing came to a grinding halt when, not only did some of the fellows turn in old engines that belonged to Korean nationals for new ones, but they got extra greedy and would turn in a case of rocks which were then sent back to Japan for rebuilding. Of course, it's easy to understand the consternation of the troops in Japan when they opened the case with no engine, just a bunch of rocks. Perhaps that was a good thing because it seemed to me that the biggest part of that stuff was being sold on the black market.

Another wacko thing that I never completely understood was the lack of green money in Korea. I used this to my advantage on many occasions since I managed to keep a pretty good supply of the green stuff around. The official explanation was that the green money could fall into the hands of the enemy and they could use it on the black market. Utter nonsense. With hundreds of millions of Americans handling green money stateside everyday, I'm confident that if the enemy chose to get their hands on it, that wouldn't be a problem. But nonetheless, because of this we had what were called "military payment certificates" known as MPC's. As memory serves me, there was a $10 bill, a $5 bill and a dollar bill and paper currency for a fifty-cent piece, a twenty-five cent piece, and perhaps for a nickel. I'm not sure about the nickel, but in any event, that is what we used for currency.

From time to time the government would change the MPC, let's say from yellow to red for the sake of discussion. The idea was to catch the black marketers, the whorehouses, and so forth with their pants down because they all accepted MPC's in exchange for their product or services. The way this worked was that they would keep military people restricted to quarters inside a base and then there would be an orderly change of currency. Twenty-four hours later the old MPC was valueless and the new stuff was the order of the day, the idea being to stick the aforementioned entrepreneurs with tons of worthless certificates.

Because of the nature of what we did for a living in the Air Force it would be difficult, almost impossible, to restrict us to quarters. As a consequence, I prayed for an MPC exchange. I would be able to go downtown, and for a penny on a dollar, acquire the old stuff, which would be exchanged for the new currency. Clearly, an instant millionaire was in the making. They had such an exchange very shortly before I arrived overseas. While I was in Japan and Korea for a total of eighteen months, there was no change of currency, another lost opportunity. I sure did hope there would be one, just one, and then the Williams' fortune would be made.

When I got back home I was able to drive a relatively new convertible and have a decent selection of cashmere jackets. Not a bad stunt on $75 a month.

Liquor was very easy to come by in Korea. If memory serves me, you could buy a case of what we would generally call today "well booze" for twelve to eighteen bucks a case. The good stuff, the bonded scotches (name brands) were difficult to come by.

Not out of character, I had a connection through the diplomatic corps to get my hands on a fair amount of supply of good booze. It should be noted that when I was in Japan and Korea I seldom drank anything more potent than Coca-Cola. This lack of alcoholic consumption, would you believe, got me in much trouble. I had always coveted a Russian pistol. Nine millimeters and they looked a bit like a 45, but much lighter and obviously because they were in short supply they were the envy of those who owned them.

A friend and I decided we would go up to the First Marine Division one sunny day in August and see if we could trade some of my good Scotch whiskey for a Russian pistol. It should be noted that they were carried by only field-grade officers, so the guy providing it would had have to nail himself a full colonel or above, not an inconsequential task.

The two of us went as far as we dared into the combat area in a Jeep. We didn't want to lose the vehicle. The driver dropped us off and we started to hitchhike. We were walking along the Han River on a sunny, summer day, as picturesque as one might wish. Birds chirping, not too hot, altogether pleasant. Suddenly a jeep appeared on the scene and asked us where we were going and we told them we were looking for the First Marine Division. They said, "Get in, don't you know what's across the river?" We acknowledged we did not. "That's held by the Chinese." Not exactly a John Wayne idea of a front line, but there it was. Our side held one side of the river, the Chinese the other. I asked the driver why they drove so slowly, and he said, "If you drive very slowly you don't leave a big plume of dust behind you, which oftentimes will excite the enemy gunner on the other side to knock you off for sport." Not exactly the front line I envisioned when I was younger.

We got dropped off at the staging area. The First Marine combat points were called Able, Baker and Charlie sites (what a lack of imagination). We caught the chow truck up to Able site and talked to the guys up there. They had plenty of weapons to trade but not what we were looking for. They offered to buy our whiskey, but that's not why we were there. We went to the Baker site. A very young second lieutenant came out and asked me who I was. I told him and I told him what I wanted.

He very casually reached into his holster, pulled out a 45, pushed a round into the chamber, put it to my head and said, "You're under arrest." I looked at him, pushed the gun away from my head and said, "Lieutenant, where am I gonna run to?" I guess he figured that was probably true and cleared his weapon. I asked, "What are we under arrest for?" He told me, "Bootlegging whiskey." My reply was, "I have no intention of selling this whiskey." He said, "That's not the way I heard it from the guys at the last site." At that point he confiscated my whiskey.

Now, in all the years since I've graduated from high school, I've run in to someone with whom I graduated on only two occasions. One was at a speaking engagement in Pittsburgh, Pennsylvania, and the second was about to happen in Korea. They put me under guard with a fellow I played football with in high school. Hard to believe! He then took us to the staging area where the officer in charge sternly lectured us. As I recall, I think he was something like a captain and he didn't like these airmen running around "the front." He decided our hair was much too long and took us to a barbershop, where a young Asian lad in rubber shoes was holding forth. I made the mistake of calling him "boyson." Turned out he was a Filipino Marine. My hair came off right down to the scalp. Not that it mattered very much, it's not like I had any impressive dates coming up.

We were then taken to a major who vowed that he was about to put a stop to these airmen coming up to "our front" — note the possessive adjective. We were put in a tent and were supposed to be under guard, but it was pretty loose. The young Marines were impressed by us, taking no nonsense from senior non-commissioned officers. There wasn't a whole lot they could do to us. They knew it and we knew it. After going down for dinner, we were returned to the tent for the night and then were told there was a possibility of combat since the only time the Chinese and the Marines made any contact with each other was at night. Fortunately nothing came of that.

The next morning we were taken to the colonel. He gave us a lecture about the airmen coming to his front. (With the major calling it "our front," I wonder what possessive a general might use.) He asked us who our commanding officer was, and I responded "Major General Lynn." Of course General Lynn was back in the United States and our commanding officer on site was a captain, but the Colonel didn't have to know that.

He kind of looked a little flustered for a moment and said, "Well, you'll have to send an officer back if you want to get your liquor back." I knew they had consumed it the night before, and wasn't too concerned about it. They decided to turn us loose and give us a ride to a safe area. We hitchhiked back to our squadron area, where we got an interesting reception since we were walking around with very closely cropped heads. We were also technically AWOL for one day. The old man decided he would do some kind of punishment on paper so somebody later on down range couldn't bring any action against us. It was kind of a fun arrangement because nobody paid a whole lot of attention to military rules in security service, which is perhaps why someone like me wound up there. As it turned out, I never did get that Russian pistol.

Ultimately, my time in the service ended. Somewhere about six or seven months before my discharge date, which would have been February 25, the Air Force came out with another regulation, bless the regulations. In essence, if you could demonstrate that you could be admitted to school but if your regular discharge date precluded that so you'd miss a year, or if there was a job position available to you now that would not be available three months later, you could get out of the Air Force ninety days early.

I am sure to most of you, and to me as well, today ninety days either way doesn't sound like very much, but for a kid in the military who wanted out, ninety days seemed like an eternity. Immediately I set to work to think how could I make this happen? The school angle had no worth to me because I was being discharged in February. At the very most, I would have got out a couple of weeks early to start school. That was quickly scratched; the job angle was something else again!

I talked to my brother, Walter, who in turn, turned me over to Joe Cassini, the son of the attorney mentioned earlier. I had a Cassini at each end of my enlistment. One helped me get in and one was going to help me get out. He owned, among other things, a construction company working on the Garden State Parkway. Joe said, "You write the letter, I'll sign it."

When I got done with the letter on Joe's stationery it became clear that the entire Garden State Parkway project would go right into the dumper unless this young man was discharged immediately. The letter suggested, among other things, that while experience was certainly desirable and I had that, most important I was acceptable to the local unions. The Air Force accepted my letter, via Joe, and I beat them out of three months. As a matter of fact, I even got a few extra hours because I was discharged on Thanksgiving Day 1954. Because it was a holiday, instead of waiting for the end of the day at 4 o'clock, I was discharged at 10 a.m.

Unbeknown to me on that exact same day, at about the same hour, Mike Thompson, whom I have mentioned here on other occasions, came into this world.

I returned to New Jersey and was reunited with my old friend, Bob Geyer. When we were discharged, Bob was married and had kids, so he had to find employment immediately. I was a little more fortunate to the extent that I was only looking out for me.

We went into several businesses together. One was Pleasure Island Products — there's a name. Bob had been stationed in Hawaii for a period and made some business connections there for such items as jewelry, stuffed animals, perfumes and shoes, so we went into the business of "importing" products from Hawaii.

What we didn't know about importing and selling things would have filled volumes. For our business phone, we used his home phone number which, would you believe, was a party line. Well, to make a very, very long, sad story short, we lost our hat and shoes and tail. (As an aside, one of the products, the thong shoes, took off like a rocket about a year after we were forced out of the business.)

We took our entire inventory to Long John's Auction Market (yes, the talk show host), which was analogous to today's flea markets, and unloaded a portion of our inventory. At that time, I was working for Wesson Oil, driving a company car, and had a load — and I mean a major load — of these stuffed animals jammed into my trunk so I could go to the auction after work. As luck would have it, my supervisor, John Charles, decided to ride with me that day. I thought, no problem, he's not going to want to go into the trunk. But he did. He wanted to pick up a couple or three cubes of margarine to deliver to a customer, and as I started to load it in the back seat, he said, "Oh no, no! Let's put it in the trunk." He grabbed the keys, opened the trunk and the thing blasted open with a couple of hundred stuffed animals. Keeping my job took a lot of explaining.

For some reason, Bob and I decided to go into the ice cream business, meaning the vending business. We picked up an old Chevrolet truck. The roof of the truck had a rack screwed onto it for carrying ladders, so rather than trying to take it off and repair it, we built a peaked roof like a cottage and put shingles on it, not knowing that was the trademark of an ice cream company in New York at the time. We built the back of the truck out of wood, insulated it and put in 55-gallon drums to make freezers where we would put dry ice.

Why we didn't make a square box out of wood is something that to this day I don't understand, but we decided to use the drums, which were a bit cumbersome. We bought our ice cream and dry ice from a wholesaler. Ice cream pops cost us a nickel each and the ice pops I think were 2 cents or thereabouts. We sold the ice cream pops for 13 cents or two for 25 cents, which was a couple of pennies under our competitor, Good Humor. We never made a ton of money, but we made some.

Bob had to work in the daytime where I did not, and as a consequence, I was paid more than he, but I depended on this for a living, where he did not. I had no responsibilities. We kept the truck in a garage across the street from my parents' home on North Walnut Street in East Orange, where I was living after my discharge from the Air Force.

Most businesses take a direction of their own. You may decide to carry a certain line of merchandise, but your customers will ultimately dictate many things, such as, what you carry, how much it costs and so forth. If you don't go with the customer, pretty soon you are out of business. That has been true of my broadcast career and, in general, it's a truth that should never be neglected. You go with the flow.

One of the things that we found rather quickly when we were selling ice cream was that you sold a lot more ice cream in the poor neighborhoods than in the better suburbs. It doesn't require a genius to figure out why. In the poorer neighborhoods, on hot summer nights the kids were playing on the street. In the better neighborhoods, they were away at summer camp or down at the shore or maybe in bed after 7 p.m., but not out buying your ice cream. Oh sure, you do some business there, it would be disingenuous to say otherwise, but the poor neighborhoods were where the money was. And very quickly, when I ran my evening route, I started running it through the poor, essentially ethnic and, in many cases, largely black neighborhoods. At 11 o'clock at night, those kids were out and they had a dime in their hand.

That just proved the truth of something my Father always used to tell me. He didn't leave much money behind, but he constantly told me a couple of things that stuck with me. The first was, "If you want to live with the classes, you work with the masses. If you work with the classes you will live with the masses." In other words, there are a lot more people eating at McDonald's than there are at Twenty-One. Buy a McDonald's, and dine at Twenty-One.

The second thing he told me was, "A fast nickel is better than a slow dime." In other words, don't be an oink-oink. If there is a profit, take it, but don't try to squeak the last bit out of every deal. Good advice to be remembered.

I remember meeting a young black guy. I used to stop at his place. I called it a delicatessen then, but today you would probably call it a bodega. While we never got to be close friends, we talked a lot about opportunities. We were both the same age, we were both hustlers. I mentioned something in passing one day about South Orange, which was the next town up directly on South Orange Avenue from where we were having this conversation. He said, "I've never been there."

"You gotta be kidding me," I said, "it is only four or five miles away. What do you mean you've never been there?"

"I'm too busy here," he said. "You have no idea how much opportunity there is here in the middle of this Negro (black) ghetto. You see that fish store up the street? I own that. The tavern on the corner, I own that too.

"There are so many needs to be met here, why in the world would I want to be messing around up in South Orange?"

That lesson has always stayed with me. There is much more money to be made in the poorer neighborhoods than in the wealthy neighborhoods, simply because the poorer neighborhoods have needs that are constantly going unmet. If you wish to succeed in any endeavor, look to the areas that are not prospering. There is a classic buck to be made there. I have used that to my advantage throughout my entire life.

Driving that ice cream truck was a good introduction to peddling and I've done a good deal of that during my life. I've done a good deal of driving, too, and eventually I went on to driving a taxicab, as I have recounted.

However, the hours were impossible, and especially with a family to support, I was always looking for some other way to support them. And, it was one of my failures that contributed to my finding a much better way.

I mentioned elsewhere that Bob Geyer and I bought Remley's Pharmacy after poor Mr. Price had a heart attack and it was closed. We didn't buy it for a drugstore, but to turn it into a restaurant and soda fountain, which, as the outcome demonstrated, we were clearly ill equipped to open and manage. However, everything that you do contributes to who you are and, although that experience in itself was very negative, it contributed to another job that got me much of the way through college and taught me a great deal.

The drugstore property was not owned but rented by Mr. Price's wife for very little money. The electricity had been off for at least three or four months, and when it went off the freezers were full of ice cream. You can imagine what that smelled like after several months of fermenting inside a closed freezer cabinet. Bob and I sucked it up, dumped this witch's brew into the sewer outside the store and managed to scrub the freezers clean. We had to clean out the store and we threw out, by today's values, probably hundreds of thousands of dollars worth of stuff. Thousands of apothecary bottles and glass stopper bottles went into the trash and the contents were emptied down the sink, which I'm sure would be an environmental no-no today. Hundred and hundreds of metal cigar boxes crammed with prescriptions went into the garbage. Bob asked if I had any interest in a huge mortar and pestle and I said, "No." He gave that to a physician friend of his. I believe that the druggist's equipment, which even at that time was antique, would be worth a mint today.

The basement was crammed full of World War II tie-in merchandise. What was tie-in merchandise? If a merchant wanted a case of hard-to-get merchandise during World War II, he was frequently required to buy a dozen or more cases of stuff that he didn't want. Examples being toothbrushes or, as I found both at the Service Drug Company when I worked there and at Remley's, hundreds of cases of very poor-quality sanitary napkins. They probably had been sitting around warehouses in the 1930s until the suppliers found a good way to get rid of them during World War II. The same was true with cigarette brands that failed and were sitting around warehouses.

During what was probably an artificial shortage in World War II, they were forced upon merchants who toward the end of the war were glad to get them. Anything was better than nothing.

We inherited this basement full of all of this old-time merchandise, including, I recall, several hundred bathing caps. Bob and I took all of that stuff up to Long John's Auction, rented a place for a weekend and sold it for a couple of pennies on the dollar, realizing some profit.

We opened BruBobs, (wow, what imagination) the only air-conditioned luncheonette in the area, which was quite an innovation in those days. We lost our shirts. Bob, once again, was working at a full-time job. I was working also at a job and trying to run this place. Fortunately, we found a live one who wanted to buy a business for her son and managed to get ourselves out with a reasonably whole skin. We were now ex-restaurateurs. We knew a lot about the business, or so we claimed.

When I decided to go back to school, the college was located in Newark, New Jersey: Newark State College on Broadway. The state had acquired a piece of property from the Kean family, who were a major force in New Jersey economics and politics, and of which, former Governor Thomas Kean, was a member. They were moving the college out to Union, New Jersey. I'd become friendly with one of the professors, Everett Howe, who was put in charge of the Student Union Building. Newark State College, now Kean University, is a huge institution today, but at that time it was one academic building, a power center, a library, and an administration building. The student center was home to the cafeteria and space for a snack bar. I say space, because that's all there was at the time. Mr. Howe said that he had heard from some of the other kids that I had some restaurant experience and, of course, I was quick to embellish on that. By the time I got done, I was certainly capable of handling at least a dozen Horn & Hardarts.

Mr. Howe asked if I would be interested in running the college snack bar. The idea of a job on campus had a great deal of appeal. I told him I would be very happy to. As it turned out, there were artist's renderings of the snack bar, the permanent installation and tables and booths, but when we got out to the campus, there was absolutely nothing there other than a room. Not even the plumbing had been completed.

I built the snack bar entirely on credit and a little bit of money of my own. We put contact paper on the wooden counters, bought coffee urns with timers so when we got there in the morning we would have hot coffee. The doughnut racks were hand-made and the refrigeration hand-me-down — nothing very professional, but we made it work. We scrounged up tables and chairs at the old school and moved them into our snack bar area, but not without some difficulty. Among other things, we were not allowed to lock up anything at night. Good ol' Tex Wilkins, the president of the college and a nice gentleman, (but a bit naive), said, "College students don't steal." Unfortunately, not only do college students steal, but so do faculty members, janitorial employees and others. We had an extremely difficult time just breaking even because of theft.

By the way, when all of the equipment finally was delivered some two years later, they found an outside manager who promptly locked up everything and put up iron gates, because "college people don't steal" but we might as well discourage them a little bit. The college then spent at least six months trying to prove that I was stealing during my management adventure.

I was the only one who wasn't, but there was a major sign that I was. Of course, they couldn't read the sign. The registers balanced every day. They balanced because I was smart enough to figure out that these rascals sooner or later would be looking at me because of the losses, so I kept a little slush fund. If the register was over by $6, I put the money into a cup in the safe. If it was under by $4, I took the $4 out of the cup, so

159

every single day our cash register was right to the penny.

Now anybody in the retail business knows that's a sure sign that somebody is monkeying with the receipts. Not necessarily stealing, but certainly monkeying, and I confess that my bookkeeper, fellow undergraduate Bob Alloway, and I manipulated those books every day. They almost never came out — how could they? With hundreds of transactions and four, five or six cashiers in the course of a day, how could they be expected to come out? But I knew that in their naivete, the college officials would want to see the registers balance, so I gave them what they wanted. But I tell you now, guys, long after the statute of limitations would free me from any responsibility, I never took a nickel. Manipulated? Yes. But I never took a nickel.

The man in charge of the snack bar did me a lot of good — although through the back door. For reasons that escape me, Dr. Fred Arnold was placed in charge of the snack bar. His sole experience with restaurants was even leaner than mine. He had worked in a drive-in theater snack bar when he was working on his degree. I had Dr. Arnold for a class on only one occasion but I still remember the example he gave. He asked us to do some very simple math problems and then he timed how fast we got them done. He then handed us another page with similar math problems, but just as we began doing the computations he went around the room like a crazy man banging on things, making all sorts of noise, demonstrating what distractions can do to you. The lesson was well taught to me.

Sometimes distractions cannot be done away with but we can condition ourselves to work under stressful conditions and outperform those who are less prepared. Score one for Dr. Arnold.

Once the faculty that governed the building had a meeting, I asked for a raise. I was making $80 or $85 a week and I wanted $100 a week. Dr. Arnold and I were walking down the hall. When I asked about my raise, he said, "You have grandiose ideas. You will never be worth $100 a week." I remembered that as I was progressing. Every time I was close to giving up, I would think of that pompous #!*!# saying, "You have grandiose ideas. You will never be worth $100 a week."

Years later when I was visiting the college, I was walking down the hall and I saw his name on the door. I stopped and I was going to knock on that door and say, "Well, here I am, Dr. Arnold, with grandiose ideas. I make more money in a couple of weeks than you make in a year." Then I thought why would I want to make an older man miserable? To what purpose? In reality he did me a kindness by telling me I had grandiose ideas. He inspired me when I was really down. I thought about him and I went on my way.

Sometime later, that anecdote was quoted in Pat Williams' book. Pat is the senior executive vice president of the Orlando Magic, and the title of this book is *Go For The Magic*. I sent the book to Dr. Arnold. He was very put out and wrote me back. I wrote him a tongue-in-cheek letter, I thought, saying, "I was worth more than $100 then and still am." He wrote back, "In my opinion you weren't worth $100 a week then and maybe not now. After all, some faculty members weren't making that much." There's something we slip into. Because one person isn't making it, does that make another worth less? I was worth more (in dollars) than the faculty members and have proved it. But because a faculty member wasn't making $100 a week, I wasn't worth $100 a week? What utter nonsense.

Despite all that, I earned a living to support my family for a couple of years within the college community, which was a bit easier than driving a cab. The negative experience with Dr. Arnold telling me about my "grandiose ideas" provided the stimulation that helped me succeed. For this, I owe him a debt. I pointed out to him in my letter that the primary function of an educator is to exert a positive influence on those charges that they, however briefly, touch. That is their only excuse for existing. In this instance, he was a success, even though he hadn't planned it that way. He has my thanks.

While I was running the snack bar in my junior year of college, my staff consisted entirely of other undergraduates. They came and they went. One of the things that I did on the side was to bid on college functions and, once again, I did whatever I had to do to survive. Among other things, I would get hold of the other bidder's bids, open them and always underbid them. Pretty soon, nobody else bid, and I had a lock on the business.

I would charge all of the food and groceries to the college. I didn't have the kind of money to order that amount of food — 150 pounds of roast beef, say — but I always intercepted the bills and paid them in cash so they never got into the system. I used the college's credit but never abused it. I also used all of the college's facilities to prepare things.

Two of those projects were noteworthy. The first was the dedication of the college library. Dr. Vaughn-Ames was in charge of this. Parenthetically, you know you have been around for a while when people you know have passed away and have their names on buildings. The college now has a Vaughn-Ames Hall.

In any event, Dr. Vaughn-Ames contacted me to cater the dedication of the library, which required some 1,500 lunches, which seemed like a pretty good bunch at that time. For each participant — and I believe she overestimated their appetite — she wanted a couple of sandwiches, one turkey and one tuna fish, a dessert item and a piece of fruit in a box. I won the bid and I got my fraternity brothers together to work all night to put these lunches together. You learn something every day and one of the things she wanted was one slice of white and one slice of whole wheat bread. But I found in a hurry that evening that whole wheat bread goes stale a lot more quickly when exposed to air than does white. It was necessary to always put the whole-wheat side down and then put mayonnaise on the upside to keep the bread from going stale too quickly.

Dennis Swanson, one of my fraternity brothers with whom I am still in contact, now a college professor and superintendent of schools, was one of the workers that night and thought it was really funny to tell disgusting jokes. Jokes that would upset your stomach — you know the kind. After about two hours of telling these jokes, only one guy got sick. Dennis had to leave the room with the food smells as he tossed his cookies. How sweet it is.

We made a minor error the evening when we catered this little affair. We forgot to defrost the turkey, so now I was stuck with solid frozen turkey that had to be sliced and put into sandwich form in a matter of a couple of hours. We solved the problem, however recklessly, by tapping into a live steam line that was used to heat the building from the powerhouse. We then scalded our turkey. I'm surprised that no one has continued to use our slicing method. Rather than slicing the turkey like bologna is traditionally cut, for that's what it looks like when you slice it, we cut the turkey into about 4-inch chunks of roll, and then sliced it from the side, thereby giving it a look of freshly sliced turkey, rather than bologna. Restaurateurs, note.

We catered many a college function and it was easily done because I could hire the kitchen staff from among my colleagues. There were lots of coeds with blue skirts and white blouses, or tan skirts and white blouses, and the guys with chino pants and white shirts. It worked out. They got paid in cash and everything was done well. We gave them ample portions of groceries at a price they couldn't match elsewhere. It was a win-win for everybody that helped me keep the wolf from the door and I learned a good deal about doing affairs for 500 to 1,000 people.

However, we did have some screw-ups. One involved sheet cakes, which were always precut. You cut the cakes into squares and then put the icing on top of the cut cake. That way, you could just break off individual pieces and you were ready to go instead of having to slice it and make a mess. The only problem was that one of my girls didn't know that. She saw these beautifully iced cakes and proceeded to slice them through the icing, not knowing they were cut underneath. We wound up with a whole bunch of crumbles. We solved that problem by crumbling it up even more so that the icing and the cake were all mixed together, and then serving it in a receptacle designed to hold puddings. As a matter of fact, it didn't taste bad.

On another occasion, we had Charlotte Russe to serve at one of the class functions in the evening. Unfortunately they got behind in their scheduling, and the first thing you know we had the curfew, and we hadn't had a chance to serve dessert. I, of course, was using the college cafeteria refrigeration facilities, but the next morning, when it was time for Mrs. Smith and her crew to come in and serve the regular meals, my stuff had to disappear. I was stuck with 1,000 or more Charlotte Russes (ladyfingers that have been split, put into a cardboard container and then filled with whipped cream and topped with a cherry). I drove home with my station wagon loaded with Charlotte Russe, giving trays of them to the turnpike toll collectors, my neighbors, and whomever. I was too parsimonious to throw them out. I couldn't sell them and certainly couldn't eat them, but I had a great time giving them away.

One day, one of my classmates came into the snack bar and asked me to cash a check. The check was for $240. I looked at it. It was drawn on a bank in Pennsylvania. I couldn't believe it: $240! I was working for $80 a week. That was three weeks' pay. I asked, "Where did you get this from?"

The guy said, "That's what I made last week."

"Last week?"

His name was "Marvin."

Marvin was a decent guy. He went on to be a football coach, a basketball coach, and the head of a special school. But Marvin was not the most ambitious guy in the world, and I don't think he would argue with that, even today.

I looked at that check and said, "Okay," and I told the girl to cash it, but I put the check in my pocket and took it back to my office. I called the company that issued the check, World Mutual Health and Accident Insurance Company, King of Prussia, Pennsylvania. The guy's name on the check was Bob Yarnall. I called them and asked for Mr. Yarnall. They put me through to him, and I said that I had this check drawn to Marvin so-and-so, and he said, "Yes, it's good."

"I know it's good, I already called the bank."

"Why are you calling?"

"I don't know what Marvin does for you, but I understand you paid him this much money for one week's work. Well, if he's worth $240, I'm worth $1,000, 'cause I'm four times the man he'll ever be."

There was dead silence on the phone. Mr. Yarnall said, "Are you for real?"

I said, "I couldn't be more for real. I'm as serious as a heart attack."

"So, why don't you come out and see me?"

I drove down to Pennsylvania and two weeks later I was Marvin's boss.

I left the snack bar to go to work for Bob Yarnell and the president of World Mutual, Blaine Scott III. This was another one of those quasi-legal endeavors that I was involved with when I was younger. World Mutual was in the business of selling hospitalization, accident, and health insurance to all manner of clients, but in particular to clients who were elderly.

They had a neat way of making sure their salespeople were out there hustling all the time. If you lived in Pennsylvania, you'd work in New York. If you lived in New York you might work in Virginia. The point is, you weren't working in your home area. You didn't go home at night; you went back to a motel. So there was no reason for you not to be out hustling to sell your products. The problem was that the sales people had to have leads that could be developed and were cost-effective. Bob Yarnall had worked out a system to do this, a system that you would never get away with today and, even then; we were always trying to stay one jump ahead of the local constabulary. We called it "dropping."

It works something like this. Bob had a print shop on the premises where he printed return mail postcards with a coupon that you could fill out. We put them on relatively light paper, and we printed them by the hundreds of thousands. We loaded up our car with these postcards. We used to count them out, but I got to the point where I could reach in and grab a stack of 100 or 200 at a pop — no problem at all after you handle tens of thousands of them. We took a town such as Bayonne, New Jersey, and started on one side and just drove up one side of the street and down the other until we had covered the whole town. When we saw a group of children, somewhere between seven and ten years old, we would call them over to the car. Can you imagine doing that today? But, even then we didn't call over little girls, just boys. "Hey guys, we're running a little advertising program in this area, and we'd like for you to help us out."

"Yeah, what do you want us to do?"

"What we'd like you to do is take a little package of cards like this, take them in your neighborhood — we don't want you to go out of the neighborhood — and put them behind every mailbox in the area. Now, you heard me say 'behind' so that it sticks out, or even in the screen door, but you're not allowed to put it in the mailbox, 'cause that's against the law, and just keep going until you are finished. Now, you have to promise us that you won't throw them away, that you'll do the job. In return, we're going to give you a brand-new ballpoint pen."

As it progressed we handed out yo-yos, wallets and other premiums, but the pens were the big thing at the beginning. I got paid a quarter for every kid that I got, and on a decent Saturday I could go out and get 200, 250 kids. You have to remember; this was a time when you could hire a grown man for $3 an hour to work in a factory, so this was major league money. Then, of course, I moved on to hiring other guys to do it. I paid them 20 cents, and took a nickel override, so I might have as many as ten people scattered around. Then the returns would come in. We averaged a consistent three-tenths of one percent, or three cards of every thousand that we put out, would come back in as a lead. The closers would close one in three. So, we had to put 1,000 cards on the street, or ten kids, to result in one sale.

We really had no great problem with the police. I used to go to the same cities time after time. I do recall being in upstate New York in the Glens Falls area, sitting in a diner one day and hearing on the police radio — the officers would leave all of their windows open — a description of my car and some guy who was having kids take stuff door-to-door without a license. Depend on it; I was out of Glens Falls in a heartbeat.

The only time I actually ever got arrested was in Spring Valley, New York, as I remember. They took me in and I had to pay some kind of a fine. A little nip and tuck here and there, and the legality, I suppose, could be questioned but, again, you did what you had to do. I don't recall anybody ever suffering from what we did. I often wonder how many of those thousands of kids remember the guy who pulled up wanting them to help out with an advertising campaign. They would be pushing 50 today.

Toward the end of my college career, I had to pick up some money. I was finished with my job at the snack bar. I saw an ad for Mr. Softee, a soft ice cream company in Newark looking for drivers. I applied. I was rejected. The operator told me that they wanted a black guy because the route was going to go into the black neighborhood on the hill in Newark. I said I was perfectly willing to do that. He said, "No, you'd never survive up there." I gave him my name and address and told him, "Well, if something turns up, I'd like to hear from you," because I really needed the money.

At that point, we had three children, Matt, Mark and Robbins, so income was important. About a week later I got a call back. The guy wanted to know if I was still interested. I said, "Yeah." He said, "We can't find a black guy who is willing to go into that neighborhood." This was not exactly a walk in the park. It was a tough area. I was twenty-eight or twenty-nine years old, reasonably well built and far too cocky, and I said, "Sure, I'll do it."

Working in a soft ice cream truck was quite different from the hard pack that Bob and I had operated. You stayed inside the truck. You had machines that made the ice cream from a mix. You could make sundaes and milkshakes and all that sort of thing. You had a big generator in the back that was propane-powered and allowed you to have air conditioning. A little store on wheels — I'm sure you have seen them. You attracted the patrons by playing a tape over and over. I can still hear it in my mind: "Whenever you want an ice cream cone, look for Mr. Softee, S O F T EE, Mr. Softee."

There was no established route. I went out and built one up and down the streets. From the time I left the garage to the time I came back, except for a very occasional service person or someone passing through rather rapidly in a car, the only white face I saw was my own. There was antagonism between the races, nowhere near what we have today, but I knew I was going to have trouble sooner or later, so I figured I might as well get set for it. There was no point in locking the door, because if someone wanted in badly enough he could get in the front door and into my truck, so although I frequently left the door closed, I always left it unlocked.

Then trouble came. I pulled up in front of a tavern on Bank Street in Newark, and suddenly a guy who was half blasted was coming into my truck. I really don't know what his intent was, but probably to teach Mr. Softee a lesson or take his money. I kept a roll of dimes on the console in the truck, and when he started getting into the truck, I picked up the roll of dimes. The long and the short of it was that I worked him over and worked him over good. I'm sure I broke some of his ribs and messed him up pretty badly, attracting a crowd in the process. I dropped him off into the street a lot worse for wear.

I looked at all the guys standing around there, and I said, "I want you to pass the word around the neighborhood, I'm not looking for trouble, but don't ever f--k with Mr. Softee." They looked at me for a second, and a couple of the guys started to laugh and one of them said, "Right on, brother," and that was the end of my problems. I used to get out of the truck and play softball with the kids, leaving the door open, but nobody bothered me. I was the #2 truck in the state from the second day I was out there and #2 until I left.

I could go out at 11, 11:30 p.m., play my songs and find kids sitting on the stoops. They were the poor, and I was comfortable with them because I was one of them. They were out buying ice cream at 11 o'clock at night. If you were to go up into the suburbs at 8 p.m., the fathers would come out with shotguns.

We are a product of our environment and our experiences. I don't think anyone would question that. One of the experiences that made a big difference in the way that I function personally took place in 1963. Today it would be very out of character for me to go to the store for a newspaper without $500 in my pocket and likely closer to $1,000. I certainly wouldn't go out for the evening with anything less than that. I always have a substantial amount of money in cash in addition to a couple of credit cards with high limits. Also, taped in the back of my address book there is a hundred dollar bill. Just in case all else fails, I've got that hundred bucks. This may seem grandiose. I assure you, that it was not something that I had planned. Here is the experience that changed my pocket money habits.

Years ago, when we first moved into the building where Lane Robbins School was operated for so many years (it is still a school today under a different name) we had neighbors, almost directly across the road, but sitting way back from the road. Lillian and Wendell Forbes owned the large farmhouse. Wendell Forbes was a gentleman to his toes. He had served on the planning board of our community long before I came to town. He was a chief corporate council for Mobil Oil in New York City. Lillian Forbes' formal education ended in high school, but she schooled herself in many of the arts, and her manners, with one or two very interesting exceptions, were impeccable.

Their home was a showplace. Everything in the home, with the exception of appliances such as a waffle iron and hair dryer, was an antique: the utensils, the pewter plates. The silverware all predated the American Revolution, and all were authentic pieces. In the dining room, the chandelier was entirely dependent upon candles to shed its light. The home itself was from that same period. They also had, across the way, a barn that was finished to be a very cozy apartment.

Renting the apartment was somewhat restricted. You had to be a full-time student at the Princeton Theological Seminary in order to qualify to move into Wendell and Lillian's barn. Given the fact that the Forbes' were childless, there are a significant numbers of Wendells and Lillians born to pastors of that persuasion. Lillian was considered the grand dame of the area. It was also a custom to invite the young bucks and their wives, like Ruthann and me, Jack and Ann Joyce across the road, and others including a guy I became very close with, Albert S.

DeVries.

Albert and I were tight for the better part of thirty-five years. Unhappily, he passed away on December 30, 1996.

Albert started out after World War II with a wheelbarrow and a couple of shovels and built them into a very substantial landscaping enterprise. He was way ahead of me in terms of establishing himself as a player. He was my senior by some six or seven years.

We were all attending a very elaborate cocktail party at Lillian's. The guest list, as I remember it, was like a who's who in industry and the local peasantry, i.e. neighbors. For example, I was instructed to take a drink out to Mrs. Penny. I believe she was the widow of James Cash Penny. If memory serves me, one of the Sarnoff family was at this particular soiree. You get the picture. We did serve the drinks, move the cars and the rest of it. I remember pulling up in my Volkswagen bus, next to a Rolls Royce. Somehow I didn't think it fit but I had to leave it someplace. The affair was pleasant.

After the festivities somebody suggested we all go up to the "Grill" and have a drink. The "Grill" was the Franklin Park Inn. The building and the restaurant are still there, but under different owners and different names. This building, a stagecoach stop on the New York to Trenton run in Colonial days, has operated as a restaurant and bar without interruption since that time. It was the local hangout and had a big fireplace where we'd sit in the corner and talk. A fellow named Freddy Reck was running the place. His ninety year old mother was the cook, and she made the best turkey and the best mushroom soup that ever teased a palate. It was fun to go in there for dinner, and we ate there on a fairly regular basis.

There must have been a dozen or more people that went up to have a post-mortem about the party we had just attended. I remember so well to this moment, Albert saying, "Let's have a drink, this round is on me." Well it's ordinarily expected if someone buys a round, the other guys do the same thing. I have been accused of many things in my life, but not picking up a check isn't one of them. I go out of my way to, perhaps because of this incident or maybe because now I can afford it. The fact was on this occasion there was no way I could say, "Have a round on me." I simply didn't have the money and I cannot tell you how bad I felt. It obviously wasn't a question of making a choice. This was in a day before credit cards became ubiquitous. I had enough in my pocket to buy a drink for my wife and me, maybe even two, but certainly not to buy an expensive round. I got over the pain, but I decided that was never going to happen to me again, never!

Now with credit cards that's all one needs to be able to buy that round. Beyond that, given that I have the ability to have a couple of dollars, I simply do not ever go anywhere without funds in my pocket. Call it my security blanket. That would be a fair analysis. Call it a weakness, perhaps. I am never secure unless I have far more funds available to me when I'm traveling then would ever be necessary.

Once I discussed this incident with Albert. He had no recollection whatsoever because for him this was just an ordinary thing and, very candidly, over the years it has become a very ordinary event for me. That cocktail party, and the little get-together at the Franklin Park Grill afterwards, truly had a profound effect on my feeling toward money. "This is never going to happen to me again," I promised myself, and it has not.

I have always said, "Don't sweat the small stuff," and I stand by that. In other words, don't let the little things get you down. Deal with the big problems. The little ones will resolve themselves. On the other side of that, I have been aware since I was a very young child that little decisions can alter your entire life. (Not putting a seat belt on, for example.)

I remember the little decision that made me aware of that and has stayed with me for a lifetime. I was twelve years old wandering down Fourth Avenue in East Orange, going home to North 15th Street. I was on the corner of Fourth and 19th and for whatever reason, I pondered whether I should walk down Fourth Avenue down to 15th and over, or over 19th to Park Avenue and down. A major decision for a twelve year old. As the fates would have it, I decided, for no particular reason, "Oh, I'll go down Fourth Avenue." Well, no more than 40 feet down Fourth Avenue, I passed Bonnaforte's Market and saw a help wanted sign. This was at the tag end of World War II, when warm bodies were hard to come by. As it turned out, they wanted a delivery boy for a fat $5 a week. I took the job, which led to my working in that area and finally working for Mr. Price at Remley's Pharmacy and going on to Sam and Joe's.

In other words, the whole course of my life was altered because I went down Fourth Avenue and took that part-time job. I have often wondered, suppose I'd gone down 19th Street, what would life have held? I'll never know.

8

Getting Ahead in Business

Surviving and prospering in business take the application of all the lessons I have talked about until now and then some. While each business has its own circumstances, challenges and opportunities, some lessons apply across the board.

Obviously, in this space I cannot go into every type of business and every contingency that might arise. However, from my own experience I can point out some pitfalls anyone getting into business can avoid, and some prudent steps that one can take to safeguard his investment and make it grow.

What I am about to say arises from my own experience, which has included everything from selling ice cream myself on the street, to owning operations with many employees. One thing I have learned is that many of the same principles apply to all of them. Here they are:

Never get complacent.

Never. No matter how well you're doing, no matter if you're raking in the money faster than you can count it, never stop watching the competition. Never take your success for granted. That is the fastest way to turn today's moneymaker into tomorrow's disaster.

In the early 1960s, my wife and I opened a nursery school and then a day camp, Lane Robbins, in Somerset, New Jersey. In the middle '60s we were the place to be. We had a waiting list to get in and we had to make little effort in terms of advertising. We did advertise, but not as much as we should have because we had more people than we could accommodate. That situation leads one into a feeling of complacency.

One summer, a young couple purchased a defunct overnight camp and turned it into a day camp. I remember when they wanted to arrange some intercamp athletics. I said, "Well, I'm not too sure you guys can play us, since you only have 70 or 80 kids over there and we are in the several hundreds." But we were very happy to accommodate them and I must say, at this late date, that I was a bit condescending. What a mistake that was.

They had a good operation, but more importantly, they were aggressively promoting their operation. For a good many years I added a new attraction every summer but, once again, with the disease of complacency, I had started to neglect that activity. In any event, that first summer they had their 80 kids. Two years later when they came to play us, you can imagine the shock I had when I saw that a great many of "my kids" were suddenly their kids. They became the place to be. I saw my enrollment starting to drop off and had to scramble like crazy just to keep even.

All of this was totally unnecessary.

Sure, we had our loyal cadre of customers and we were very happy for that, but we were not out there every day telling our story. If it is not necessary to do that, please explain to me why McDonald's spends hundreds of millions of dollars a year on advertising. The fact is that there was only one company that ever achieved national greatness without advertising, and that was the Hershey Company. Milton Hershey didn't believe in advertising. After Mr. Hershey's demise, the folks running that company joined the rest of the world and became advertisers.

It's funny how things come full cycle. Steven Spielberg's company offered Mars and Company the rights to put M&Ms into his movie, *E.T.* Mars declined. Hershey stepped in with its Reese's Pieces, and so it was Reese's Pieces that showed up in one of the biggest hits of all time. It was the sales of Reese's Pieces, not M&Ms, that went up 30-odd percent. What a great investment for Hershey. What a bad call for Mars.

The point is, no matter how good you are at what you do, no matter how dominant your particular endeavor is in your industry, never get complacent. Always look ahead. Always look to improve your product and your image. Let people know who you are. I am constantly reminded that while millions of people listen to my program, the overwhelming majority of people in the United States have never heard of me. That's the good and bad news together. The bad news is that they are not listening, but the good news is that my potential market is still out there to be expanded. You can bet your life and your first-born child that I do everything I can to expand my audience and my impact. You can't stand still. Either you go forward or you go backward. Those are the only two choices. Choose to go forward.

While you go forward, however, never forget to bring along the people who got you to where you are now. Those people are your customers. And that leads to lesson two:

It's easier to keep a customer than to find one.

Somebody told me the ratio is about 20 to 1. It costs you twenty times as much to find a new customer as it does to hold onto one you have, and yet, so many businesses don't take that into account.

Here's an example of what I mean. We had been in the rose business for a long time. We get down and dirty when we sell roses: a dozen roses for $15, sometimes two dozen for $20 —

well under our competitors. We do not arrange them. We put them in green wrappers, throw in a little Baker fern, and out you go, cash on delivery.

Oftentimes, the people who bought roses from us were not the traditional $60 or $70 a dozen rose buyer. Many were Joe Six-Pack who had a fight with his wife the night before, taking a peace offering home. Sometimes these guys would come in, pick out a dozen roses and flip them into the back seat of their car, forgetting that it was twelve degrees below zero outside. Then they would decide to fortify themselves before the trip home, stopping for a couple of shots and a beer while the roses languished on the back seat. You can see where the scenario is going. The next thing you know the roses were frozen black and when the package was opened, both the recipient and the giver were upset. Back they would come to our store. Well, the easy thing for the clerk to say was, "Hey stupid, you left the roses out in the cold and they got frozen. Roses won't take that kind of treatment. No flower will."

You could say that and tell them that if they wanted more they would have to pay for them. They might even buy them, but that would be the last you would see of that customer.

We took a different tack. Our gals and guys were instructed to say something like the following:

"Hold up your right hand."

"Hold up my right hand?"

"Yeah, hold up your right hand. 'I solemnly swear, *I solemnly swear* to go right home. I will not pass go, I will not look for the $200 and I will give these roses to whomever they are intended for.' And if you do that, I will give you the roses at no cost."

"Okay."

On that kind of deal, we probably broke even. We haven't lost, but we haven't made money. But at the very least, we do not have someone walking around bad-mouthing us for the next twelve months. And, more importantly, the likelihood is that the next time this guy screws up at home, and he will, he'll come to our joint instead of somewhere else because we took good care of him. We have taken a negative and at least made it neutral, and possibly made it into a positive.

That sounds like a simple thing, and it is. You'd be surprised, though, by how many businesses, small and large, have never learned it.

Once I went to a stockholders' meeting at a bank where I have a small investment. I stood up at the meeting and said that I appreciated the remarks that the chairman had made in his statement to the stockholders about consumers and how service is the most important thing we had here. However, it was my contention that the noise of what he was doing and, more importantly, what his subordinates were doing, was drowning out what he was saying in his message to the stockholders.

I had the following experience. I called the bank and was given an officer. I had a very simple request. I had what was called a "zero balance" account in this bank, among others — perhaps a dozen accounts in all. "Zero balance" accounts are operating accounts into which you put in enough money to pay whatever checks you have drawn, but you keep no balance in them. But we did have money market accounts, corporate accounts that had substantial balances, and sent well over seven figures through the bank in the course of a year — not a bad account. We were profitable for the bank. In any event, from the zero balance account it was our custom to deposit a check to cover the payroll 941 Federal Deposit obligations. (The 941 is the money that is due the government for Social Security taxes, both the employee's and the employer's share, and any money withheld from the employee's pay for federal income tax. This is a very routine proposition, known to every employer.) The problem was that the check to cover these items was drawn on a "foreign" bank — in other words, a bank in a different state — so that the 941 check would clear immediately, the foreign check would not be collected yet, therefore the account would be technically overdrawn and, although the bank would pay it, it would charge us a service charge.

The manager, who recognized that this was stupid, would always wipe away the service charge. The point, though, is that it was being done. If it were not for that manager being on his toes, I would have been a very unhappy camper. I called an officer at the home office of this bank — it had about 28 branches — and explained my situation. The woman on the other end of the line said, "What do you expect us to do? Do it for nothing?" The cost of supporting the float here, if indeed there was any true float, would have been about 15 cents per day. Figure three days, 45 cents, twice a month, 90 cents, or something on the order of $12 a year. Now, that is the outside cost of the float.

But for that, she put in jeopardy one checking account that had an average of more than $30,000 at all times, which the bank had the use of without paying interest. Figure that one out. When I talked to her, she just couldn't understand that. I said, "Let me talk to another officer." She gave me a senior vice president, who told me he would look into it. He must have been taking a penetrating look, because by the time of the stockholders' meeting, seven months later, I had yet to hear from him.

The point I was trying to make — and I did embarrass this gentleman in front of the stockholders — was that while he may have had good intentions, his subordinates were screwing up the works. I pointed out that a bank he had recently acquired, at a premium price, had lost about 25 percent of its deposits, and I had to believe that at least a portion of that was due to the very foolish way the customers were being handled. (I had stock in his bank because I was a stockholder in the smaller bank that had been absorbed.) He sputtered a bit and looked embarrassed. I did not think things were going to change.

Now, why would you tick off current customers? It's so much easier to make them happy than to find new ones. If you are starting a business or running a business, understanding this principle can make the difference between profit and loss and, indeed, between success and failure. Remember, no one ever won an argument with a customer. Sure, you win the argument, but you lose the customer.

Here are some more examples:

On a recent Sunday, I visited a Sears Roebuck store in New Port Richey, Florida. As some of my friends along my various party lines know, I own a 1964 Ford Mustang convertible that has been completely restored from the ground up and obviously requires loving care. Since it is stored in my garage in Florida and Florida enjoys high humidity, it's imperative that the garage be climate controlled. My dehumidifier gave up the ghost and, although I guess it was repairable, I thought it was easiest to go out and buy a new one and get it over with.

I stopped at my friendly Sears store and found four different types of dehumidifiers. Given the fact that I was just going to stick this in the garage and let it crank, there was no reason to get anything but the bare-bones model, which was on sale for $179.99. Sold. It took me at least 15 or 20 seconds to pick it out. I'm a tough sell. The salesman came back and apologized and said, "I'm sorry, we're out of that one and since it is on sale we can't let you have the floor model." Terrific. I wanted to get this job done that Sunday. I said, "Well, what's the alternative? I'm out of here on Wednesday. I'll be out for a week or two and I've got to get this done." He went through his computer and after he tap-tap-tapped for a long time, he said, "Okay, we can get one in here on Tuesday." I said, "That will be fine." He wrote up the order and tap-tap-tap — oops!

Between the time he wrote up the order and the time I asked about availability, it slipped forward to Wednesday. I said, "Terrific, I can't come on Wednesday, I'm out of here on a plane. I'm going to have to go somewhere else and that really is aggravating. Either you sell me the one on the floor here, or find a way to get one to me by Tuesday." He said, "Just a moment, let me talk to the manager." He came back a minute later and told me the manager said there was nothing he could do about getting another one here, but he said he would sell me the next grade of humidifier at the sale price. The next one cost $249.99 but was sold to me for $179.99.

That store kept a customer. That manager knew exactly what he was doing. I don't know how much difference there was in the actual cost of those two products, but I can tell you this. In the next six months I spent upwards of $10,000 in that Sears store. By being smart, he kept a customer. Sears spends a ton of money, including a lot of money on my radio program, to attract new customers, and that's as it should be. But why antagonize an existing one, particularly one who spends a lot of money? This guy knew exactly how to handle that. Maybe the store took a little bit of a hit. It's possible there was no profit on this sale, but there would have been no profit anyway, since I would have had to walk out and go buy my dehumidifier elsewhere.

Chasing customers away, sometimes literally, is easy. Just forget why your customers trade with you. Service Drug Company, where I learned so much, provided a sad example. Sam and Joe, well after my leaving, decided to sell the drugstore. Whether it was to retire or not, I do not know. But I remember the guy they sold it to. His first name was Manny. Manny was a salesman for one of the drug companies, and he was going to shape up the store. The first thing he determined was that nobody made any money on newspapers, so the newspapers left. The next thing was that the postal substation was more trouble than it was worth, and so that went. In short, he was getting rid of everything that was not a part of a definable profit center. He was going to have an ethical pharmacy, not a place to hang out. Don't worry about a great cigar selection, and the soda fountain could easily be dispensed with. It's easy to see why, in about two years, Manny had bankrupted the place.

The drugstore worked because it was what it was, a place where people could congregate, where customers could be certain of finding whatever they needed in the days when supermarkets were relatively rare, the shopping mall had not yet been born, and the term "strip mall" had not yet entered our vocabulary.

When he ripped away everything that made it what it was, all in the name of higher profits, he took away all the reasons people traded there, and he doomed the business.

There are other ways to chase people away. Governments are notoriously guilty of that. For a good many years after I got into the broadcasting business, I maintained an office in New Brunswick, New Jersey. My then-manager, Bill Lally, was a reverse commuter. He lived in New York City, came out to New Brunswick and worked in the daytime, and went back to New York in the evening. As a consequence, we could oftentimes drive together into the city and talk over the affairs of state. Shortly after Bill left, my daughter, Kelly, became my business manager and worked out of the same office. From time to time we had talked about moving to a more user-friendly area.

One of the problems at that time was the great difficulty in hiring competent help. Often when you put an ad in the newspaper, all you got was a bill from the paper or, in the best-case scenario, a nineteen year old whose first question was, "What is your vacation policy?" and whose second was, "What are my retirement benefits?" Still, inertia is a difficult thing to overcome. We did have a staff, the office was furnished and we were comfortable. Even though from time to time we discussed relocating to a user-friendlier environment, nothing much ever came of those discussions.

One evening, one of the young women who worked for us was picking up the mail to take it next door to the post office. Because of the nature of our business, our mailings can be very substantial, sometimes a bag or more of mail for just one day. The young lady went to our third-floor offices, via the elevator, to pick up the mail and parked her car out in front. The building was serviced by a doorman. A New Brunswick patrolman came by and looked over at the car. The doorman said, "She'll only be a minute. She just went up to pick up the mail." The cop's rejoinder was, "Then let her pay," and he wrote out a $20 ticket. We ate the $20 ticket, but that was the straw that broke the camel's back.

We immediately began to search out a new venue for our business. We settled, ultimately, upon our current locale, New Port Richey, Florida. Before we made the move, we ran a test on the availability for help, having satisfied ourselves that there would be no problem in finding office space. We ran an ad in a local newspaper and gave the address of a Holiday Inn for interviews. We had no fewer than forty women apply the first day, certainly twenty-five of whom were perfectly acceptable. That made up our minds for us! I am certain that my leaving did not dramatically upset the economy of New Brunswick, New Jersey. On the other hand, a half a dozen jobs disappeared, the landlord had to find a new tenant, and on balance, the police officer's attitude of "let her pay" is one that I believe communities cannot afford.

In retrospect, I suppose I ought to send the cop a gift of some kind because he certainly did me the greatest favor of "encouraging" me to look elsewhere. I have never, for a moment, regretted our move to Florida.

Similarly, I recently stopped at my Lincoln dealer because my car came under a recall. A switch had to be changed, a switch that Ford first said was no problem and finally, without admitting it caused fires, agreed to change in millions of vehicles. (You be the judge of that one.) So after standing in line for twenty minutes at the service writers, I was told it would take at least an hour and a half, and the average time I believe is something on the order of twenty-two minutes to install this switch.

On top of that, my secretary had called and told them to also schedule the replacement of a mirror, and the dealership agreed. When I got there, they told me it takes ten to twelve days to order a mirror. The upshot was that I was going to have to return to the Lincoln dealer and buy the mirror because that is the only place that had this particular product. Why in the world would it take twelve days? It might not be the dealer's fault, but someplace, somewhere in this mix, somebody is responsible for a situation in which it takes twelve days to order a lousy mirror. In a world of overnight deliveries for a modest price, you will never convince me that it's necessary to take all this time.

In that vein, I often wonder, when I go to the dry cleaners, why some dry cleaners want more for same-day service than one-week service. It's hard for me to believe that they spend any more time cleaning, pressing, and hanging up my pants if they are there for a week, or for six or seven hours. I doubt that the clothes get any more tender, loving care. It might be a tad more convenient for them but, in the long run, it's my judgment that this is a way to lose customers. The cleaner that I have selected to do business with does a good job. If I get it in by 10 a.m., it's out by 4 p.m. at no extra charge, and the establishment is thriving.

The point is this. Hang onto your customers, however you can. Don't kick them away. There are probably as many ways to do that as there are businesses, but one thread holds them together. Give the customers the best you can. Here's an example of what I mean from my radio show.

When I first began doing my show on WMCA on Sundays, I obviously coveted a better and a more regular time position. The unchanging fact is, there are only 24 hours in a day and if some new programming comes on, somebody's got to go. I learned a very valuable lesson with my first experience at WMCA.

The fellow on in the afternoons from 2 to 4 o'clock, if memory serves me, was Garry Knul, who did a health show. Garry decided he was going to take a vacation. He went to London over the Christmas week of 1978. I was asked by Mrs. Strauss and Mark Mason to fill in and do his show during that week. Of course, I jumped at the chance. To make that proverbial long story short, when he came back, they decided my show was doing a lot better than his show and all of a sudden he was looking for work.

That taught me a very valuable lesson. There is no problem with taking vacations and taking days off — as a matter of fact, I look forward to it — but I'm not about to let my replacement audition on my show. That's why I do my own replacing.

I believe I was the first to do this, and it works so easily and so well, thanks to my loyal audience. Instead of playing an old show, (with rare exceptions such as holidays) the public deserves what we call "a virgin program," one that has never been heard before. Yet how do you do that and still take a vacation from time to time? It seemed to me to be pretty easy, and it has worked for me over the years. We simply announce that we will be taking calls off the air for four or five hours, from 10 p.m. to 3 a.m. And, I've done it for as long as 9 a.m. to 6 p.m. The public, my friends on the party line, have been very, very generous and remember the times either later that day or the next day, and give us a call.

It's called an "accelerated recording." In other words, the weather, the sports, the news, the commercials — all of the things that you have come to depend upon radio for — are inserted later. With the commercials, what would ordinarily be a twenty-two minute and ten second time period suddenly becomes nineteen minutes and five seconds accelerated. When we do an "out cue" — "I'm Bruce Williams" — the little machine goes "Beep, beep, beep," and I start with my next call: "Hello, Toledo." That way, we can do six hours of recording in less than five hours.

It does work and, as a matter of fact in my view, it adds a new dimension to the program. There are many people who may be working or otherwise engaged during our regular live hours, 7 p.m. to 10 p.m. Eastern, but are free to call either earlier in the day or later that night. Then too, since the program is delayed, particularly in many West Coast locations, this gives the person on the West Coast an immediate stimulation because they can figure out that we are now taking calls off the air.

We do get a little different flavor of calls during a recording. Does it lose any character? I don't think so. If one is doing a show tied to current events, clearly this can be a bit of a problem, but since the vast majority of the things discussed are seldom related to time, we can do our shows a couple of weeks in advance with nothing lost.

The proof of this pudding is that a few years ago I was in the hospital for an entire month. Every program during that month had been recorded earlier and all were "virgin." Of the almost 400 radio stations that were carrying the program at that time, only one station executive called my office to say, "Is Bruce on tape?" And, he called, not because of the content or listening to the shows, but because I had canceled a special program and he knew that I would cancel only if I was absolutely forced to.

I talked to one general manager, who had been in the business for 35 years, and he thought he could pick up on a taped show right away. For the whole month my program was on tape, he, nor anyone else, knew. No one complained, and no one suffered. So much for the business of "You've got to be live."

If you have to be live, what in the world makes television work? There are virtually no live TV programs today. Do you think for a moment that Jay Leno and David Letterman do their programs live? Of course not. They are taped and then edited. I'm not suggesting that radio should always be taped, but for the purposes I've outlined, it works, and no one suffers. I think there is a major value in that.

It is my contention that radio should be consistent. In other words, if you turn on a station WXXX at a particular time of day, you should know what to expect. There shouldn't be "I wonder what they are playing today" sort of thing. And, frankly, if you are really interested in one particular talk show host, the likelihood is, you don't want to hear a substitute.

There is a school of thought in the business, however, that sticking a substitute on once in a while will make the listeners appreciate the real stuff. I know a talk show host who is a master at picking incredibly bad substitutes. His listeners are very happy to get him back.

One thing few of us can disagree about, though, is the value of a first impression. That's the one that lasts, but an amazing number of businesses forget that, so the third lesson is:

You never get a second chance to make a first impression.

One company that never forgets this is the Disney Corporation. I have attended almost every opening of a new Disney facility, of any consequence, that has been held in the past two decades. I am constantly amazed at how well the Disney organization does things and how it brings them in on time when the odds seem hopeless.

I visited the site of the MGM Studios perhaps four months before it was scheduled to open and took one look at this huge hole in the ground and said, "Absolutely no way! Can't be done." I was there for the opening of the MGM Studios at Walt Disney World in a heck of a rain, with 8,000 guys running around in their penguin suits. New umbrellas were as common as fleas on an unwashed dog. Everywhere you looked, somebody was handing you a brand-new umbrella. Tarpaulins covered mountains of shrimp and dozens of young people all dressed in evening clothes were using brooms to push away the water.

On another occasion, I was to do my broadcast from the Grand Floridian Hotel and — talk about getting things done at the last minute! — they were still painting upstairs when they were handing out lemonade in the antebellum lobby downstairs.

I went to my suite to change before doing my program live from the hotel, and found out to my horror, that I'd been painted in, literally. Somebody had painted the doors and shut them tight. King Kong couldn't open them from the inside. Happily, the telephone did work and that little problem was resolved. That's the sort of thing one expects, but I must tell you, those are the little glitches that make stories.

And the big glitches make bigger stories. I attended the premiere of *Dick Tracy*, which was opening on property but not at a Disney facility. It was one of the two hotels not owned and operated by the Walt Disney organization. It really was a crazy affair. I checked into the hotel. There were relatively few people staying there, given the fact that it was brand new and really not prepared to be open to the public.

That aside, there were still a number of celebrity guests, who required, in someone's opinion, a high degree of security. The rugs in the hall at that time were meant to look like beach sand, but they went out of the way for realism, inadvertently. The air-conditioning system was so out of kilter that the rugs in the hallway were soaking wet, so slogging down the hall was like walking down a wet beach. Talk about realism!

I called to inquire as to how I could turn down the air-conditioning in my suite. You could have hung meat in my living room. The sweet young thing on the telephone said, "Not to worry, Mr. Williams, all you do is open your balcony door. The air-conditioning is connected with the door, and upon opening the door, it will stop, warm air will come in and your problem is solved." Neat.

A little later I called her back and said, "I've got one minor problem."

"What's that, sir, won't the doors open?"

"Not only won't the doors open, but there are no doors."

"What are you talking about?"

"There is no balcony or lanai in this suite."

"Mr. Williams, please look again," she said. "Every room in the hotel has its own private balcony."

"Let me check again."

Somebody had made a minor goof. The suite had no private balcony, hence no air-conditioning cut-off switch, hence I could continue hanging meat. As it turned out, if you left the front door of your room open (now there's a security breach), then the air-conditioning would shut down.

I called and asked the engineering department what they could do about the air-conditioning situation, and they said they were sorry. There was little they could do because there was a computer that was triggered by occupancy, and since there was such a small occupancy, this caused the problem.

I said, "To rephrase this answer, what you're telling me is that because there is no one registered in these rooms, your computer is giving you a problem."

"In essence, that's the problem."

"Why not just check in 100 or 150 mythical John Does? Tell the computer the rooms are occupied and the problem should be solved."

Dead silence. Then he said, "Son of a gun, let's try it."

He called back in a little while and said, "It works!"

Didn't figure that took a rocket scientist.

I then decided to take a swim in the pool. In every elevator, in the literature, and in some places even in the halls, there were signs leading to a pool. We will call it the Dragon Pool (I've forgotten the name long since). I sauntered down the hall and took the elevator to the appropriate floor. When I got off the security guard asked where I was going. I said, "I'm going to the Dragon Pool."

He looked at me rather strangely and said, "Do you have identification?"

"Well, rarely do I carry identification in a bathing suit and no, I do not."

"Sir, there is no Dragon Pool. There's no pool here."

"Don't be ridiculous. Come right into the elevator and look. Here is the schematic telling me how to get there."

And he somewhat warily came into the elevator and said, "I'll be darned." Every elevator had a sign leading you to this pool area that didn't exist. The pool area had been wiped out of the plans two years ago, but nobody told the sign makers.

This was a perfect example of Murphy's Law: What can go wrong, will. The crowning problem came when we went down to the dining room late at night to have something to eat. When it came time to pay, we were told that the computer (here we go again with those ubiquitous computers) would not accept a house charge card. We suggested that we were not about to pay cash or put this on another credit card because the meals and expenses were being charged to the house under the terms of the broadcast. This entailed getting a manager out of bed at 1 a.m. They also had no guest checks, which was part of the charge problem.

All of this added up to a bad first impression. The manager of the hotel was understandably upset when I reported during my program what had gone on. If good things happen, I talk about them; if bad things happen I talk about them as well. To the credit of the executives at Disney, when I brought the manager's criticisms to their attention (which were noted in a letter to me), he was quickly told that I had every right to say exactly what I thought about the way things were being run. And in no way was I to be inhibited just because I was broadcasting from their property. If I didn't like something I was free to say so.

Disney makes an impressive first impression. Some other operations don't. Whose customers do you think will keep coming back? Who will prosper, and who won't?

The fourth lesson makes it possible to hold onto your customers and make that all-important good first impression:

Take care of your employees. Failing to do so can be catastrophic.

I have observed on many occasions, both in print and on the air, that no matter how skillful you are, no matter what great abilities you possess, the overwhelming likelihood is that you are never going to be very successful and, certainly not very wealthy, unless you have people working with you.

The good Lord put one severe limitation on all of us. We have only twenty-four hours in each of our days, sixty minutes in each of our hours, and sixty seconds in each of our minutes. As a consequence, it's absolutely essential that we have folks working with us. You'll note that I said "with us" rather than "for us," although technically, if you're signing the paycheck, I guess the folks do work for you. The reality is, though, you have to have them working *with* you.

Management and management techniques are absolutely essential in order to make things happen smoothly and cost-effectively. I've met people who are absolute bears to work with and still managed a high degree of success. But consider how much more successful they might have been if they had better management techniques. I don't in any way suggest that I am a particularly good manager, but I try to treat my employees, when possible, in a way that I would like to be treated. Now, this may be just my personal management style, but oftentimes one can illustrate a good practice by showing a bad one. Let me give you an example that happened recently.

A woman was asked if she would like to participate as a guide on a cruise. While she was not to be paid, she would receive a free cruise, be able to take all of the side trips, such as visiting active volcanoes and all manner of things that would certainly be instructive. This would be particularly useful to her since she was teaching elementary school. A year or two before, she had taken a year's sabbatical and traveled around the world, gathering all sorts of material that had clearly proved useful in her classroom. She had been commended by her superintendent on the unusual materials and perspective that she brought to her classroom, given the experiences she had during her travels. She shared these and made teaching about these areas and incidents so much more interesting because she had firsthand experience, as opposed to just the kind of knowledge that she had gathered from a book.

This cruise opportunity presented itself somewhat suddenly. She had a decision to make. She had many sick days accrued, more than 100. She could have lied and just called in sick or had someone in her family do it for her. In all likelihood, the school would have called in a substitute and that would have been that. She didn't want to do that because it would have been dishonest. Clearly, she knew that she could be fired if she was caught, but more importantly, she thought it was inappropriate. She was raised to believe that honesty is the best policy, and if a sign said, "Keep off the grass," she kept off.

She wrote to the superintendent, telling him that she had been teaching some twenty years in the system, was at the top of her salary grade, and had several personal days coming in addition to the 100 sick days. She indicated that she would like to take advantage of this opportunity and that she would be visiting many areas that were already incorporated into the year's lesson plan. Having visited them, she would be able to teach more clearly, with recent, firsthand knowledge. She wrote that she planned to take photographs and bring back souvenirs to share with her students. She offered to take no salary at all during the cruise. At the time, she was earning more than $50,000 a year, so this would have been a salary reduction of well above $1,000 for the week. Alternatively, she offered to pay a substitute on her own, out of her own resources, or to take her personal days or whatever combination was satisfactory to the superintendent and the school district. If the superintendent had taken her up on the offer, the school district would have had a substantial savings.

The woman discussed this with her principal, who had no objection. The letter was hand-delivered to the superintendent, who said he would consider it. He got back to her some forty-eight hours later, saying that he regretted turning her down, but that substitute teachers were not the same caliber as regular teachers. He said she belonged in her classroom and, most importantly, this would have established a precedent that he didn't wish to have.

Let's analyze this. The superintendent could easily have let this woman take her trip to the betterment of her class at no cost to the district. Of course, she would have signed off on the lesson plan, so there would be continuity of teaching. The argument that a precedent would be established is probably the weakest, given the fact from the management perspective that instead of having a now-hostile employee, one who likely will stop participating in any extracurricular activity for which she is not compensated and not required to do under her teaching contract, they would have created a gung-ho employee who would have been very happy to go out of her way in return for the accommodation.

The argument that substitute teachers are not as desirable as a regular teacher truly fails. In many districts the substitutes are people who have taught before, raised a family and now are returning to the profession via the substitute route. They are certainly as experienced as the younger teachers just coming out of school and often more experienced and more qualified.

Now, the superintendent has a teacher who is unhappy and is going to continue to be unhappy and probably will be a lot more militant in her union activity. The word will get around that the administration is unbending, and so a great many people who don't want to have any confrontation will simply not make the overture and will instead just call in sick. The sick days, which under another administration might never have been redeemed, now will be. The administration has forced people to compromise themselves in order to accomplish what they would like to do rather than do it in an honest manner. Everybody loses, financially and morally.

I cannot emphasize it enough. Take care of your employees. They are often the first to suffer from your complacency or neglect.

When my wife and I owned our nursery school, I had a long-term, faithful secretary — one of several, I should add. She, like many of the others, labored long and hard to make the business a success. While her duties included answering the phone, typing letters and the usual clerical details that one would expect from someone in the position, she did a great deal more.

When it came time to prepare for open house, on her own time, she planted flowers and decorated the school so it would give the best impression. In short, she did a great deal to make the business succeed, as did all of my employees. I have never forgotten that there is no way in the world that you can do it alone as a boss. While loyalty is not an absolute prerequisite, as I'm sure many successful employers are hated by their employees, it sure makes it easier when they are working because they want to achieve a common goal. In any event, this gal certainly did that and more. I want to emphasize, she was only one of several.

One day, after many years of employment, she abruptly handed me her resignation. There was no explanation whatsoever, but she had accepted a position with another firm and would be leaving after the customary two weeks' notice but would be happy to leave immediately, if I so desired.

To say I was thunderstruck would be an understatement. I couldn't imagine what I had done or what had happened to suddenly make her determine that she had to leave. She steadfastly refused to tell me the reason for her sudden departure. To compound matters, when I said that if she didn't want to put the two weeks in, it wasn't necessary, she immediately dissolved in tears and raced out of the building.

Other employees, seeing her leave, immediately rushed to the conclusion that she and I had an affair and that a lovers' quarrel had taken place. Nothing, absolutely nothing, could be further from the truth. While we had worked closely together for many years, nothing more than a friendly smile had transpired between us. There was no point in trying to convince other people of that, but that is the absolute truth, spoken more than a quarter of a century later.

It was many years later that I found out why she had left, and I experienced the same emotion in somewhat different circumstances, as an employee. In 1978, after bombarding WMCA with literally thousands of phone calls and hundreds of letters, I was contacted by the then-program director, Mark Mason, who offered me a Sunday afternoon position.

Subsequently, I was given a "full-time" job of a 2 to 4 p.m. shift Monday through Friday and Saturday mornings from 6 to 10. Among my colleagues at that time was Sally Jessie Raphael, who went on with me to Talknet and then on to considerable fame in television.

At various times, Barry Farber, Bob Grant, Steve Powers and others who have done very well in radio, worked there. Ellen Strauss, whom I mentioned earlier,. was running the station. She was a lady from the tips of her hair follicles to the tips of her toes, imperious, demanding, obviously born to the purple, and, from my perspective, quite competent.

When Mrs. Strauss was running the station, we were achieving a very respectable showing in the Arbitron ratings in New York City, which is a formidable task, given the competition. Although at times I disagreed with Mrs. Strauss' management decisions, there was no doubt about her focus on the job and she made some very, very good decisions with regard to personnel and management. Not the least of her good decisions was the selection of Mark Mason as program director. Mark has demonstrated over the years his talents in this endeavor, having worked for NBC and WFAN, among other high-profile positions.

Something was happening at WMCA. The term today would be "downsizing." When I arrived at the station, each talent had their own office. We occupied an entire floor of a New York skyscraper and it was, in short, what one expected a major broadcast facility to be. After a time, a major portion of the floor was sublet, and our offices were consolidated. The office for the talent was now called the "bull pen," where four or five desks were in the one room. I suspect, from a purely objective position that was adequate.

One incident sticks in my mind. I reflect upon this with some fondness. Though I suspect Mrs. Strauss may not have recalled it with the same emotion, for she was certainly displeased at the time.

I have, I think, some strengths and, of course, many, many weaknesses. I have been accused of a great many things, but being a good housekeeper is not one of those things, particularly when it comes to maintaining a desk in an office.

As a matter of fact, in my office in Florida now, I do not have a desk. I solved the problem simply by using the table in the kitchen area when I come into the office. When I am finished it has to be cleaned off so the employees can have lunch.

But I did have a desk at 777 Seventh Avenue, and it was completely covered with debris. In my own defense, I should say that I knew where everything was, that I answered my own fan mail, and that I did whatever research was necessary myself, all of which was not required by the job. I was paid only to be on the air at that time, two hours in the mid-afternoon, and Saturday morning for four hours. Anything I did above that was gratis.

It was my custom to come in around 1 p.m. for a 2 p.m. show, open the mail and whatever, and then after the show hang out until about 4:30 or 4:45. Then I would catch the subway in order to catch the train back to New Brunswick, New Jersey.

One day, Mrs. Strauss walked past in the hall, took one look at my desk — which, admittedly, could have passed for an adjunct to the village dump — and walked in and announced that my desk was unacceptable. She felt it would be embarrassing to her since she had guests coming in the following day. I was to clean it up and not let this happen again. She said she would be back to check.

I looked up and said, "Mrs. Strauss, it won't be necessary to come back. I'll clean it right now." I took my arm and swept everything, and I mean everything on the desk, including the telephones, into a trash basket, put the chair under the desk and walked out.

The following day I returned and found my desk reasonably neatly stacked and the telephones in place. From that day on, even though the desk returned to the village dump condition very quickly, there was no mention of my cleaning it. It's really amazing what management will put up with from talent when they are making money.

Mrs. Strauss, who was of the *New York Times* Sulzberger family, was married to R. Peter Strauss of the Macy family. Peter was an active Democrat who supported Jimmy Carter in the 1976 election and, as a consequence, was rewarded by being allowed to run the Voice of America in Washington. The Strausses were Washingtonians in their hearts, if not physically, and maintained an apartment in the capital as well as in New York. Mr. Strauss spent almost all of his time there and the task of running WMCA and Strauss Communications, which R. Peter had inherited, fell to Mrs. Strauss.

Then came the election of 1980. Ronald Reagan was in and Jimmy Carter was out along with his appointees, so Mr. Strauss returned to the station. The night he returned, a meeting was held with all the employees in Studio D and Mrs. Strauss very graciously said her interim stewardship was over and she was returning the helm of the station to her husband.

While Mr. Strauss had many strong points, when push came to shove, Mrs. Strauss did a better job than he did at the station. Over the next few years, we went from a very strong position with good ratings to a very weak position. The talent schedule was rearranged and some talent was fired, including Sally Jessie Raphael, although she was still pulling a 4 (which is a good rating) as I recall.

Mark Mason was replaced by the Strauss's daughter, Jean, who was a very pleasant young woman but who, in my view, was thrust into an impossible, no-win situation. Not only was she her parents' child and, as a consequence, received little respect, more importantly, she had no experience in this job. Their son, on the other hand, went off to one of the smaller stations, did all the jobs and learned the business from the inside out. Today Eric Strauss is a qualified, respected professional.

All of us at the station could see it going downhill, and there was nothing we could do about it — which brings me to my point.

My secretary left because she saw me tearing apart a business that she had helped build over the years. For many years, a new attraction was added every summer, and I was diligently trying to expand and improve the enterprise. After about 10 years, I had just had it. I guess today's expression is "burned out," but it was a little more than that. The new additions every summer stopped, my attention to detail diminished, and the business started to slide.

After watching this for a year or so, she couldn't take it anymore and resigned. I found this out through a mutual acquaintance years later. I could now identify with her feelings, because the same thing was happening at MCA. The station was being consolidated, positions eliminated, ratings were going down, and talent was either being rearranged or was leaving altogether. And, in short, while we were still being paid, something that we had labored so hard to build up was being destroyed through no fault of our own, and nothing we could do would help save it.

When I was offered a position at NBC, I jumped at it. I probably would have done so under any circumstances, but I felt relieved to leave, as it was painful to watch an enterprise that we had worked so hard to build up, foundering.

There's a lesson for everyone in business. When you are fortunate enough to have employees who are pulling for you and trying to build up the business, don't work against them — doing nothing is, in fact, working against them.

With regard to my own personal experience, I guess it proves the adage, "What goes around, comes around." It is a mistake I do not intend to repeat.

For a good many years I had my hair cut at Joe's barbershop in Kendall Park, New Jersey. The owner, Joe Sagi was fortunate. He purchased the shop from another guy named Joe — how many times is that going to happen? As bad luck would have it, Joe Sagi developed a problem with his eyes and after cutting a couple of heads of hair, his eyes gave him a great deal of difficulty. Understandably, Joe decided he was going to sell his shop. To protect the guilty we're going to call the other barber in the shop Jim. Jim started his barbering career at this shop and I had known him for many years. He was concerned that when the shop was sold he would lose his position. Because I had known this fellow for a long time, I suggested that he consider buying the shop. I would finance it and he could pay me back over a period of years. He didn't feel comfortable doing that but suggested that I buy the place and he'd manage it. So I did. All of a sudden I'm in the barbershop business. After purchasing it, we spent almost the same amount of money to renovate the shop, bring it up to speed in terms of brightness, painting the walls and so on.

After a few months it occurred to me that there was a serious problem. This shop supported Joe, the original Joe and his family for a good many years, and then Joe Sagi for a number of years. Now all of a sudden it's losing money!

An examination of the books and keeping a close look at what was going on clearly indicated that we had a partner that we didn't count on. That partner had to be Jim. When confronted with this he first denied it. And then muttered, "You have to do what you have to do," and some comment like "You could afford it."

Mr. Sucker that I am, I still wanted to try to protect him and so I offered him and the other barbers a proposition. They could rent the chairs. In other words, pay me a flat amount of money per week, and everything after that was theirs, knowing that it would be impossible to steal. Bear in mind that Jim was reporting in his statements to us that he was doing one-half the amount the other barbers were grossing. One of the other cutters piped up rather quickly, "That wouldn't be fair to Jim. He cuts twice as much as we do." I never could figure out why this would have been unfair to him.

We told Jim we'd give him one more chance, and I'm sure you

can guess after a short period of time he went back to his old habits again, showing on the books only a very small percentage of the heads he was servicing. Here I bought the place to protect his job, offered to finance it for him, and then after catching him stealing gave him a second chance. Finally, to put the last nail in his coffin we put marked bills in the register one evening in such a fashion that we would know exactly what was going on. True to form, some of the marked bills were missing. We simply told Jim to take off and never stick his nose anywhere near our business again. Certainly the profits went up again and since that time, the shop has always been mildly profitable. I still have no desire to be in the barbershop business, but as long as it is showing a little bit of a profit, with very little stewardship, I guess it's OK.

The point is that I went out of my way to do a kindness and received nothing but abuse. What is most tragic is that I'm sure that Jim himself feels misused. In his own mind, he is the victim. Go figure.

9
Staying Ahead in Life

Everyone thinks his life is unique. Everyone likes to think he faces special circumstances unlike those faced by anyone else. To an extent that's true. But after all these years taking questions on the radio and in my syndicated newspaper column, *Smart Money*, I can see a lot of similarities.

The same questions come up again and again. Sometimes the particulars are a little different, sometimes very different, but the same issues come up again and again, no matter who is calling or writing:

> *How can I get ahead when I have no money?*
>
> *Am I obligated to keep a contract, even if it is inconvenient for me?*
>
> *How can I afford to buy a house?*
>
> *What can I do about my pesky neighbors?*
>
> *How much insurance do I need?*
>
> *How should I invest the money I have?*
>
> *Do I really need to consult a lawyer about whatever it is that I am about to do?*
>
> *Do I really need a will?*

The answers to those questions point the way to several general principles and rules about making it in your personal life. In the first section of this book, I covered the qualities of character I think are necessary for a successful life.

In this chapter, I will talk about applying those virtues to more specific circumstances and give some advice based on my experiences.

One of the most common complaints I hear — wrapped in a question — runs something like this: "I have a job that doesn't pay much, not much education, and too many responsibilities — spouse, children, chores — to have time for the education it would take to get ahead. What can I do?" I don't know what those callers expect for an answer, but I know what I tell them, time and again. **If you want it, you can do it. But *you* have to want it and do it. You have to want it more than anything else.**

Everyone has the time to advance himself if he will make the time. If you work days, take night classes. If you work nights, go to school during the day. If you have children, see if your spouse or a relative or a friend can watch them while you're in class. If you're short of money, check into loans or take a second job until you can pay the tuition. You may not be able to afford Harvard University, but nearly every area has community colleges.

The point is: Do it. Don't make excuses, don't procrastinate, just do it. The sooner you start, the sooner you will finish.

This may entail some sacrifices. In fact, it probably will. You will have less time for a social life — perhaps none. You will have less time for rest and relaxation — again, maybe none. But almost all gains in life entail some sacrifices, and the payoff is worth it. After a few years, you can get a better job that pays more and gives you a better life.

With married couples, that will probably mean that both spouses work. Many of us remember a time when the husband's income was enough to support a family. Those days are gone for most people, and the income from two people is often necessary to maintain a lifestyle that most would consider acceptable.

In all cases, and especially for those with a low income, budgeting is absolutely essential. Little, spur-of-the-moment purchases can add up fast. It is absolutely vital to keep a firm rein on them so there will be money left over. After fixed expenses, like housing, are taken care of, put aside some for savings.

Savings take care of emergencies. Savings take care of down payments on large purchases such as cars and houses. Down the line, savings will take up the slack as age cuts into your earning power or retirement stops it. Social Security and pensions are all very well, but for a comfortable old age, we need to save starting as early as we can.

Many of my listeners and readers are living paycheck-to-paycheck, and that's a recipe for disaster. What happens if one, just one, paycheck doesn't come in? One of the answers is budgeting. It may also mean a spouse with a full-time job takes a part-time job too. It may mean a spouse with no job may have to find one. The payoff in peace of mind now and a better life down the road is incalculable.

There is no quick fix. There is no other way but hard work and a determination to succeed. People often ask about schemes that promise a big payoff for a small amount of work or capital: stuffing envelopes, providing scholarship information, whatever the vogue scheme of the day is. But the old saying holds true: If it seems too good to be true, it probably is.

It's not glamorous, it's not attractive, it's not always fun and it's never easy, but there is no substitute for hard work and a determination to get ahead. Period.

That is true even when life seems to hand you an opportunity to cut corners. It can be as small as an undercharge at the grocery store cash register or as large as an undeserved credit on a bill.

Don't try to cheat your way ahead. It's not worth it. It may be illegal and it is certainly immoral.

You have to keep your word. In many cases, such as applying for a job or an unsecured loan, all you have to offer is a promise. You make a promise that you will do the work, and a promise that you will repay the loan. And, if you don't keep your word, your promise is worthless.

Sometimes promises can get you into hot water. That doesn't mean you can sneak your way out. A common question I get is about deposits. If I have put down a deposit on a lease, a service or a purchase, am I obligated to pay the rest of the contracted amount?

The answer is yes. Your deposit is your promise in the form of dollars to fulfill a contract. If you have promised to use a certain photographer for your wedding or to rent an apartment or to buy a house, your deposit tells the seller that you will keep your word. Sometimes we find out after making a promise that we could have gotten a better deal somewhere else. Aside from such considerations as any cooling-off periods, or provisions in the contract for withdrawal by either party, that's just too bad.

Look at it from the seller's point of view. He has promised these goods or services to you and no one else. How would you feel if on the day of your wedding, the photographer didn't show up because he got a better offer somewhere else? How would you feel if you went to move into that apartment and found it had been rented to someone else who promised to pay more rent? Sellers are obligated to keep their promises, and so are buyers.

Keeping your word is important on a personal level, as well.

During the summer between my freshman and sophomore years at college, my Mom insisted that I go to a family picnic with all of the cousins and uncles and aunts, in-laws and outlaws. Most of them were from my Mother's side of the family. Among the attendees was my cousin Ralph, a guy who, despite this little anecdote, I remember with some affection. He had served in World War II in the American Field Service as an ambulance driver. He was 4F with regard to the regular military. He had shown a great deal of initiative in going back and getting educated and moving right along with his company, Mobil Oil. He ultimately wound up running their operations in several African countries.

I had just completed my freshman year and had my son, Matthew, who was a few months old at the time. Somewhere during this social event, Ralph said, "Well, you know if you ever get that college degree, you come and see me and I'll take good care of you." An offhand remark, but one I remembered. Unhappily, it was one he did not. When the time came three years later, I did call him.

Suddenly, he was out to lunch and too busy to talk to me. I mention this in passing for those of you who are in similar positions. Don't make offhand remarks that you can not, or will not, follow up on. I must tell you that I was very disappointed, not in the lack of opportunity, because I knew I could do that for myself, but rather I was disappointed that a guy I respected let me down.

What you say can and will come back to haunt you, and often the people around you.

Three or four days after I regained semiconsciousness after my airplane accident, I was in the Intensive Care Unit of the Princeton Medical Center. My head was swollen to the size of a basketball and my eyes were swollen shut. I could hear clearly even though I couldn't see and signs of consciousness apparently were difficult to determine. Moreover, a good deal of the time I was lapsing into some kind of a twilight zone, which was merciful. In any event, I remembered distinctly hearing two physicians standing near me and talking. I recognized both of the voices and I will generously not identify them any more than that. One physician said to the other, "Hey, when are you going to do his leg?" The question was addressed to an orthopedic surgeon who had been brought in to consult. His rejoinder was, "I don't think we're going to bother. Why put a good leg on a stiff? This one ain't going to make it." When you are the guest of honor that is not the kind of conversation that you wish to overhear. My point is that anytime you are visiting someone who seems to be unconscious, don't bet on it. I heard a number of things that were not meant for my ears. It doesn't hurt to say to someone, I'm here for you. I love you. You may never know if they heard you, but you will know that you didn't do any hurt.

This is particularly true for those of you in the health fields that are continually working with people in this position. Clearly, you are not emotionally involved in most cases, but equally clearly, you have a professional responsibility to think before you speak.

Now let's look at more specific applications and problems that arise in our personal lives.

Buying a House

The biggest purchase most of us will make in a lifetime is a house. The larger the deal, the more complexities associated with it, and for most people, buying or selling a house is confusing and frustrating.

I have dealt with this is my book, *House Smart: A Step by Step Guide to Making the Best Deal in Buying or Selling a Home* (Radio Merchandise, Inc., and Nathan Rosenhouse, P.C., Publishers, 1995). But here are some tips for getting started:

First, get a lawyer. Buying or selling a house requires you to agree to a contract that may be very complex. Your lawyer can guide you through these complexities and, what's more, will do so for your advantage because, unlike most brokers, he works for you.

Second, figure out what you can afford. *House Smart* offers ways to figure out what you can afford, and you need to figure that out, because it is very easy to get in over your head.

Third, be sure what you are buying. Surveys and inspections by professionals can seem cumbersome and expensive, but believe me, they more than pay for themselves in the long run. More often than I can count, my listeners and readers have gotten themselves into trouble with inaccurate or outdated surveys, or problems with the structure that a professional inspection would have uncovered.

Independent Contractor

Let's talk a little bit about independent contractors. Now, why do employers constantly try to confer independent contractor status on people who would clearly be, under almost any definition, employees? The answer is simple. It's economics. It is cheaper to have independent contractors, on balance, than it is to have employees. How so?

Let's consider what the average employer has to do and frequently does, for employees. He must contribute Social Security in the approximate amount of 7.65 percent on the first $60,000 of employees' earnings. This can amount to as much as $4,590 per employee. Now, clearly if the employee earns less, then the employer's "contribution" is less. In addition, in many states the employer will be obliged to contribute to state unemployment insurance, state disability insurance, and on all occasions, to federal unemployment insurance.

Additionally, the employer will be obliged, in almost every jurisdiction, to carry workers' compensation, which can be very, very modest in the case of clerks and low-exposure employees, to very, very high premiums for people in risky occupations such as construction or the use of power tools. These are the mandatory expenses. Over and above this, many employers have arrangements whereby they provide hospitalization, life insurance, profit sharing, retirement, etc. All of these are very substantial cost items. Now, what does the employer provide for the independent contractor? Nothing. That's it. No Social Security contribution, no workers' compensation, no unemployment insurance, no pensions. In short, nothing. You can appreciate why it is so attractive for many employers to convert their employees to independent contractor status.

Well, if it was so simple, we'd all be doing it. Why in the world should we have this extra expense? The facts are, however, that the Internal Revenue Service sees things a little bit differently. It has many standards that it applies and if you fail any of these standards, then you are not a true independent contractor. How do you know which is which? Check the table on the next page.

Follow these guidelines to find out if you are an employee or an independent contractor.

Factor	Employee	Independent Contractor
Relation-ship	Ongoing relationship, even if it has irregular intervals.	Relationship ends when the job is completed.
How paid	Usually hourly, or salaried.	Paid by the job.
Profits	Receives a set wage.	Makes a profit or loss.
Full-time hours	Spends full-time hours at one job.	Spends less than a full-time workweek at each job, or runs own business.
Hours of work	Must work hours set by company or firm.	May work any hours he chooses.
Job instruction	Must comply with job instructions as to where and how to work.	Responsible only for end work product or job completion.
Service offered to	Offers services to one person or firm.	Offers services to general public or contractor.
Services rendered	Performs job personally and does not hire assistants or staff.	May hire any workers needed to accomplish the job.
Right to fire or quit	Can be fired at any time and can quit at any time without liability.	May not be fired as long as he produces the agreed results. May not quit without liability unless the job is completed as agreed.
Training, tools and facilities	Any needed must be provided by the company or firm.	Any needed to accomplish the job are the responsibility of the contractor.
Capital investment	Does not have a significant financial investment in the company or firm (not including stock).	Has a significant financial investment in his business.

What do you do, however, if your boss suddenly says, "Beginning Monday you are an independent contractor"? You can kick and scream, hold your breath and turn blue, but the chances are you will lose your job.

It's not much of a jump from independent contractor status to owning your own business, and so many people call me, write to me and otherwise ask, "How can I get money to start my business? I've got the greatest idea since sliced bread and ice cream, but I haven't got any money."

Unfortunately, unless you are a major-leaguer and playing for the big bucks, raising small money for high-risk enterprises is an almost impossible task unless you are fortunate enough to have friends and relatives who love you, have confidence in you and are willing to take a shot. There are a variety of reasons for this. Some are solid business reasons and others, are more difficult to nail down.

From the point of view of a lender, there are two things that he has to consider. How solid are you, and even above that, how are you going to repay the loan? You can be a very solid citizen with a great credit record, but unless you can demonstrate where the money is going to come from to repay a loan, the lender is going to be as nervous as a pheasant during hunting season.

Banks are not in the risk capital business. They are in the business of loaning money with an almost certain expectation of being repaid, hence the relatively modest interest rates. Venture capitalists, on the other hand, expect to get burned and, as a consequence, not only do they want extremely high interest rates, but they also want a piece of your business and perhaps a lien on your first- and second-born children. And, believe it or not, they are entitled to it. Because they lose more often than they win, they have got to win big. Furthermore, I mentioned that the lender, even on a solid deal, is not interested in small loans. There are good business reasons for this as well. It doesn't cost any more money to process a large loan application than a small one, but the large loan generates decent revenue, while the small one does not. In short, if you can't reach into your pocket and find the capital, the likelihood is that you are going to have to go to someone who loves you.

Oftentimes, I will talk to young folks, and I'll say, "That's a good idea; what are you willing to invest?" "Well, I don't have much except my house." "How about hocking the house or selling it?" Well, sometimes one partner will say, "Yeah, I'll even do that, but my wife or husband won't let me." My next serious question is, "If that's the case, are you prepared to divorce them?" And, 99 percent of the time, they say, "Of course not." Well, I'm not suggesting that you should, but that's the kind of dedication and willingness to gamble everything that is frequently required to have a reasonable shot, not a sure one, but a reasonable shot at success.

Neighbors

In his poem "Mending Wall," Robert Frost has a bad neighbor saying, "Good fences make good neighbors." Well, I think good surveys go a long way toward making good neighbors. Often I get questions about driveways or mailboxes or trees encroaching on a neighbor's property.

The short answer is always the same. Establish exactly whose property the structure is on. If you don't have a survey, get one. If both of you have surveys and they conflict, get a more recent one.

If it's you whose structure is encroaching on your neighbor's property, see if you can work out an accommodation. Buy a few feet of his property, for example. If no accommodation is possible, though, you may well have to swallow your pride and a fairly large expense. The law is strict about putting things on other people's property.

Pesky Pets

One problem that apparently is almost universal is pets straying into other people's lawns and gardens. Now, I can appreciate why that can be a problem, having had a dog in the house throughout my childhood and all of my adult life. Happily, the current denizen of the Williams' household, Pistol, is not a roamer; besides, my yard is well fenced and Pistol has no propensity for leaving the yard. Similarly, the fences keep the neighbor's dogs out if they are allowed to roam. This is not always true in many areas.

Oftentimes, thoughtless neighbors allow their dogs to run without regard to leash laws. They frequently intimidate children, defecate and urinate in unseemly places and, in short, become a large nuisance. What to do? Well, you can talk to the neighbor and ask him if he'll keep his hound under control and, if necessary, talk to an animal control officer about keeping him under control or having him picked up.

Oftentimes, neither of these remedies has a long-lasting impact. One of my callers, however, suggested a remedy that several of my listeners have used and told me works like a charm. It goes like this. You take advantage of the dog's natural instinct to establish territory. Anyone who owns a dog knows that if there is something that is really filthy, dirty, smelly and disgusting, a dog just naturally has to roll in it and make it his own.

Taking advantage of this propensity on the part of your canine adversaries, pick up a mesh sack, similar to the ones that onions are shipped in. Then collect as much decaying material as you can find. Fish work especially well, (include the entrails if you can, as well as decaying meat). In short, use anything that when left out in the sun for a couple of days really picks up a stink. When you have a good supply of this, put it into the bag, leave it outside, keep it moist so it decays appropriately. Then, when the decaying process is at the top of its game, place your bag in an area where your neighbor's dog loves to visit. It's almost guaranteed that the dog, when smelling this surprise, will roll in it and cover his body with this delightful concoction. When he goes home and runs into the house smelling like this, your neighbor will have a formidable task of cleaning up the hound. After two or three trips, I suspect your neighbor will get the picture: "I'd better keep my dog home." My correspondents tell me it works every time, and it's fun to watch the neighbor out in the back yard scrubbing off Fido after an excursion into the next door neighbor's yard. Revenge, indeed, is sweet!

Insurance

I can't imagine anyone who likes paying insurance premiums. On the other hand, when disaster strikes, the first thing we ask is, "Who's going to pay?" Let's talk a little bit about insurance.

Probably the most common insurance is automobile insurance and it is, perhaps, one of the more misunderstood forms. The insurance policy has many facets but there are two essential ones: covering the other guy for what damage you may do to him, and covering yourself and personal property.

The "other guy" part of the policy breaks down into two parts: bodily injury, meaning physical being, and property damage, something that the other guy owns, such as a car or a building. Bodily injury is pretty easy to understand. If someone is injured in an automobile, he has received a bodily injury and you may be responsible for making him as whole as money can. Property damage is a little broader. It could be the automobile that someone is riding in that you clobber, but it is not limited to that. For example, if you fall asleep and run off the road and hit a utility pole, you will have to pay for that utility pole. This is where the property damage part of your insurance policy comes into play. People ask, "So how much damage could I do?" A car is only worth $40,000 or $50,000 tops. That may be true, although in today's world there are cars that are worth even more. Suppose you turn the local drugstore into a drive-in and in the process the building catches on fire. You can easily cause several hundred thousand dollars worth of property damage. Having a scant $50,000 or $100,000 of coverage can leave you very much in the lurch. You should always carry at least $1 million worth of coverage.

Oftentimes, people say to me, "But Bruce, I don't have a million dollars, why should I carry a million dollars worth of insurance?" The problem is that while you may not be worth a million, you can clearly do a million dollars or more worth of damage.

Most states require insurance, but very, very little. Often, people say, "I carry what the state requires." What the state requires and what you should carry to protect yourself have almost nothing in common.

It is my contention that everyone needs at least a million dollars worth of liability insurance and perhaps two or three. While you may think that this is an excessive burden, more often than not, it isn't. This can be accomplished by purchasing what is called an "umbrella" policy. Visualize a couple of gears, you know, wheels with teeth, that have to mesh together. This is what an umbrella policy and your regular insurance must do.

Your underlying policy, the regular automobile policy, and the liability portion of your homeowner's or renter's insurance, and the umbrella must all work together. If you have, for an example, a quarter of a million dollar liability policy on your car, and on your home, then the umbrella policy will have a quarter of a million dollars deductible. First quarter-million, the umbrella company has no liabilities. After a quarter of a million, up to one, two or three million dollars, should the award go that high, the umbrella carrier will pay. How much does an umbrella policy cost? It will vary from place to place and from risk to risk, but ordinarily no more than $125 or $150 a year. Very little to pay for that extra protection.

216

There are any number of other coverages that are available from your automobile carrier. Whether or not you should carry them is a matter of personal judgment. They are not obligatory in most cases. I contend, though, that personal injury protection covering you and the people in your car, and uninsured and underinsured motorist protection, are absolutely essential. There are experts who argue that uninsured motorist insurance is a luxury coverage. I don't think so. If someone hits me and is socially irresponsible and does not carry adequate insurance, I want to know there is enough money there to make me whole. If I have to pay a little bit for the privilege of feeling that comfortable, I am prepared to do so, and I think you should be as well.

If your state is a no-fault state where you must collect from your own carrier, be certain to understand what your rights and obligations are. In some cases, in return for relinquishing some of your rights, your premium goes down. Trial attorneys will argue that this is a poor buy. I leave that to you to make that decision. If you pay the lesser premium, you are restricted from collecting for pain and suffering until a fairly high threshold or plateau is reached. Whether or not you choose to take this risk for the luxury of a lower premium is purely a personal consideration. You are not betting the family farm on this in most cases, but by carrying inadequate liability insurance you definitely put everything that you've ever worked for in jeopardy, including future earnings. If you don't have adequate insurance and you cause an accident, it's very possible that your salary will be attached unless you go through the pain of a bankruptcy, and no one wants to do that.

I am constantly appalled about how many people carry collision and comprehensive, that is, physical damage insurance on elderly automobiles. Let's take a look at this. If you were to have a $24,000 car insured for collision and comprehensive, it might cost you upward of $1,000. When that car is reduced to $2,400, or 10 percent of its value, you can depend on it, the collision and comprehensive premium will not have been reduced by a factor of nine or down to $100 or less. Further, let's assume that you have a $200 deductible. $200 against the $24,000 value is a very tiny percentage. But $200 against $2,400 is indeed a very significant percentage.

The older the car gets, the poorer such insurance becomes. If a car is worth under $3,000, carrying collision and comprehensive is like flushing money down a toilet. It can be argued that if you have an accident you'll be glad it's there, but the value is so small that it's my feeling that you are far better off to be "self-insured" for these relatively modest losses.

I never cease to be amazed at the number of people who will carry low limits of liability but nonetheless carry collision and comprehensive on an old car. Understand this, you can kill somebody just as dead with a twenty year old, $50 car as with a brand-new, $50,000 car, and your liability is no less just because the car is older. To my mind, it's a crime that insurance agents continue to issue these policies without, at the very least, advising their clients that this is a very poor buy.

Personal Finance

Personal finance is so involved, with so many variables that change from person to person and from day to day, that giving general advice in a book can be difficult. There are, however, some principles that apply to most people and most situations, along with the more specific tips that I will give throughout this section. The most general rule can be summed up simply.

Know your options and compare them. Many of the questions I am asked stem from confusion about the merits of particular uses for money. Should I pay cash or borrow? Should I invest in mutual funds or savings bonds? CDs or individual stocks? Should I go deeper in debt to buy what I want now, or wait until I have more cash?

The particular answer I give each time varies, of course,

according to the questioner's circumstances, but the guiding principle is that you should put your money where it will work the hardest for you. The return from an investment varies inversely with its risk. The safer it is, the less you'll earn. You have to weigh your circumstances and your temperament when deciding where to put your money. If you are near retirement age or just have a low tolerance for risk, you probably should shy away from risk, putting your money where it is safer but less productive. If, on the other hand, you have decades until retirement and won't stay up nights fretting about a chancier investment — in mutual funds that invest abroad, for example — you should consider accepting a greater chance of losing some of your investment in hopes of a much larger return on your capital.

Paying Cash vs. Borrowing

When buying a car or other big-ticket items, many people still think there is an advantage to borrowing the money as opposed to paying cash. There was a time when that was true, when all the interest you paid was deductible from ordinary income tax. No more. Nowadays, the only interest payments most can deduct are for first and second home mortgages. That's why paying cash now can make more sense.

Let's look at an individual dollar. Right now, you have it invested at, say, 9 percent, which is a very good return in these days of low inflation and low returns on investments. Let's say you're in the 33 percent income tax bracket. That dollar returns 9 cents, of which you pay 3 cents to the feds, so you pocket 6 cents.

The auto lender is offering a 10 percent simple interest rate, meaning that you pay him 10 cents on the dollar per year for using his money to buy the car. You leave your money invested. You get the 6 cents for the investment, but you pay 10 on the loan, for a net loss of 4 cents. If you had taken the dollar out of the investment and paid for the car, you'd save 4 cents on a dollar.

In this example, you would have to get a 15 percent return on your investment just to break even on the whole deal, and 15 percent can be pretty hard to achieve.

In other words, in some cases, paying cash for big purchases is the better way to go.

Sometimes the riskiest but most rewarding investment you can make is in a business of your own. When making your decision about going into business for yourself, you should consider the payoff from your own success as part of the equation. Will working for myself be more satisfying? Am I the kind of person who wants to call the shots?

Partnerships and Corporations

People going into business with a partner often wonder if it's better to stick with a partnership arrangement or incorporate. In most cases, incorporation is better. It's easy, it clarifies ownership of the business's assets, and it separates the partners' personal finances and responsibilities from those of the business.

In either case, though, several rules hold. You should work out on paper:

> *What each partner's (or corporation official's) responsibilities will be.*

> *What happens in the event of one partner's death. (Life insurance can usually take care of this).*

> *What happens if one partner wants to leave.*

After the agreement is worked out, take it to a lawyer and sign it formally. You may be going into business with your brother or best friend, but businesses can put unimagined strains on the best of relations, and it's best to have everything worked out, legally, for everyone's protection.

Collectibles

We all read stories about people who bought a few cheap things in the 1950s or '60s that turn out to be worth a fortune. But, not all of us hear about the thousands of people who lose their shirts on collectibles.

Collectibles are an extremely speculative investment. Who knows what the price of anything, be it pork bellies, stamps or Beanie Babies, will be tomorrow, much less a few decades from now? People who do make money in collectibles tend to be those who put a great deal of work into the project, as much work as many people put into a regular job.

The potential for losing a lot of money quickly is heightened by the presence of unscrupulous operators who solicit customers. They promise high returns on collectibles with a guarantee that they will repurchase them at the buyer's convenience. The operators vanish, of course, leaving the buyer with a collection for which he probably paid several times the actual value.

An old saying holds true for all sorts of collectibles. "If you don't know jewelry, know the jeweler." If you do plan to invest, study up on the market as much as you can — many publications are available, along with a variety of sites on the World Wide Web — and find a reputable dealer, preferably in your area. And remember another old saying, "Let the buyer beware." Typically, losses on collectibles are the sole responsibility of the purchaser.

A question I'm frequently asked about collectibles arises when someone inherits a collection from a relative. Whatever the collection is, there almost certainly is a dealer specializing in it. The Yellow Pages in any major city can usually point you to a dealer, as can publications about that kind of collection or the

Web. The local library can be a big help and can point you to associations of people who collect whatever it is. Often, the publications and associations can point you to a trustworthy dealer in your area. Many dealers will provide an appraisal free of charge, but never take the first appraisal you get. You would be surprised how widely appraisals can vary.

Wills

Everyone needs a will. I have said this on many occasions and so many people take exception to it. They ask, "But Bruce, suppose I have a trust. I was told I didn't need a will if I had a trust." That simply isn't true. Now, it is true that a living trust may very well be advantageous for you. But that's a matter between you and your advisors. There may or may not be some tax savings. The principal advantage of a living trust for most people is that it avoids probate and is a private document. Probate has been made into such a bogeyman that people are willing to go to any length to avoid it.

I still don't understand why it's such a big deal. It is true that one of the advantages of having a trust is that it's a private affair and then all one might need is a pour-over will where everything goes into the trust upon your demise. It's impossible to figure all of your assets at any given time since most of us are acquiring things a little or a lot, depending upon our station in life or our age.

However, the most important parts of a will are frequently not addressed elsewhere. That is, if one has minor children, the will would be an appropriate place to appoint the guardians of those minor children should both parents die unexpectedly or prematurely. If you fail to have a will, you are deemed to have died intestate and then the state you die in will provide that will by applying the laws of intestacy. Someone will have to apply to the surrogate court, (called the Widows and Orphans Court in Pennsylvania), to be appointed administrator of the estate. A bond will have to be posted and then the law of intestacy guides the administrator. It is so much easier to you to spell out precisely what you wish done with the assets that you have worked so hard for, but most particularly the appointment of a guardian for your minor children.

Many times people say, "My parents will take the children," but the problem is that your parents may be a little older and it's possible the judge would not consider them appropriate because of their age. If you name them in your will, the likelihood is that the court will go with your choice.

A will is a living document and should be reviewed and upgraded from time to time. Conditions change. The names of your heirs change. A will need not be a complicated document. Simple, everything-goes-to-my-spouse wills, called reciprocal wills, should do it for the greater number of people, especially the younger folks. As you mature and acquire more property and objects, a will can become more complicated.

Why not sit down with your children, if they are to be the heirs of your estate, and discuss with them how you intend to leave your money? Explain there are certain things that cannot be divided up, such as Grandma's china, silver and so on. Ask who might like these objects, and then leave them to the one of the kids who wants it the most. The perfect balance is never achievable. You should be able to divide the things up so everybody gets his fair share. Don't feel a bit guilty if one or more of your offspring is completely independent and requires no financial assistance from you, while others need that boost.

So many people are seduced by the idea that a will is very expensive and that they can copy an old will and that will be fine. Some will write out simply what they want to do and have it notarized. Nothing can be further from the truth. Let me disabuse my readers of a notary public authority. A notary simply says that the person named did actually sign a document in his or her presence. It doesn't make the document less or more legal other than that. Another source of wills could be a will kit. I know they have been advertised on my show repeatedly and I know the sellers have sold millions of these will kits for a few dollars. It's my considered opinion that you are very foolish to use one of these kits. Yes, they may be perfectly valid. On the other hand, you won't know if they are valid or not 'til after you're dead, and then it is impossible to have them changed.

There are a number of things that should *not* be in your will. I handled an estate of a lady who put instructions for her burial in her will. Often the will isn't looked at for several days, and clearly, the funeral arrangements are made right after your demise. Directions for funeral arrangements should be made to whoever is handling your affairs, but not in a will.

In short, a will need not be expensive, it is absolutely necessary, and if for any reason there are not any assets to be distributed, the will could simply be filed, but not probated. In the absence of the will, one thing is certain. More of your money will be spent than is necessary.

Funeral Arrangements

One thing is absolutely certain in this life: none of us will get out of it alive! Given that homily, one of the consummate acts of love, as I view it, is for the individual to work out the details of his or her own funeral. I'm not suggesting that you 30-somethings race out and buy a funeral, but if you are on the wrong side of 70, it may well be that it's time to consider the fact that we all are going to leave.

If you have never purchased a funeral, then you'll have a difficult time understanding what I am getting at, but most of us have done so at some time in our life. You are making a business decision under the very worst possible circumstances. You're making a judgment for someone whom you clearly have been close to, usually someone you love. How much will be spent? Where will he or she be buried? How long and where are the funeral services?

Wouldn't it be so much wiser to make this decision for yourself without the pressure of the moment? The chances are you will spend less money and, more importantly, make it so much easier for those whom you leave behind.

My aunt passed away on Christmas Eve and so my son, Matthew, and I spent a portion of Christmas Day arranging for a funeral — not a happy event. Furthermore, since my aunt did not have the foresight to purchase a cemetery plot, and obviously on Christmas Day cemetery offices are closed, we had to postpone all of the festivities for several days. That not only extended the difficult period between passing away and the final services and all that goes along with it, it also incurred some modest increases in expense. Knowing the parsimonious nature of my aunt, I think that would probably have troubled her the most. Spending money unnecessarily.

Similarly, some years ago, I had a close acquaintance who, a short time before she passed away, named me as her personal representative. Among other things, it was my duty to make funeral arrangements. The problem was, she didn't share all of her desires with me. Upon her demise, I purchased a cemetery lot and had the grave opened. This lady was Jewish, so I instructed the funeral director, in keeping with her faith, not to have her embalmed. I said I would have her interred the following morning.

About midnight, when I sat down with her attorney in an all-night restaurant, I found out that (a) she wished to be embalmed, religious considerations notwithstanding, and (b) she wished to be placed in a mausoleum rather than in the ground. The next morning found me scurrying around arranging for the mausoleum, undoing the deal by having the grave closed and filled. In short, I was picking up all sorts of pieces that would have been totally unnecessary had she, at the very least, confided her wishes to me or, better, made the arrangements herself. She was clearly capable of doing all that.

225

I view this as the consummate act of love.

Many funeral directors and associations have arrangements under which you can prepay. You receive the benefit of the interest that your money is earning and you lock in all of the costs at the prices charged when you make this decision. As a consequence, inflation is not a factor. If you change your mind, or perhaps move to another location — say, you make the arrangements in Massachusetts but then decide to retire to Florida — the entire package can be either refunded to you at your pleasure, or transferred to a funeral director at your new address. Often a swap on the lots can be worked out. The whole key to this is that you are working in an unpressured environment as contrasted with "We have to get it done today," which is the way the overwhelming majority of us approach death. This is not a particularly pleasant topic, but on the other hand, the adage, "None of us are leaving this world alive," clearly applies.

Too Late To Classify

In many publications they will have a section called "too late to classify." In other words, it's advertising that would have gone into a certain category but because it was received late, they just printed it in any order. When I first began this little endeavor I wondered if I would have enough material to flesh it out, but I have reached the point where now it is a question of what material can make it in and what material has to go. I have had a number of random thoughts and observations that do not fit anywhere special and rather than struggle to find a place or make a place for them to fit; I think this category will work out just fine.

10

Reflections

Embarking on this little enterprise has been an interesting adventure. It has required me to think about things and remember times that hadn't crossed my mind for better than fifty years. It is clear that the world that I grew up in is quite different from the one that we inhabit today. Here are some examples of this, some memories of a time long gone, and some observations about things that endure.

Old Neighborhood

When I was about six years old I moved from one house in South Orange, New Jersey, to an apartment in South Orange. I was born at the height of the Depression. At the very beginning my Dad did well. The Depression didn't affect our family. We moved on three occasions, in the better part of five years, and each move was to less expensive quarters. When we moved into the apartment my Dad's fortunes were on the decline, and therefore money was a bit tight. I would emphasize that we never went hungry, although I remember eating a lot of fricassee chicken, which to this day I detest.

Unlike others, we always had food on our table, but we didn't have a whole lot of money left for frivolous activities. I remember distinctly when I was between seven and eight years old exploring empty homes in the neighborhood. In South Orange there were a great many large homes that nobody could afford. As a consequence, they were uninhabited. We could enter a new house every day for weeks and never enter the same house twice. We never stole anything of any consequence, but one thing that I do vividly remember doing was collecting any old clothes that we could find that had been abandoned in the house. These we sold for a few pennies.

Hard as it is to believe, before World War II, horses and wagons were actively used in commerce. I remember, as clearly as if it were yesterday, a man coming down the street with a wagon pulled by a horse, yelling, "Hey, junk man." That's all, just "Hey, junk man." We used to call him "fish head." The junk man came down the street religiously a couple of days a week. We kids would collect rags and old newspapers and sell them for a few pennies. I recall going door-to-door asking people for their newspapers, bundling them up and waiting for the "junk man."

He spoke very little English but knew enough to evaluate what the bedspring you found was worth, or the newspapers and rags. He would reach into an old leather purse and pull out a few pennies. Can you see today seven year olds going door-to-door collecting rags and newspapers?

Another thing that I marvel at was that routinely, during the warmer weather, we would hitchhike several miles up to the park. Remember, we were seven years old. Our parents never gave it a thought to be worried, nor did we. I went out recently and drove the distance — of course, distances become magnified with passing years. My odometer doesn't lie. Two and half miles of travel between the park and my home in South Orange, with never a random thought of danger and indeed never an incident at any time.

The old neighborhood is remarkably the same sixty years later. Yes, the vacant lots have long since disappeared and the place where we built the tree house is now apartments. But on balance, it is one of the few places that I remember that had the least amount of change over that period of time. It is also a testimony that age does not mean that neighborhoods have to go downhill. The homes are still in good condition and the apartment house that I lived in is remarkably unchanged from the time that I lived there.

Glens Falls

For the couple of years I lived in Glens Falls, New York, we had no major problems. My Dad and Mother both worked and made enough money so there was never a question about food on the table. Extras were another thing.

In general, for whatever reason, I was not particularly happy in Glens Falls. It was, in my eleven year old mind, a hick town, and I was looking forward for the time we could move back into a more urban area. One of my distinct memories is me walking down into town and stopping on South Street. South Street was the home of the Trailways Bus Terminal and I sat and watched people get on and off of those buses going somewhere, anywhere. I determined in my own head that, as soon as possible, I would be on one of those buses.

As it happened, when we left Glens Falls, we did take a bus, a Trailways from South Street, back to the New York-New Jersey metropolitan area. I even recall the places the bus stopped on the way. I wonder how many other kids sat by a railway station, or bus terminal, or perhaps watched airplanes go over and said, "One day I'm gonna be on that bus or train." How many of them made it? I'm so glad I did.

Selling Seeds

Another of my money-making adventures, that was okay for a little kid, was selling Burpee seeds door-to-door. During World War II everyone had a Victory garden. Vegetable seeds — lettuce, carrots, radishes, and tomatoes — were an easy sell for a little kid. People had to buy them anyway, so why not buy them from the kid at the door if the price was right? I didn't make a lot of money, I don't remember how much. I got the seeds through advertising in comic books. In the backs of comic books there were coupons asking you to become an agent of their company, for either prizes or money. If memory serves me, I always selected the money.

Camp Kiamesha

In 1940, 1941, 1942 and 1944 I attended Camp Kiamesha for the entire summer. It may seem like a contradiction to say that my Dad was struggling and yet he found money to send his son to camp. There was a reason for that which had nothing to do with wanting me to learn about outdoor activities. The simple fact was that in those years every parent lived in constant fear of his or her child contracting polio.

These were the days before we had a polio vaccine. It was generally accepted that polio was transmitted much more readily in the summer months than the colder months. During the summer, most families would not allow their children to go to the movies, public parks, swimming pools — any place where there was congestion. For whatever reason, they felt that the close proximity was not a factor out in the country, so if it was at all possible, your kid went to sleep-away camp.

I attended Camp Kiamesha in the aforementioned years. As one who operated a summer camp, I am amazed at the freedom we were allowed. Often in the morning we would go up to the chow hall, get a loaf of bread, three or four cans of tuna and a couple of other snack items and disappear for the entire day. No one, including our counselors, had any idea where we were. Nothing very exciting was happening.

We would go out into the woods, hike up to what we called Bald Rock, make our lunch, and gather blueberries. When I was operating the camp, if a kid was unaccounted for, just for about three or four minutes, we really got into a panic. We wouldn't dare allow children that kind of latitude. Was it a question of their not caring? Were we better able to care for ourselves? Were there fewer hazards than there are now? I suspect that it's a little of all these things. Once again, it was a different world, and I don't remember anything remotely untoward happening in those years.

Working On The Farm

When I was thirteen years old, between seventh and eighth grades, a radio really got me into trouble. I was listening to whatever, and there was what we would call today a "public service announcement" making the case that most of the able-bodied men in the county had entered the service in one of the four branches. There was a huge shortage of able bodies.

This was being felt particularly in the agricultural section of our economy. In short, they were looking for people to go out and work on the farms. It was your patriotic duty. Would you believe I called, went down and was interviewed and immediately given a job on a farm!

I had to take a bus to the trolley (to the end of the line) where a truck picked me up to take me out to the farm. I say "me," but there were a bunch of other guys all about my age. Remember, we were just young teenagers! As I remember, they had us out hoeing beets the greater part of the time. For a kid who never did this kind of work, it was hard, hot, and dirty. And we weren't paid a whole lot of money.

One day at lunchtime, one of the farm agents came up to talk to us all and said he had a real opportunity for us. There were farms out of the area where we could go and live for the month of August. Good pay, great food and so on. I listened to the pitch and went off at thirteen years old to work on the Adams farm in Frenchtown, New Jersey.

No, my parents didn't drive me. I got on a bus and went out to meet these people. It was a very unusual situation. The father and son ran the farm as partners and they ate together, but two entirely separate meals were served on the table. The meals the older Mr. Adams and his wife ate, and the meals of the younger

Mr. Adams and his wife and children, were very different. The latter ate a whole lot better. Since Grandpa Adams employed me, I ate with those folks.

The smokehouse had washed away in a recent flood, so meat was a very rare occurrence on our table, although the younger family had it every day. I was allowed either a glass of milk or a cup of cocoa, one for breakfast. At that time, I was a heavy milk drinker and this was a dairy farm, yet they would allow me to have only one glass of milk. I retaliated by going down to the icehouse and drinking pure cream. Now, of course, this was during World War II, and rationing was a factor.

These guys had me doing stuff that even in that world — never mind today's world — was probably illegal. Here's an example that certainly was too dangerous for a kid or anybody else for that matter. We used to string barbed wire. We would attach one end of the wire to a tree and then pull a hundred or more yards tight with a tractor. We would then go in and set the posts and attach them to the tight wire. Could you imagine what would happen if that wire ever let go? It would decapitate you. Nobody was worrying about OSHA rules. That's just what we did.

World War II ended while I was on that farm. I remember the day like it was yesterday. We were bringing in hay bales. We used a big hook in each hand and hooked the bales and threw them on the wagon. By the end of the day, my right hand had a hole right down to the bone where the hook had worn into my hand. To this day, I still have a scar on my middle finger of my right hand from using those hooks that summer long ago in August.

At the end of my indenture, I was paid the princely sum of $35 for the month. I was told it would be at least $35, with probably a bonus, but Mr. Adams never let the word "bonus" pass his lips. To say they were a parsimonious family would be much too charitable. They were downright cheap. I'm sure they felt they were doing the right thing, but one of the things I told myself at that time was if I ever had people working for me; I would never treat them the way that family treated me.

Grandma Kate

World War II had a number of effects on our economy. One of them was that automobiles went to war. They became tanks and jeeps. In 1942, '43, '44, and '45 no civilian automobiles were built. The purist might remark that there are a few 1942s, but for all intents and purposes, we had four years without new cars. As a consequence, after World War II there was a very competitive automobile market. Not only did you pay full price (what could be likened to sticker price), but you were required to pay under the table. The public remembered the dealers who extorted money in that fashion and most of those guys are no longer in business. The more forward-thinking dealers took care of their customers without any under-the-table stuff, and many of those dealerships still prosper.

My brother, Walter, a veteran now discharged, got himself a 1946 Chevrolet. This was a great achievement to acquire a car so quickly after the war. He and I were going up to visit my maternal Grandmother. I say mine, rather than ours, because Walter and I are actually half brothers. We both have the same Dad, but different Moms. We were riding up to the county store that my Grandmother Katherine operated. It was truly a general store and I remember distinctly that the soda was kept cold with ice. There was an icebox, truly an icebox where the iceman used to leave ice.

During World War II, as a very young child, I was appalled at the way some of my Grandmother's relatives took advantage of her. They would go up to see her from the city and then buy all manner of very scarce items, (cigarettes and certain meats), depleting her inventory. To my parents' credit, while they would purchase these things, they would buy all of their groceries from Kate, allowing her a decent profit, unlike the leaches that just took the hard to get stuff and only came for that purpose. I loved my Grandmother, actually my step-grandmother, married to my widowed natural Grandfather. She was known locally as Aunt Kate.

Walter and I were riding down the country lane that led to her place. It is less a country lane today but the road still retains much of its character. As a kid about three years away from a driver's license, I pleaded with my brother to let me drive the car. I argued, "There's nobody out here" and so on — you know the drill. My brother, would you believe, let me drive, much to his regret. The trip down to my Grandmother's place was relatively uneventful until I overtook a car in front of me. I, in my panic, instead of hitting the brake, hit the clutch, so we were still rocketing right along. (The clutch, by the way, for some of you younger readers, is part of a manual transmission. I am sure many of you have never driven one.)

I swung off to the left to pass, but lo and behold there was another car coming, which I ran right off the road! There was enough of a shoulder where he could turn without any damage to himself or his automobile. You can believe he made a snappy U-turn! A short time later my brother and I arrived at Grandmas, pulling in under a tree. Right behind us was the sheriff. As you have guessed, I had run the sheriff off the road.

The sheriff came over and said to me, "Let me see your driver's license." Now a driver's license was years in my future, but I squawked in my pre-pubescent voice, "I have a learner's permit, sir." "Well, let me see that," he replied. "I don't have it with me," I said. He continued, "You're not old enough for a learner's permit and you" — he looked at my brother — "you should go to jail, and I just may take you guys in."

About this time, Grandma came out and said, "Hello, Sheriff Smith, what's going on?" He explained it to her, and she said, "You know, sheriff, these are my grandsons." He said, "Kate, I don't care who they are, this kid shouldn't been driving the car, this other guy shouldn't have given him permission to drive the car, and I'm taking them in." My Grandmother said very sweetly, "I'm sure that's what you should do, and I'm not going to fight about that, however, before you leave, about your bill?"

You see, my Grandmother had everybody on the arm. A lot of them never paid. The whole neighborhood owed her two, maybe three months pay each. When she passed away, it was hard to find somebody in the entire area who didn't owe her money. So when she said to the sheriff, "About your bill, I'm sure you're going to want to come in and settle your account before you take my grandsons down to the station," he got the message. He stuttered, "Maybe I should think about this a little bit."

Two minutes later Sheriff Smith took off, leaving my brother to chew me out and my Grandmother smiling benignly. That was a microcosm of the world. She had juice in her area, in this case because of finances. Everybody respected her. She was fair, and in many cases, more fair than she should have been.

Some forty years later, I was in that same area. I found the foundation of the home that my Grandmother once occupied. That was all that was left. At the time I was looking to purchase a couple of travel trailers for a business venture. I saw one for sale not too far from her place. I walked in and looked at it. The seller was not a young man so I asked him, "By the way, did you know Katherine Paddock down the road? That was my maternal grandmother's name." He said, "You mean Aunt Kate? Everybody knew Aunt Kate, she was the best. When you didn't have any money she made sure you ate." So forty-odd years later, at least one guy remembered who she was and then, of course, there are my brother and I, which makes three. If the sheriff is still with us, I have a feeling he makes number four!

Mr. Bodenschatz

In our freshman year of high school, like all freshmen, we were feisty and uncertain of our environment. I clearly remember the day we walked into Mr. Bodenschatzs' class. One of the first things that he did was take a roll of the kids in class. Bodenschatz was not too tall, on the stocky side, his hair was thinning but he was certainly fit. As the kids stood up to give their name, Bodenschatz looked a little surprised. One fellow stood up and said, "My name is Dick Tracy," another, "John Smith" yet another "Tom Collins," and still another, "Jack Frost." Of course, Bodenschatz thought that he was being put on, but indeed I did have a classmate named Thomas Collins, another Richard Tracy, both of who have passed away, a Jack Frost and a John Smith.

As he tried to straighten this out, one of the kids in the back of the class started cutting up a little bit, giving him some "stuff." Bodenschatz stopped immediately, looked at the class and said, "My name is Bodenschatz, Arno Von Bodenschatz, recently Major Von Bodenschatz. During the war I killed a good many men; one more will not matter in the slightest." He walked over to the kid who was "cutting up," held him over his head and threw him out of the window. Needless to say there was no more "stuff" in Mr. Bodenschatz class. A great many of the teachers were veterans coming back from World War II, and these guys were glad to be back to civilian life, but they didn't want some "snot-nosed kid" screwing around with them. Perhaps we need more of that in schools today.

Yokohama Harbor

I left the United States on November 17, 1951, on a ship. The *Randall* sailed from San Francisco bound for Yokohama, Japan. For the first three days, if they had been handing out cyanide pills, I would have been the first one in line because I was so sick. Forty men were stacked five high in a compartment that was about the same size as the suite that I occupy on a cruise these days. How things have changed! After three or four days, however, almost everyone got over the seasickness and the balance of the voyage was reasonably pleasant.

When we entered Yokohama Harbor, we were impressed with the sight of Mount Fuji, which we all had come to associate with Japan during the war years. Almost immediately, after we arrived in Yokohama, the ship was besieged by two to three hundred men and women in pajama suits swarming all over the ship chipping paint. They were not paying the least bit of attention to these fearsome troops brought over from the United States. As I watched these folks chipping away, I believe I experienced an epiphany. These were the same people whom, a few years before, my brother and his peers had been committed to obliterating. The people, whom we would be fighting very shortly, if we made it to Korea, had been the allies of my brother and his peers. It occurred to me, at the tender age of nineteen, politics shift very quickly.

I made up my mind that I was going to stay alive. That is not to say that I wouldn't do my job, it isn't to say that I wouldn't do anything that I was called upon to do, including taking the life of a North Korean or the Chinese. But I can say truthfully, then and now, I had no antagonism towards these individuals. I got to thinking that they are probably just like me, being told to go somewhere by their government, and just like me, they would probably like to stay alive.

Since I did survive, I have come to see reconciliation with the Chinese and now under way, reconciliation with the North Koreans. It's a good thing that we generally send young men and women to war. Anybody older than twenty-five would have figured out that wars are created by old men for young men to fight, and that today's friend is tomorrow's enemy.

Bruce Eats Crow

Some years ago, I was on one of my many cruises to Alaska with a fair number of listeners. We were on the inaugural voyage of the Royal Princess. It indeed was an exceptionally fine ship and, of course, when it's brand new, it's a real pleasure to be part of that break-in process. The trip began and ended in San Francisco. As I recall, it was a ten-day cruise. Ordinarily, when I go on these trips I have several people with me: my brother, his wife and my staff. But, for whatever reason on this particular trip, I was all alone, just me.

I came to find out that I was the only single male passenger on the ship. I couldn't even find a guy to have a drink with once in awhile. Frankly, traveling alone is not much fun and I really had every intention of ending the trip prematurely. I did have an obligation on the sailing day for a party and I knew of one other. Several days into the cruise, on a day at sea, I spent the afternoon with a young lady whom I met. She worked for the airlines and was traveling with her mother. She too was a bit on the bored side and we commiserated at the bar at the stern of the ship for a considerable amount of time.

Five or six o'clock came and it was time to go to our cabins to get cleaned up for dinner. When I arrived at the second seating for dinner, one of our lady listeners came over to me and with a very unfriendly look asked, *"Where were you?"* "Mrs. So and so where was I? When? What? I had no idea what she was offended by!

As it turned out, the party that I was to host was held ninety degrees around the corner from the bar where I sat wasting away the afternoon, no more than fifty feet away. I had no idea and, unlike my ordinary trips when I have somebody to remind me of my responsibilities, it completely got past me. There was nothing to do but have another party, and this one was on me. As I remember, it cost me something in the order of $1,500 to host it. The name of the party was *"Bruce Williams*

Eats Crow." We had the chef make a matzo pan crow that I devoured ceremoniously at our party. Since we had to arrange this little gathering, I wasn't able to jump ship. I had to complete the entire ten-day cruise. I will attest to this however, traveling alone on a pleasure cruise, such as this, is not a whole lot of fun. While it is possible to meet someone, if I were giving advice, I would strongly suggest anyone taking a cruise of this kind to bring his or her own companion.

I will leave it to your own imagination as to the suggestions from my cruise guests as to what part of the crow I should have eaten first.

A Pal Across The Years

One of the fellows I hung around with toward the end of my tour in Korea was from Memphis, Tennessee. But he never said Memphis, Tennessee. It was "Memphis bygod Tennessee." His name was Julian Jeffries. Jeff worked in the Angry Twenty-Six (Radio Shack) along with Harry Bruns and a couple of other fellows and me. He was one of the guys who got rotated a little earlier than I, which put a little more working pressure on me.

Jeff and I became good friends. For a short time he was transferred up to Chodo, an island on the wrong side of the Chinese lines. Most of our conversation was encrypted but from time to time it was necessary to go into plain text. As we were interfering with the Russian and Chinese broadcasts, even to the extent of persuading the Russian pilots that we were their controller, we were obviously very sensitive to the fact that the other side could do the same to us. Therefore, when we got a plain text communication from Chodo, we were suspicious of its origin. That was cleared up very quickly when Jeff got on the line and said he was calling from "big-foot country." Jeff wore size sixteen shoes, and it was very hard to believe that the enemy would have known that "big foot" was on the other end of the line.

Jeff and I hooked up again in San Antonio when we were both stationed there. By that time, Jeff was married to Betsy and things were moving along in an orderly fashion, but we were, as usual, hungry for a buck. Another of my failures in the business world had its genesis in San Antonio.

We decided to go into the mail order business. We were impressed with all of the classified ads in *Popular Mechanics* magazine and figured if these guys could make money so could we. We wound up doing two things. We'd acquired, from a source that I have long since forgotten, aprons, which were made to be worn while a person was barbecuing. Our ad read something to this effect: "Host apron covered with witty expressions and humorous cartoons, $2.50, Box 1918, San Antonio, Texas." I believe we may have sold at least two, possibly three aprons.

Another venture with the same box number that was a bit more successful was setting up a San Antonio re-mail. This allowed people to send a letter for a dollar. That letter would have a San Antonio postmark on it. If the sender wanted to hide where he was from, it could not be traced by the postmark. Some of these communications would simply be a joke being played by one person on another. Others would be a surreptitious way to contact the addressee without them having a clue as to where the letter came from. We charged one dollar for re-mailing the letters, which is a pretty easy bit. Open up the envelope, put the buck in your pocket, and drop the other guy's letter in the mail. While we didn't get rich, we might have made a couple of pennies on this operation. But it was more trouble than it was worth, and very shortly Jeffries and Williams Mail Order ceased to exist.

Some forty years later I was doing a phoner with our new Memphis, Tennessee, affiliate. (A phoner is simply talking to one of the local hosts over the telephone, on the air.) After we chatted for a time, I mentioned my good friend Jeff and I said,

"Wouldn't it be great if we could find him." The host said, "Sure, let's talk about it," and so I mentioned his name and the fact that he lived in Memphis years ago. Not ten minutes later the host got me during a commercial break and said, "You're not going to believe this. We got his wife on the phone." Great! They said, "Hello, you're on the air with Bruce." "Hello, Betsy, it's been so long," and she said, "This isn't Betsy, it's Betty." I said, "Golly, I always remember you as Betsy." She said, "Oh no, he dumped her years ago, I'm his second wife Betty, but Jeff died six years ago." End of the reconnect with Jeff.

Beach House

I was doing the Saturday morning show on WMCA in New York from 6 to 10 o'clock. After the show in the summer months, I would immediately depart the studios, grab the A train down to 34th street, take the New Jersey transit to New Brunswick and drive to our home at the shore. I remember being at the shore and griping about having to carry things down to the beach. At that time, we had a house, one house away from the beach (subsequently we bought the house on the beach and owned the two of them). We had to walk at least sixty or seventy feet to get established on a private beach where, on a crowded Sunday, there would be as many as ten to twelve families.

When I picked up the A train at Columbus Circle, only a couple of stops from 34th street, I noticed families loaded down with beach paraphernalia going out to Coney Island — a good hour ride on the train. Then they had to lug their things down to the beach, some considerable distance, and then stake out a few square feet as their own for the day. Upon reflecting on this, I had some feelings of guilt regarding my bitching and complaining about lugging the kid's stuff just a few feet.

It was not always so, however. I remember going with my

friend Bob Geyer, to take the Park Avenue bus down to First Street. We would then pick up a trolley car (in New Jersey called the City Subway) because it went underground into downtown Newark. Taking the trolley car, Number 29, to the end of the line was a good hour ride up to Caldwell. We got off at the end of the line and walked down a long hill a couple of miles to a swimming pool called Sunnyfield. We would spend the day and reverse the process at the end of the day. In other words, we traveled some three hours, and then some, in order to go for a swim, not even considering that we had to walk two or three miles.

It's amazing how our perspectives change. Maybe we just get soft as we get a little more affluent. I would like to think that there is a little more to it than that. My folks had a car, but unlike today's generation, I don't remember one occasion where my Mother or Father drove us up to Sunnyfield. It was always the bus, trolley and walk. Perhaps we appreciated it a bit more.

My Growing Family

We bought a house in Old Bridge, New Jersey, a portion of East Brunswick, when I was a sophomore in college. My son, Mark, was born the first semester of my junior year. Our neighbors, Joe and Dot Skurka, were going to baby-sit for Matthew while my wife was in the hospital and I was at school. In those days, mercifully, a woman got to spend a few days off in the hospital, rather than being pushed out the door half an hour after giving birth. Obviously, it is a matter of economics not medicine.

I remember as if it were yesterday, telling Matt to go down and see Aunt Dot and Uncle Joe. While he was on his way down two houses, at the tender age of a year and a half, I scooted out the door and on to school. You can bet your life the next day I didn't get away with that story. As soon as I told him to go down and see Aunt Dot and Uncle Joe, Matt went ballistic and said that he wasn't going. I had to carry him down kicking and screaming. It is amazing how little incidents like this stand out in your memory.

I went to Orange Memorial Hospital in Orange, New Jersey, to pick up my wife and our last child, Michael. Four kids were in the station wagon with me. When I told them that Michael was in the box full of things that I had brought from the hospital and we would open it up when we got home, you can imagine my kids, "Get him out of the box!" But I was insistent that he stayed in the box until his Mother came out from the hospital. Of course, when she was finally discharged, she carried Mike in her arms, and the kids were somewhat relieved.

Friends

We throw the word "friend" around far too loosely, in my opinion. A youngster will say "all of my friends at school" or "I met so and so years ago and he's my friend," that sort of thing. I have tried not to use the word "friend" loosely. By the true definition of the word, I think any person on this earth who has had a half-dozen friends, outside his family, has been very blessed. In my lifetime I have met many people and had many casual acquaintances and casual friends. But when I think of true friends, I can think of six and six only.

Of the six, two have passed away: Albert DeVries and Nate Rosenhouse.

Albert DeVries was a bomber pilot while he was still a teenager. He made the very tail end of World War II. After returning to college in a small upstate New York school, he showed up in New Jersey with a shovel and a wheelbarrow. With these implements, he built himself a multi-million dollar landscaping business. Al and I became friends in the early 1960s and this friendship continued through his death in the late 90's. We played racquetball when it was not trendy, enjoyed Friday night poker sessions and Al was a member of the group that went to Las Vegas for our annual excursion. We spent hours discussing business, politics, and in short, ruminated about life in general. He was stubborn, acerbic, but a very important part of my life in Franklin Park. The last time he and I were together before he was hospitalized was our trip to New York City. The high point of the trip was tossing a coin to see who paid for dinner. We would go to the most expensive restaurant we could find, flip a coin and put the coin underneath the plate so that the coin toss was settled but neither of us knew who the winner was. Then we would order the most expensive things from the menu hoping to stick the other guy. I think I speak for him and say that both of us would have preferred to win that wager than make a major business coup. It is probably unreasonable, but, from time to time, I still get angry with both Al and Nate for leaving so early.

I became acquainted with Nate Rosenhouse in the early 1960s when his daughter was enrolled in my nursery school. Throughout the years, we became close friends and he has been my attorney for over three decades. Unfortunately, Nate had a stroke at a relatively young age and subsequently passed away. During the years that we played together and worked together, we became very close associates. He is sadly missed.

My oldest friend is Bob Geyer. He and I go back to our first encounter at five or six years old. Aside from my brother and a distant cousin, Bob has known me longer than anyone on this earth. I think we think of each other more as brothers than we do as friends. He knows that if there were anything he needed, I would do my best to provide it. I am also sure that the same is true of him. Back in the early days in school, when I was desperate for money, I did borrow $500 from Bob for a relatively short time. It was a lifesaver. And of course, he was repaid. I can't think of anybody else who was able and would be willing to lend me the money at that time. He is indeed a true friend. It's a friendship that I cherish.

Another fellow, who is mentioned in the book, is Ken

Langdon. Ken and I became acquainted through Indian Guides. Both of our eldest sons were involved. Indian Guides, you may know, is a father and son operation. You can't just pack off your child; you have to go with him. Ken and I started out in that relationship and it has grown over the years. We have helped one another in business, had a lot of fun together, worked together in politics and, in short, he's the kind of guy I admire and love. Kenny is one of the most resourceful people I have ever met.

Abe Sudam, a neighbor, would be fifth. Abe is from a farming family of considerable wealth. They at one time said they came from Brooklyn. Of course, they failed to mention that they came from Brooklyn in the seventeenth century. Abe and I go back to the time shortly after I moved into Franklin Township, back in 1961. Abe is in the insurance business and has handled a big part of my insurance needs during that time. But more importantly, he has been a good friend and has been there when I needed him, and I think, on occasion, I was there for him.

These are the five guys whom I have been close to. Certainly, there are many others that I am grateful to have known. As I said, my definition of friend results in a very short list.

Rounding out my team of six close friends of a lifetime is Arthur Maccini. Art, his wife, Margaret, and I became acquainted during those days when politics was still fun. Margaret was my campaign manager in my happily unsuccessful attempt to become part of the New Jersey Legislature. While I talk to Art on the phone from time to time, we see each other infrequently, but I have to believe that this is a guy who, if I really needed a friend, would be the first to be there. Of course, I am here for him.

That, my friends, rounds out the last of the six. We met over the course of six decades. I count myself very fortunate in having six true friends, and I believe they value my friendship as I value theirs.

About Susan

My wife, Susan, and I have been married for over two years at this writing. The relatively short time that I knew Susan before we were married and since our marriage, has proven to be a wonderful experience. If you were to see Susan and me, you would be quick to note that this is a May-December marriage. Susan is younger than three of my children. I believe I speak for her and, certainly for me, saying I have absolutely no regrets and that we have thus far found a great deal of satisfaction in being together. We are grateful to our families, who obviously had to swallow hard in the very beginning on this one. Both families have become very accepting. My kids hold Susan in the highest regard and her family has been most gracious in taking me into their family.

My Children

Many of you have asked, "What are your children doing now?" As of this writing my number one son, Matthew, is self-employed in Longview, Texas, where he lives with his three children. Mark, my number two son, who is a trained and licensed physical therapist, has made over 5000 skydives as a skydiving instructor, as well as a tandem master. He is now flying airplanes as a commercial pilot, which seems to be his true love. He is enjoying himself in this capacity. My daughter, Robbins, is a managing partner in our nightclubs and is doing a remarkable job working with the personnel and putting systems in place. She commutes regularly between Orlando and Atlanta, as does Michael, my youngest son, who is also a partner in this enterprise. Michael began as a piano player and singer working with the entertainers. Unhappily, he has a problem with his voice and no longer entertains but is showing remarkable talent for being an executive. These two of my children run this multi-million dollar enterprise with remarkable acumen. Kelly, my second daughter, is a practicing attorney in Longview, Texas. After several years working with me as my manager, she decided to go to law school and is now working independently in her own practice. All five children are productive citizens and all five make me proud.

Peer Recognition

I was a nominee on two occasions for an award by the National Association of Broadcasters but had absolutely no hope of winning simply because of the process. What in the world would a young kid running a rock n roll station or a hip-hop station know about talk radio, and yet he is able to vote in the NAB selections if he's a member. Knowing that, unless you have gained a reputation through either doing stunts or would you believe through television, the likelihood is that it's just a matter of guesswork and the big edge goes to the guy at the head of the alphabet. With a "W" you know where I'm going to wind up. It always seemed to me so much more reasonable to have the elections done by categories. In other words, religious stations would vote about religion, talk stations about talk, different kinds of music about music. However, that would take a lot more work, and so far to my knowledge, it has not been broken down that finely.

In November of 1999, I was very pleased and honored to be inducted into the Radio Hall of Fame in Chicago, Illinois. This honor was particularly rewarding since my wife and all of my children and grandchildren were there to share with me that memorable evening.

My thanks, then and now, to Bruce DuMont, the president of the organization, and to all those folks who were generous enough to check their ballot for me.

My induction into the Radio Hall of Fame was an honor that I didn't take lightly, given the fact that there are a huge number of real celebrities who have been so honored. I have enclosed a list for your edification:

The Radio Hall of Fame Inductees

Ace, Goodman & Jane	Freberg, Sam	McLaughlin, Edward
Allen, Fred	Freed, Alan	McLendon, Gordon
Allen, Mel	Godfrey, Arthur	McNeill, Don
Ameche, Don	Goldenson, Leonard	Morgan, Robert W.
Arden, Eve	Goodman, Benny	Morrow, Bruce
Armstrong, Edwin H.	Gordon, Gale	Murrow, Edward R.
Barber, Red	Gosden, Freeman	Osgood, Charles
Benny, Jack	Guild, Ralph	Owens, Gary
Berg, Gertrude	Haas, Karl	Paley, William S.
Bergen, Edgar	Harvey, Paul	Pate Jr., Edward
Biondi, Dick	Harwell, Ernie	Payne, Virginia
Blayton Sr., Jesse B	Hinkley, Gordon	Phillips, Wally
Block, Martin	Hope, Bob	Quello, James H.
Brickhouse, Jack	Imus, Don	Sarnoff, David
Buck, Jack	Jack, Wolfman	Schaden, Chuck
Caray, Harry	Jackson, Hal	Scully, Vin
Carter, Andrew	Jordan, Jim & Marian	Skelton, Red
Clark, Dick	Joyner, Tom	Sklar, Rick
Conrad, William	Kasem, Casey	Smith, Kate
Correll, Charles	Kaufman, Murray "the K"	Stamberg, Susan
Corwin, Norman	Keillor, Garrison	Stanton, Frank
Crosby, Bing	Kent, Herb	Steele, Bob
Daniels, Yvonne	King, Larry	Stern, Bill
Dees, Rick	Kyser, Kay	Striker, Fran
DeForest, Lee	Limbaugh, Rush	Thomas, Lowell
Dorsey, Tommy	Magliozzi, Tom & Ray	Tremayne, Les
Dunbar, Jim	Marconi, Guglielmo	Welles, Orson
Dunphy, Don	Marx, Groucho	Williams, Bruce H.
Edwards, Ralph	McCarthy, J.P.	Williams, Jerry W.

Information Provided By: www.tribads.com/mbcnet/rhofmembers.htm

11

Contemporary Observations

One of the greatest difficulties everyone faces in this country today is the denial of opportunity that over regulation causes. Sometimes it seems that no good idea goes unpunished by the government. Although the people in Washington and your state capital can do plenty of damage, sometimes municipal government throws up the worst obstructions. It's a subject I know something about.

Winning and Losing in Politics

For reasons that I have totally forgotten, I decided in late 1964 or early 1965 to attend a Council meeting in my community, Franklin Township, Somerset County, New Jersey. I was upset about something. The mayor, whom I had met on one previous occasion, was George Consovoy, a guy I got to know very well in succeeding years and developed affection for. He came out after the meeting and introduced himself, and I said, "Yeah, we met when I first came into town." He commented, "You're upset." What the reason was, I don't remember. He finally said, "Well, if you're so upset, why don't you get on the Council? Why don't you come after my job?"

Shortly thereafter, I decided I'd like to get on that governing body at age 33. I knew I could settle the affairs of state. Unhappily, a Republican occupied the seat for the ward and I was, and still continue to be, a Republican. Although today, I am less partisan than I was then, as I have come to the conclusion that the differences between the parties are nowhere near as pronounced as I once thought them to be.

The councilman for the First Ward, where I was living, was a gentleman — and that is the appropriate term, gentleman — J. Leonard Vilet, a farmer, craftsman, a genuinely decent man. I took exception to some of the stuff he did. Of course, he was older and old was to be discarded. I had the usual disdain for age that youth seems to carry with it. I went before the nominating committee and, of course, J. Leonard received the nomination, as he should have. I decided to run as an Independent.

There were four individuals running for the office: Mr. Vilet; me; the Democrats' nominee, a farmer from up the road, Alex Pinter; and, finally, the council gadfly, Armand Petrillo, a barber. Although small of stature, Mr. Petrillo had the voice of a Nineteenth Century orator. He didn't need a PA system or a megaphone. You could hear him anywhere. The four-way race would have to be settled by a runoff, given the fact that it was unlikely that anyone would receive a majority of the votes cast since the votes would be so fractured.

Here I was, an upstart, living in town for only three years and presuming that I knew more than people who had been there for twenty. Maybe I did. Maybe I didn't. I published position papers with my campaign committee, which consisted of a good friend, Jim Zonino, who passed away recently, and one dissident Norwegian, the late Hans Voge. I mention his ethnicity because the area where J. Leonard was strongest was a section of our community called Griggstown. Recently, a street in Griggstown was named after Hans.

Griggstown consisted of former summer residents from Brooklyn, New York, who over the years started to move out to the country to retire. The community was almost entirely Scandinavian. The church was Scandinavian. Eddie Tornquist operated the one general store in the area. More importantly, this was J. Leonard's strong area. In the wintertime, he would plow people's driveways and keep the streets in good repair. Because of these good deeds, in the Griggstown of that era, J. Leonard could do no wrong.

The ward was subdivided into four districts. The one that I lived in was largely rural. The district adjacent to mine, the most heavily developed, was almost exclusively black, (then called colored). Neither party paid much attention to the area, not because this was a black area, but because the cold hard facts were that almost nobody voted. With a potential voting population of some 800 or 1,000, a large turnout would be fifteen to thirty souls, clearly not worth spending a lot of time on. Griggstown, in contrast, would always turn out 90 percent or more of the electorate — a good place to be popular.

The long and the short of it was that my campaign consisted of knocking on doors. I visited every home in the ward in a four-month period. I spent every night introducing myself and, when it was too late to knock on doors, Jimmy and I would deliver position papers to the rural mailboxes. Of course, there were the candidate's nights, which everyone attended. But the thrust of my campaign was door-to-door and the mailbox route with Jimmy.

I sneaked through, and while J. Leonard ran No. 1, I was No. 2. I forced a runoff with Mr. Vilet. The runoff became a tad acrimonious. We did have some words both during and after the election. Happily, that rift was healed and we became close associates before J. Leonard's passing. In the runoff election, I carried three of the four districts, but did I get murdered in Griggstown! If I got more than Hans' and his wife's votes, I don't recall. The overall win was about 35 votes of several thousand cast, but all you need is one extra, and J. Leonard kicked my butt.

I remember July 1, 1965, like it was yesterday. It was the

swearing-in of the new council. I remarked that day that this could have been a very special day. As it turned out, two years later, July 1st was a special day. I ran with the party for an at-large seat and won after going through another runoff, starting with 13 candidates for four seats, and reduced to eight. I ran second in a field of eight, and took my seat on the council on July 1, 1967. I was re-elected in May 1971 and chose not to run in the next election in 1975. During my councilmanic career, I served as mayor, deputy mayor and, of course, councilman, and member of the Planning Board and other committees.

I will point out something that became extremely clear to me in this and then other areas of my life. If you're going to play, you can win and you can lose. I have experienced both in politics and other endeavors. I can tell you this, if we have a scale of positive and negative, one to 10, a loss can be a negative 10; a win possibly a positive 2 or 3. Or, put another way, the pain of losing is geometrically larger than the joy of winning. I found that to be true in so many areas. Maybe that's just human nature.

The Sports Rip-Off

It seems to me that one of the phoniest bills of goods that have been sold to the American public and their communities is that sports teams are good for their economic health. Let me say at the outset, and let there be no mistake, I have no problem with professional sports teams locating in a given community any more than I have a problem with any other business enterprise that has been designed for profit. I have a great deal of antipathy toward the proposition that sports teams are different from any other business enterprise and therefore should be supported not only by the patrons — and Lord knows there are millions of those both in the seats of the stadiums and arenas and watching on the tube as well as listening on the radio — but also by the taxpayers.

It seems to me the height of imbecility that millionaires with their toys should be subsidized with tax dollars in the form of a stadium, parking areas and concessions that generate the revenue. I have absolutely no quarrel with them owning their teams, building their stadiums and charging whatever the traffic will bear to get in. However, to ask that the citizenry build the stadiums with tax dollars or give heavy tax relief for a number of years so that the multimillionaire owners can have sky boxes to sell to other millionaires or to businesses who, in turn, will deduct that expense from their taxes, further increasing the subsidy that they receive, is wrong.

It should be understood that professional sports, like any other business, chase discretionary dollars. If, for example, a fan goes to the stadium and eats three hot dogs, the likelihood is that he will not go to McDonald's that afternoon and buy a Big Mac and some french fries. There are only so many discretionary food dollars and he has only so much appetite. The same thing may be said for the couple of beers he would consume. He does not go out to his local tavern or down to the store and buy the beer. He buys it at the stadium. Once again, if he buys at the stadium, the local businessman doesn't see that money.

If you think for a moment that the majority of players and owners live in the area, please be disabused of that notion. There are exceptions where players become a major part of the community: Stan Musial in St. Louis as an example. But the overwhelming majority return whence they came, to their roots. Further, in terms of professional sports, if you are playing for one team today, you could be sold to another tomorrow, and it's pretty hard to put down a set of roots. The owners, too, for the most part, tend not to reinvest whatever return there is in the area. They, too, are multistate and sometimes multinational. I have no quarrel with that activity, but it seems to me there is no excuse for public subsidy.

Some communities are catching on. In an election in

255

Pittsburgh, a major issue was; should the Steelers and Pirates get a new stadium at public expense? The Democrats said "yes" and the Republicans said "no." The city, which had not elected a Republican for something on the order of 60 years, I believe, elected Republicans to office. Obviously, an informed citizenry rejected the notion that they should be subsidizing millionaires' toys. Sadly, the politicians and owners now have persuaded the public in the burg to pay in part for their new toys.

The professional sports community has done an enormous public relations job. In some cases, it has obtained immunity from antitrust laws and some labor laws, all at the expense of the citizens. What is really a hoot is that if "their" team makes it to the Super Bowl or the World Series, what chance does the average schlump who has purchased a season ticket at the stadium have of getting a ticket to the championship? You know the answer to that! Take a look at the roster of celebrities, politicians and others who attend only the major events. Well, those seats could be occupied by a fan, but don't hold your breath until you get it. A very small percentage of the season ticket holders of the two winning teams are going to windup with tickets to the Super Bowl or the World Series.

The leagues have also worked out a proposition in which, unless the stadium is sold out, the event cannot be televised in their area. The rest of the country, of course, can watch it. They are not going to give up the television rights going back to the visiting team's hometown and perhaps the revenue from a regional game. But again, the poor schlump in the area who either cannot afford a ticket, or finds going to the game inconvenient, is deprived of the chance to watch. They even have done their best to disable satellite transmissions into their area, so that even if you care enough to put in a dish, you can't receive the signal of your game.

The answer is clear. Every time a public referendum is offered about some type of tax relief or tax support of any professional sport, the public should immediately and resoundingly vote no! Let those businessmen, like all businessmen; invest their own money in this venture. If they make money, God bless them. If they lose money, that's the cost of doing business. And finally, there should be neither relief from the laws that control other businesses, nor any form of tax relief. I have no quarrel if they want to move their franchise every year. It's a business and they should have the right to do that, but I don't believe that they should be allowed to hold cities and regions hostage to their demands of "give us this, or we'll take our game elsewhere."

Adventures in Government

I have no regrets about my excursion into politics. The eight years I spent on the council were rewarding, frustrating and all of the things that politics is supposed to be. And, it adds to what I do on my program, because I have seen government from the inside. I did run for the General Assembly in New Jersey and, using my renowned sense of timing, I chose to run as a Republican in the Watergate year. I'm not even sure I voted for myself! The fellow who beat me, Joe Paterno, went on to spend many years in the Assembly and I went on to radio. I recently had occasion to see Joe in Las Vegas, Nevada, where he is now retired. I thanked him profusely for beating me. Had I won that election, I might have been a senator. I'd rather be a talk show host; there's less frustration and, trust me, the pay is a whole lot better.

When I was involved in local government, we had a shell of a motel on the entrance to the community, right off the Interstate Highway. The builder put several million dollars into this enterprise and then went belly up. We had tried everything we could to get this building finished. As an example, we were talking to a developer who was going to try to turn it into a nursing home. The problem was that the doors were 32 inches wide and federal standards dictated that the doors in a nursing home had to be 34 inches wide, so it couldn't be certified for a nursing home. There were several other uses that came along and the same things were true. We couldn't get the job done.

Finally, a developer from Chicago, Illinois, Ray Kuns, came in and, through sources I don't know, funded the finishing of the hotel. He then had made a deal with the TraveLodge Corporation, which was based in Australia, to take over the hotel. There was a problem, however. There are only two ways that one can create a landlocked piece of property, to my knowledge.

The first is by will. You can whack up a piece of property in your will. The second is by court order. In the second instance, due to bankruptcy, probably by mistake, the judge created a little island with no ingress or egress, other than the adjacency to a ramp off the Interstate Highway. At that time, to my knowledge, there were no curb cuts, on any ramp, anywhere, in the United States from an Interstate Highway.

We wanted to get this job done, so we approached an adjacent property owner who had done a considerable amount of developing in the area. We asked him if the developer could go across his property. He said, "Sure, don't worry about a thing," and he showed us a place where the trucks could go in and out. That was all very well, but then when the project was finished, he decided that nobody could go in and out, even though he had given his word that he was amenable to a permanent easement. This created a bit of a problem.

Among other things, as a countermove, he needed water on his property and we brought a water line within inches of his property, but not to it. He was not able to go across someone else's few inches of property to hook into the water line. A little bit of pressure.

We agreed as a consideration, because it was in the public interest, to allow him to build "100 doors," i.e., to give him permission to build 100 homes on his property. This, obviously, increased the value of his property geometrically, but that was not enough for our hero. He did agree to get everything done, and was going to do a deal, but at the last minute, he called me to cancel. His secretary said he had out-of-town friends and I explained to her that we had people coming from the West Coast of the United States, Australia and Chicago. She said she knew that, but "Mr. Levin regrets that he is unable to attend the meeting." I said, "Would you give Mr. Levin a message from me, as the mayor of the community?"

She said, "Of course."

I said, "If my memory serves me correctly, the Home for the Jewish Aged is in our community, a planned nursing home, and Mr. Levin is very interested in that."

She said, "Yes, that's true."

"It also seems to me that this evening there is a variance application in order to allow that home to be built."

"That's true."

"Then give Mr. Levin a message from me."

"Yes."

"He ain't gonna get the variance, and furthermore, tomorrow morning every Jew in New York will know the reason they couldn't have a retirement home for their older folks is because Phil Levin is a greedy son-of-a-bitch," and I hung up the phone.

Three minutes later the telephone rang: "Mr. Levin will be at the meeting at 7."

Bear in mind, all we are trying to do is get permission to go across Mr. Levin's property so this project can open. Everybody wins. The community has, instead of an eyesore, a brand new hotel, which, at the time, was something, we sorely needed.

We had a meeting at McAteer's Restaurant where Mr. Levin stalled. I looked at his attorney, Bill Ozzard, whom I knew quite well. He was president of the Senate at the time. I said, "Bill, we gotta get this job done, because I think you have to be at the Board of Adjustment meeting at 8 p.m. to represent the nursing home." He said, "That's true." I replied, "If I walk into the meeting and I've got a cigar in my hand, you'll get your variance. If I walk into that meeting and no cigar, Billy, you may as well not even make a presentation."

Well, everyone looked at me. Bill said, "This is the second time I saw somebody screw around with Mayor Williams to their detriment."

The deal got done. First of all, Mr. Levin said, "Oh, you can count on me." I said, "I can't count on anything, let's get the deal done in writing." And we did.

Later on, I didn't go to the Board of Adjustment meeting and the application was passed upon on its merits. But the postscript to this whole story is that I didn't have the votes to kill Mr. Levin's application for the nursing home. He was going to get that variance no matter what I did. But because he was so used to the fix being in, he couldn't believe that I didn't have the ability to fix the thing, so he went along with us. It's probably the only thing that I did when I was involved in politics that might have bordered on the illegal, even though our intentions were perfectly honorable. And, it was clear, I gained nothing personally.

Many years later, when I got into the radio business, I interviewed Mr. Levin's son, Adam, who was really a neat guy. He was, at that time, consumer affairs officer and I recounted the story to him, with no malice. I just thought it was a story that had I been he, I would have enjoyed hearing about my Dad. And, he did. He took it in great spirits and said, "That's the kind of guy my Dad was. He came up the hard way, as maybe you did, and he did what he felt he had to do."

I had no problem with that. I met him on his playing field and, at least that time, I came up with a win. But as a practical matter, so did he. He got his water and he got his development. Neither cost him a dime.

I don't remember quite how it happened, but we also did get a curb cut into the egress road off the Interstate Highway. That curb cut still exists today and, I'm told it was the first in the United States.

In that situation, I leaned pretty hard on a man to get something done, something constructive for the community. However, one of the problems in our society, as I view it, is intrusion of government into our lives with no productive consequence. Now, I am certain that there are many government employees who would argue with this, but let me draw some parallels between 1955 in South Orange, New Jersey, and 1990 in South Brunswick, New Jersey. Two South's separated by 35 years.

In the late fall of 1955, Bob Geyer and I determined that we would like to sell Christmas trees. We found a lot on South Orange Avenue adjacent to a small shopping area. I remember that lot well. When I was a child I lived up the street. There was an old home on that property, but the home had long since disappeared and nothing had been done with the property. Years later it became a parking lot. We made a lease arrangement with a physician who owned the property and simply handed him $35, nothing in writing, and it was rented. I went next door to the barbershop and offered them $5 to plug in a couple of extension cords so I could get some electricity. They were very happy to do it, and we were in business. No licenses, no written leases, no permits, no trouble. We sold trees for $3 apiece, made a few dollars, cleaned up the place when we were done after Christmas, and that was the end of it. Simply, no one was hurt, the people selling the trees to us made money, we made money, we spent a little bit of money in the neighborhood, the barber made a couple of bucks off the electricity, and the doctor got his rent.

The scene moves to 1990.

We are still in the Christmas tree business. It is something I enjoy. I'm not certain I make any money, but it is a ritual in my life that I maintained over a great many years, and will continue to, as long as I am able.

We made arrangements to rent a part of a parking lot from a restaurant in South Brunswick, New Jersey. The first thing we had to do was to get a merchant's license. The next thing was to have an electrical inspection. Every electrical line had to be up in the air, installed by a licensed electrician, with the appropriate amperage, fuse boxes, breakers, and all that sort of paraphernalia. Signage was closely controlled. The electrical lines to the signage had to be of a certain size and the sign itself could be only a certain size, too. We had installed a little travel trailer for the fellows working in the lot to use to keep warm. Because it was not attached to a car, the travel trailer had to have a license as a temporary building. The point is, it took almost a month and several thousand dollars to satisfy all these absurd requirements. They contributed absolutely nothing, other than to the price of our product.

As a practical matter, we didn't return the second year to that location simply because the cost of doing business was too high. However, the owner of the restaurant wanted to have us return because we created traffic for his restaurant that increased his business.

But the sad part of this whole scenario is, I am certain that when those various township inspectors went home at night they would say to their wives or husbands, "Darling, I had a terrible day. I had to work hard. We had to inspect this Christmas tree operation." They are firmly persuaded that they are doing something worthwhile when their job, in my view, has absolutely no value whatever. We could have handled it ourselves. We would have put enough wiring in for our needs to carry the appropriate amount of electricity. We would have maintained our own signs and clearly, whether the trailer was attached to a car or not, was absolutely of no importance other than to satisfy a governmental bureaucracy. If you are involved in government, take a look at what you do. Is it really, really necessary? I am persuaded that in many cases that it is not.

Work and Youth

The problem isn't just with government workers, however. We are a nation of hypocrites. What is that all about? We raise our children. We tell them that work is desirable. They should develop a work ethic. We tell a little white lie, but it's OK: "When I was your age" — you know that drill — "I walked 30 miles to school uphill both ways. We were so poor; we only had one pair of shoes. My sister wore the left shoe and I wore the right shoe. When I got to school, I got straight A's. I came right home after school, milked 50 cows and my parents knew exactly where I was."

We impress upon them the work ethic. I think it was a well-known comic who used to tell his kids that he walked to school through 8-foot snowdrifts, which was quite a feat considering the fact that he was raised in San Juan, Puerto Rico. Be that as it may, those were good white lies. We were trying to impress upon the kids that it is important to have a work ethic. It's important to have responsibilities and accept them. So far, so good. So, where does the hypocrisy come in?

On the other hand, we pass a bazillion laws that don't allow employers to employ our kids. We've got to protect them from the shirtwaist disaster of 1906. Cut me a break! Consider this. Your fourteen year old son or daughter, except in very limited situations, cannot work down at the mall in the stores. They are too young. But they can hang out in the mall and become "mall rats" in their hip-hop clothing, on their skateboards or Roller blades, which is far more dangerous than most clerking can be, and that's OK. When your daughter gets a little older, she can have an abortion without your permission, knowledge, or consent. But that same daughter can't work at the hospital because she is too young, again, except in very, very limited and controlled environments.

Your sixteen or seventeen year old who has a driver's license cannot work in a gas station and pump gas until he is eighteen because that's a hazardous occupation. But he can go down and pump gas into that 340-horsepower engine of his and whip it down the highway until Smokey grabs him, and that's legal. The ultimate hypocrisy. Your seventeen year old cannot legally cut the grass at a neighbor's house, with or without your permission, with a power lawn mower because it is a power tool that is very, very dangerous, and he could be hurt.

That same seventeen year old, with your permission, can join the Army and kill people, or be killed. Now, given the choice between my kid maybe burning himself with the grease at Mickey D's, or hanging out in the mall, I'd rather he was cooking french fries. Given the choice between my daughter having an abortion or working at the hospital, put her to work every time. Given the choice between my son pumping gas or spinning down the highway in an oversized car, I'll let him pump. And clearly, I'd rather have him cutting grass than I would killing people or being killed.

Now, why is it that we can work out a green card system for folks coming from other countries, but we can't work out a reasonable working environment for our children? Most states require working papers. I don't have any quarrel with that. When I was a kid nobody had working papers and it seemed to work out OK. In any event, let's assume that your state requires working papers.

Why not have permanent work cards? The kid has to surrender that card if his grades fall below a certain point, and even there you have a problem because there are some kids who are just not able to get decent grades. They just aren't smart enough, but that doesn't mean they can't work. Why should you take the privilege of working away from your children? OK, so he can burn himself with french fry grease, he might cut himself with a slicing machine, he might even have a tragedy at the gas station. Those are hazards that I would far prefer to see my children exposed to than the alternatives when they are not working, bearing in mind the adage about "idle hands." My kids were either privileged or cursed, depending on your perspective. You see, in general the child labor laws don't apply when you are working with your parents, so my kids could always work in the old man's business.

I did some pretty nasty stuff to my children. My eldest son, Matthew, who is now my business partner and a very close friend, was about seven years old. We were running a nursery school and day camp, and I said, "Matt, we've got a problem." He asked, "Yeah, Pop, what?" I told him it was with the septic tank, and he wrinkled his nose and said, "I know. So why are you telling me?" Seven years old and a wise guy.

He was a cute little kid, blond hair, crewcut, the usual. He looked like a typical 1960s kid was supposed to look like, *Leave It to Beaver*. (Matter of fact, my youngest son, Michael, was called "Beaver" for a good many years. I don't think Michael likes to remember that.) In any case, I said, "Matt, here's the problem. We got a septic tank. I can pump it out, but there's a stuffed-up pipe down in there and, unfortunately kid, I won't fit." (Good thing for me.) He said, "So?" So I said, "Matt, what I'm going to do is, I am going to hold you upside down, put you down into the tank, and you will see the pipe down there, and you stick your arm in the pipe." Now the kid is seven, but he's not stupid, he knows what's in that pipe. He asked, "Pop, how will I know if it's fixed?" I said, "Trust me, kid, you're going to know."

I pumped it out and took my little plunger and hung him down the tank and he had guts. He put his hand right up into that you-know-what, and all of a sudden it let go, the backpressure

265

— boom! He had this stuff in his eyes, and his nose and his ears. He was covered. I pulled him up and stood him up. The only thing that was clean now was where the tears were coursing down his face. I hosed him off at some considerable distance because this kid really stank.

When he finally calmed down, I said, "Matthew, I want to thank you for what you did. I want to talk to you for just a moment now. The chances are that I am going to be with you and see you mature into a man. I hope that's true, but just on the outside possibility that I don't live to see that happen, if you remember only one thing about your old man, remember this. No matter how dirty you get working, the dirt washes off."

I did something like that to each of my kids. I remember distinctly sending my number two kid into a crawl space to supposedly change a light bulb. He was without a shirt and sweating like a pig. The crawl space was full, full of fiberglass insulation. He must have scratched for two weeks.

Now, why did I do this to the kids? Because I wanted them to understand that the reason that they had privileges other kids didn't have — the vacation in the Virgin Islands, the cruises, and the trips to Puerto Rico — was not because of a lottery win. They did it because their Mother and their Father were working seven days a week to provide the wherewithal for those things. There is no disgrace in working. Each of my kids, from the time they were five, had responsible chores. Not make-work but responsible chores. I wanted them to understand there is no disgrace in working. Matthew now has his own children and he is planning what he will do to Brendan, Thomas and Lane when they are old enough to understand.

There are those today who would say you can't do this to kids. It's going to bend their psyches. I point out to those people that I have five normal adult children, all contributing members of society with college educations, two with professional degrees and the other three working in their chosen endeavors, making far better than average livings and, more importantly, responsible, well-adjusted adults. Empirically — that's the proof of the pudding. Kids demand discipline. Kids demand responsibility. If you don't give it to them, then it's you, *you* who are deficient.

I still maintain that we are a society of hypocrites. On the one hand, we tell our kids all of the great values of work and then we do legally everything we can do to prohibit them from working.

I recall Elizabeth Dole, former Senator Robert Dole's wife, going on television when she was Secretary Of Labor, saying, "We are conducting a raid today. We are raiding McDonald's and Burger Kings to find child labor abuses." What a load of crap. What they should have been doing was giving a medal to McDonald's and Burger King for giving these kids the opportunity, *the opportunity,* to become productive citizens.

Politically Incorrect

I have been told that I am politically incorrect in a lot of ways. On the air I have called women "honey," "sweetheart" and "baby," and I make no apology for it. It has become somewhat of an issue with some of the brass that I have worked with, but I'm not about to go to the mattresses with it. I still consider that to be part of my persona and do not find it offensive.

When confronted by some of the more activist females, I asked them a very simple question. "Which would you prefer, to be called 'Ms.' and be catered to and be called 'Ms.' secretary, or would you rather have someone like me who will call you 'honey' or 'sweetheart' but will make you a boss?" As it happens, in our own businesses, we have more females in positions of authority than we do males — not because they are female, but because they are the best we could find to fill the positions.

While I'm in my "politically incorrect" mode, I see no reason for some of the affirmative action programs or the need for forcing integration of any kind, (not only by race, but by ethnicity), on the public. Years and years ago, my boss, J. Gansky offered me his apartment in Atlantic City, New Jersey, for a vacation. I had been in to see him. I told him I needed some time off and I was really beat and maybe I ought to resign. He didn't want me to leave, so he offered my family and me his apartment to enjoy for a couple of weeks. He said he wasn't using it, and that would work. I had been around the world, a New Jersey resident all my life, but I had never been to Atlantic City. Of course, this was well before gambling changed the face of that area.

I gathered my two children and pregnant wife and off we went to take over Jack's apartment for a couple of weeks. I was pretty proud at that time that as an undergraduate, I was driving a new station wagon, one that I used in distributing cards. When I pulled into the parking lot, that was the only Chevrolet in sight: Mercedes, BMWs, Cadillacs, Lincolns, no Chevrolets. We moved into the apartment and found out very, very quickly, that we were the only Christian family in the building.

Jack was Jewish and had purchased his condominium (an expression I couldn't define at that time) in a building where the majority of the people were Orthodox Jews and the rest were Conservative. They made it abundantly clear, overtly and covertly, through remarks made in the lobby, as well as hostile stares at the swimming pool, that we were very unwelcome. (I did gain the respect of some of the younger couples the second day I was there, having been invited into a poker game, where I cleaned house.) I should add, in fairness, that the problem was not so much with the young couples as with their elders. It was obvious that, as a family, we were an irritant.

After a couple of days, I suggested to my wife that we should leave. Upon returning to the office, I gave the keys back to Jack. I explained the situation and thanked him. He went ballistic. "Who the hell do they think they are kicking you out, making your life uncomfortable? I paid as much as they did." You get the picture. "No," I said, "I don't see it that way at all." These people had picked an environment where they were comfortable. They elected to purchase and live with people who shared their beliefs, their likes and dislikes, and who was I to intrude upon that? Yes, I had a legal right to be there, there's no question about that. And, I suppose it could be argued that I had a moral right to be there, but it seems to me that I was the intruder, that I was the one making them uncomfortable.

While it could be argued that was their shortcoming, I don't see it that way. It was much easier for me to leave. Putting aside the legalities, who am I to make all these folks uncomfortable? It could be argued, once again, that they should accommodate an outsider, but it seems to me that if a group of Hungarians want to live together, they should have that right. It seems to be trendy today for black students to have a black dorm, and why not, if that's where they are the most comfortable? Yet, all white Anglo-Saxon Protestant dorms would likely be unacceptable. Why? Clearly, there should be a place where people who choose to live with a great mixture can have that opportunity.

As it happens, I have owned my home in New Jersey for some 30 years, and do not know by name more than three neighbors. I really don't care who lives in the neighborhood. I don't associate with them. It's not that they are good people or bad people. I just choose my friends by my friends, not because they happen to move in next door. The lady on my immediate left has lived there longer than I and we exchange pleasantries. Folks have owned the next house for 20 years and if a million dollars were put on the table, I couldn't tell you their name, nor would I recognize them if they walked up to me. I like it that way. I don't care who I live next door to, across the street or around the corner from. I do care that they maintain the property. It seems to me that people should have the right to live in an area where they are comfortable.

But then, that is the ultimate of "political incorrectness." What a shame.

The Boat Registration

The guy who said a boat is a hole in the water you throw money into knew precisely whereof he spoke. I am not a boat person by any stretch of anyone's imagination. But I live on the Gulf of Mexico, and my home came equipped with a rather large dock, as well as a davit for personal watercraft and an elevator that is capable of picking up a large boat. It became apparent that I would have to have a boat — if not for me, for my friends and children to use when they visit.

I sit here looking out at the Gulf of Mexico and see folks with huge boats with capable speeds just under Mach 1. I wonder why in the world they would want such a thing. One reason for me to have a boat is because a few miles off the front of my home is a very pleasant island owned by the state of Florida. Anclote Key, which has a lush beach, is available if one chooses to swim. I must admit it is fun to go out there. Keeping my needs and prejudices in mind, and rather than going out and buying some really powerful boat that would be great for ocean travel, I opted to buy a 24-foot pontoon boat which is fondly known as a "party barge." It will hold as many as fifteen people, but since I don't know fifteen people in this area, we have never put that to the test.

From time to time I do use the boat with a friend and have enjoyed it, but I can certainly attest it spends a whole lot more time at repair shop, Korman's Sunset Landing. Buddy Korman is the mechanic who has very graciously serviced this thing when necessary. I should note, that if pushed to full throttle, I might get 15 to 17 knots out of this boat. It's not exactly a speed demon and, of course, in anything but totally calm waters, it would be very foolish to drive it at anything approaching those speeds. A pontoon boat, for those of you who are not aficionados, will give you a high degree of stability in relatively calm waters but it is not the type of vessel that you would want in a storm.

I have a compass on board and a depth finder and it has been suggested that I should get a global positioning system, or GPS, such as I have on my airplane. I tell folks I have a far better way of keeping track of precisely where I am and a GPS would be of no assistance. I never, ever get out of sight of land — not even close to being out of sight of land. This is a nice little thing to play on, to even have a barbecue on, but it most certainly is not a powerful vessel.

Because the Gulf of Mexico is so incredibly shallow, particularly when the tides are running, I know the manufacturers who make propellers have seen their stock rise several points just on the basis of the props that I have taken out. The main platform is nothing other than plywood bolted onto aluminum pontoons. Pleasant, yes. A formidable vessel, I don't think so.

Late one summer I was making one of my numerous trips to Korman's to pick up the boat. As I remember, it had a tuneup and some other problems of little consequence. Korman's is located on the Pithlachascotee River and is two or three miles from the open water. As I was leaving, I was being very conscious of the speeds because on a Sunday one will find far more local constabulary and the Coast Guard at work than on a weekday.

I made my way out of the channel. I am guessing that the reason that the "no wake" zone had been extended was because of the relatively recent innovation of gambling ships coming in and out of the river. Heretofore, at the mouth of the river, one could open up. Be that as it may, given the fact that the extension was enforced, one could only drive legally at idle speeds. I was driving faster than that and captured the attention of a corporal of the local police.

271

You have to laugh at these fellows or you will cry because they are so pompous. "Captain, may I board your vessel?" Captain? I am on a 24-foot party barge but I am captain and I have a vessel. I allowed him to board my vessel. He found three or four violations, i.e., I didn't have flares on board, I had plenty of life preservers but no life ring on a rope, and no fire extinguisher. How I was supposed to know that I should have these things is another matter but that's all right, I can accept that. When he got to the registration he took a very, very hard look and said, "That is not a legal registration number." You should know that the law requires that you have a registration number on the bow of your boat similar to a license plate. When I showed him my registration, which was current, he said, "This is not the appropriate number. I don't know where that number came from. I have never seen a number like that," and he gave me a summons.

Unhappily, on the way back my shirt whose pocket contained the summons blew overboard. Those of you who have boated know that unless you are very lucky you are never going to see that item again. It is very difficult to figure out exactly where you were even seconds before and since I was alone I made a futile pass and said good-bye shirt. The following day I had my assistant call the court and ask for a duplicate copy of the summons. The clerk said they would have the corporal, who had given me the ticket, call me and give me that information. A couple of days passed and no such phone call was received. We tried again. In the end, we made several calls and were rewarded with no information.

Finally, my assistant called the State Attorney's Office, which was generous enough to advise us that we were now in contempt given the fact that we had never answered the summons. We explained that I had lost the ticket but that cut no ice. I had determined who the two judges were who hear these kinds of matters and wrote to them both asking their kind offices in obtaining the appropriate information. The one judge who responded and who eventually heard the case suggested that I call the same phone number where I was getting no information to begin with.

Finally, in desperation, I called the chief of police, who was a retired New York City police officer now working as a chief in the sticks. He was a very accommodating fellow, knew exactly what the problem was and within twenty-four hours had faxed us a copy of the summons. Interestingly, the police officer had indicated on the summons that it was not necessary to appear in court but the statute very clearly indicated one could not just send in a fine but rather must appear in court. Not the swiftest guy.

I had to appear for arraignment because it turns out this is a misdemeanor — that's a criminal act, campers. Naturally, the timing couldn't have been worse. December is a month when I spend a great deal of my time in New Jersey because of the Christmas season. I have some business obligations that require my relatively close attention. When we called the court and told them that I ordinarily spend only Tuesdays and Wednesdays in Florida during December, I was politely told, "You will be here on a Monday or a Friday because that's when we do our arraignments and we don't do them at your convenience, we do them at ours." Nice work, huh? These are public servants I am speaking with. Well, I did arrange to come in on a Monday, and son-of-a-gun, I went to the courthouse and was told, "The judge didn't come in today." Say what? "Well, he didn't come in today, but the arraignments will be done another day." This was testimony to my self-control because I really wanted to go ballistic.

I had made a 2,000-mile trip in order to be there on the day the judge was there and I found out, for whatever reason, he wasn't there that day. Happily, I got hold of the clerk of the court, who was much more sympathetic than the others. She said, "Give me a few moments, maybe we can do something." I was told that I could appear before the other judge, who happened to be

273

in the building.

Of course, they had to trot out a court reporter because this is a criminal proceeding. How did I wish to plead? Did I realize that I was entitled to representation by an attorney and if I couldn't afford one, one would be provided, etc., etc. I indicated yes, I was aware of that, and I would be representing myself pro se, which means I'm doing this without an attorney, which clearly is my right. I was then told that the sentence could be as much as six months in jail for this "capital" crime that I had committed. The judge said of course that type of sentence would not be imposed, rest assured, but I should be aware that was the maximum sentence. I acknowledged that, signed the appropriate papers and now I was criminally indicted. You may remember that this whole thing revolved around a number, the wrong number on the boat.

Here was the situation. I bought the boat brand new. When you buy a used boat in our county in Florida or, in the alternative, if you bring a boat from out of state and register it, the county very graciously hands you a brochure that explains your responsibilities, including where the numbers are to be displayed and, more importantly, what number this is.

If you buy a new boat, they don't give you the brochure. They assume that the dealer will take care of that little detail. But there is no duty on the part of the dealer to take care of that. It's just that they assume that they will. When I looked at the number, I couldn't figure out where I got it. Bear in mind, this number has been on the boat since I purchased it in 1992 and nobody had ever said boo about it. I figured out — and I believe that the less than bright corporal should have known — that I had put on, by mistake, the decal number. They give you a little sticker to stick on your boat when you pay your fees and I put down that number.

I was told, and correctly so, that if you look at the reverse of the registration it clearly tells you what you are to do. The problem is that the registration is a light blue paper with very light blue ink printed on the back and in print size only a Philadelphia lawyer could love. Without aid of some magnification there are very few of us who could read this, and realistically, how many read the fine print? It has been long held that if a parking lot puts fine print on the back of the ticket or your dry cleaner puts some terms on the back of the ticket, unless they tell you about it, you can't be held to that. It would seem to me that a branch of government should be held at least to the standard that we hold a dry cleaner to, if not higher. Nonetheless, at least we have determined a couple of things: where that number came from and that number, although not the appropriate registration number, could have been traced back to me since I paid for that decal. I could demonstrate there was no intent to deceive; the number clearly was directly traceable to me.

Finally, the day came for my time in court. Once again I was representing myself. I will tidy that little matter up in a moment or two. The state was represented by not one but two attorneys, both of whom were very nice young men who I am quite certain had reached puberty, but not by very much.

As a matter of fact, I commented on my program after the indictment the relatively young age of the state's attorney and the fact that he had only passed the bar less than six months before. After the fact, he assured me that while this may be true, he was very experienced because he majored in criminal law. Once again, I am confident that this is an up and coming Clarence Darrow, but there was nothing in the court proceedings to indicate that. And, he was positioned to be a mentor for an attorney with even less experience and a lesser ability to grow a beard. I believe his voice had changed, so that was a step in the right direction.

I was advised once again of my rights to an attorney and I assured the judge I understood those rights and I was representing myself. I had inquired to whether I could cross-examine and object, as any attorney could in the court on my behalf, and was assured that I could. The only state's witness was the police officer who accurately portrayed the incident to the extent that the ticket was issued and the number was incorrect and I was willing to stipulate that.

I had to laugh and I was tempted to object to part of his testimony in that he said I was going too fast and I was about to take out a marker — the operative term here is "take out a marker." You should know the channel markers are I-beams about 12 to 15 inches in width that are driven into the bottom of the channel. You couldn't take that out with a 40-foot yacht. You might take your boat out but you most certainly wouldn't take the marker out. I felt if that was what he wanted to say, hopefully the judge heard the irony here and I think that he did. In any event, the judge then heard the state's charge and said, "I believe that this is not a misdemeanor but rather a violation and you may move that your case for a misdemeanor be dismissed." I so moved. "You may reopen for a violation." Well, the two kids who were the lawyers protested, sputtered and cited chapter and verse and the judge smiled benignly and said, "That is my ruling." He had said to me very kindly, "You have a right to ask for a dismissal," and I so moved. This is when he moved it down to a violation and the matter was heard. I make the points that I have made to you about the small print and the lack of handing the brochure out. The junior bird-man objected to the admission of the brochure because no one was there to testify that this actually came from the county. He does have a license to practice law too, isn't that interesting?

Finally, the judge found that there was no intent to deceive and he found me guilty with no fine and a $50 court cost. I was happy with that. The judge acquitted himself well and was gracious. The two kids were trying hard and I have no personal animosity towards them. That's their way to learn. Let's face it; you don't have Chris Darden as a prosecuting attorney in a small town in Florida.

Now we come to the essence of this whole story and why I take this much time to recount it. There is no question that I could have afforded counsel and that might have been the wisest thing to do. As a matter of fact, an attorney I use regularly and one I consider a good friend, Don Peyton, offered to represent me without charge. He said he was going to be up there anyway and he would be very happy to do it. I couldn't do that. If I were to allow counsel to represent me on a matter where the maximum fine was $189 plus costs, I would be the ultimate of hypocrites, given that I am constantly telling folks on my program: "Don't let the system grind you down." There are many, many matters where clearly it is just not cost-effective to be represented and yet, unless you fight, you are going to be walked upon. There is no question that I spent multiples of that amount of money in my time preparing for and then appearing on two occasions in this matter. If I didn't do that, how in the world could I tell you guys to do it?

Principle and Pragmatism

All throughout your life there are going to be matters of principle and matters pragmatic. In the second case, often times, we make decisions strictly based on time and cost. As an example, if someone had a relatively minor accident on a piece of property that I owned and I was responsible for negotiating a settlement, I might very easily walk away with a less than satisfactory arrangement for my side just to get the matter done. The same thing might be said in most small businesses when one gets a bad check for $12, $15 or $20. Yes, there are all manner of remedies under the law, but the reality is that the remedy will cost more in terms of time and aggravation than it's worth. You simply write it off.

Conversely, sometime ago, in one of our businesses, a gentleman alleged that he was fired because he was black and overweight. Neither of these claims was true. He was fired simply because he couldn't cut the mustard. He was hired to do a particular job and was told he would have to grow into that job. We allowed that he had skills but those skills needed to be honed, and simply put, he did not make an effort to improve.

After he filed his allegations, we hired counsel and ultimately had a meeting with his counsel, our people and the state Equal Employment Opportunity representative. Initially, he was asking for an extraordinary sum of money, and just before we went into this meeting his counsel said he would settle for $5,000.

This was extortion. I said absolutely not. The hearings were nearly concluded and remember this was a preliminary hearing possibly leading to something more formal. There was some conversation across the table and I asked the woman hearing this matter if I could address plaintiff's counsel for the record. She graciously said, "Yes." What I said in substance to him was this: You offered to settle this for $5,000. I have spent more than $5,000 bringing three people from some considerable distance to this meeting today and perhaps, most importantly, coming here myself, but I want you to understand that even though I have spent more than $5,000 today I will spend twenty times $5,000 before I will give your client a nickel. This is a matter of principle.

You have alleged that I have done something morally and legally reprehensible, and this is not the case. Your client was fired simply because he was not competent in the task for which he was hired. Nothing more and nothing less. Everything else that you have talked about is fruit salad and all of these impassioned pleas about the cuts of slavery have absolutely no relevance. So I wish both of you to understand that while we could have settled this for a very little amount of money, there will not be a settlement forthcoming. If you were to offer right now to settle for 15 cents, I would decline.

We are absolutely blameless. We have conducted ourselves in a forthright manner and under no circumstance will we concede for a matter of expediency. I meant everything I said. If you can't collect a check, or negotiate a legitimate settlement claim and it has no reflection on your reputation, or character, you become a pragmatist. You do what you think is in your best interest, taking everything into account, including such things as time and legal expenses.

In the second instance, there was no room for negotiation. I felt in the boat incident that there was no room for negotiation, that I was right. I had made an honest mistake, but the mistake was compounded and perhaps the result of the inattention to what seemed to be ordinary detail on the part of the county and the state. The defense "I didn't know" usually fails on the dictum that ignorance of the law is no excuse. I asked the court in this instance how far a person should go before he or she can be reasonably confident that he is satisfying the law. I paid the appropriate fees for five consecutive years, and no one told me that which I was doing was flawed. Does not the state have some obligation to explain precisely and in detail what is expected of you? When one registers a car, in very large print you are told where to place the plates, how often, and so forth.

Brought down to its essence, if you feel that a matter of principle is at issue and that principle is worth pursuing, do it! Often we say, "It's a matter of principle," but when you come right down to it, it isn't that important. If it is a principle, then do whatever is necessary to protect your interest and the principle. On those issues where the stakes and numbers are very high, clearly competent counsel is the order of the day. On these relatively minor matters stand up for yourself — and do it right.

If you are going to court, dress appropriately. I was amazed at the outfits I saw in court: baseball hats, whose owners had to be told to remove them in the courtroom, athletic jackets, T-shirts with all manner of "Visit Fort Worth" type emblems, shorts, thongs (the shoe variety) — the works. You don't have to be dressed expensively but certainly it would pay if you are a male to wear a jacket and a tie, and if a female to wear a skirt or appropriate pantsuits, not the outfits that I saw. I suppose that the judges are inured to this, but it just seems to me that dressing appropriately cannot hurt.

Conclusion

In retrospect, a life, any life, is hard to sum up. But when I think about mine, some things seem more important than others, many of which I have recounted in this book. In this final section are my thoughts on where it all led and what the payoff was.

12
The Reward

It has always been my contention that all of us are renters. Let me elaborate. People are frequently asked, "Do you own your own home?" and they respond, "Yes." In the technical sense, they are correct. But in the long view, all of us are renters. We come into this world with nothing and we most certainly will leave the same way.

During our short tenure, we are permitted to use the planet and its gifts, sometimes wisely and sometimes otherwise.

The home that I still maintain in New Jersey was purchased over 30 years ago. It has a great many memories of raising children, trials and tribulations, election victories and disappointments, and all of the other things that contribute to our lives. That house is situated on a piece of property where the Court House of Somerset County was located during the American Revolution.

The British, on one of their sojourns through the area, determined that the Court House should be burned and did the deed. The road that I lived on was once a Lenni Lenape Indian trail. The Lenni Lenape or Delawares were the tribe native to New Jersey. The Colonials widened this trail and it became the road from Trenton to New Brunswick to Philadelphia, a Kings Highway and eventually the Lincoln Highway. I have lived on this property, had many joys and sorrows and have survived. Whether or not I could have survived on the same property 300 years ago as a Colonial, or 600 years ago as a Lenape Indian or

5,000 years ago as who knows what, is imponderable. I will never know if I could survive and prosper 1,000 years hence. Obviously, that conundrum will never be resolved.

What I have learned is that I have survived in my time and done well in the time that has been given me. Sooner or later, this property that I "own" will pass to others and then again others.

So it is with our lives. We spend a little time here, coming, and then going as we came, naked and alone. The measure, then, of the individual is how he used this gift of a tiny portion of the world. Is it in better condition or is it worse than when he came upon the scene, and is our space in general better or worse? This is the measurement to which we must all be held, and I am hopeful in my small way that it could be said of me that things are just a tad better because he passed this way. I have always considered my children my greatest success and also the contributors of some of the greatest joys and occasional sorrow. On balance, this must be the measurement and standard that we have to address.

Finally, too, there is the matter of the goals we set out to achieve, and this I can best tell by means of this anecdote.

I don't remember this incident at all, but my Father recounted it often enough to make me believe it must have happened. My Dad and I were talking when I was about twelve years old, and I said to my Father, "I love you, but I don't want to live like you are living." We lived in a neighborhood that today would be called a ghetto, but then was called "blue collar." My Dad recounted that he asked me then, "What are you going to do?" and I said, "I don't know, Pop, but I'm going to be a millionaire."

In putting this rather lengthy trip down memory lane together, it has resulted in me thinking of many things and revisiting areas that I have not considered for a good many years. I suspect that most sons, as well as daughters, spend a great deal of their time and energy trying to impress one parent or the other. I have come to the conclusion that I am no different in this regard. I am still striving to impress a man who has been dead for over 30 years.

Well Pop, how am I doing?

INDEX

Order Form

Use this order form to order future copies of this book or any other book by Bruce Williams. Or you can call 800-337-2346.

www.brucewilliams.com

Make checks payable to R.M.I., P.O. Box 547, Elfers, FL 34680

Title	Price	Qty	Total
Thanks for Asking	$19.95	_____	_____
House Smart	$14.95	_____	_____
In Business for Yourself	$19.95	_____	_____
Add S/H	$3.95 per book	_____	_____

In the state of Florida add appropriate sales tax.   _____

Name:_____

Address:_____

City, St., Zip:_____

Phone #:_____

Credit Card #:_____

Exp Date:_____

Signature:_____

Order Form

Use this order form to order future copies of this book or any other book by Bruce Williams. Or you can call 800-337-2346.

www.brucewilliams.com

Make checks payable to R.M.I., P.O. Box 547, Elfers, FL 34680

Title	Price	Qty	Total
Thanks for Asking	$19.95	_____	_____
House Smart	$14.95	_____	_____
In Business for Yourself	$19.95	_____	_____
Add S/H	$3.95 per book	_____	_____

In the state of Florida add appropriate sales tax.   _____

Name:_____

Address:_____

City, St., Zip:_____

Phone #:_____

Credit Card #:_____

Exp Date:_____

Signature:_____

Daniel Schmidt

717-439-3048